IMAGES
of America

GOSHEN COUNTY

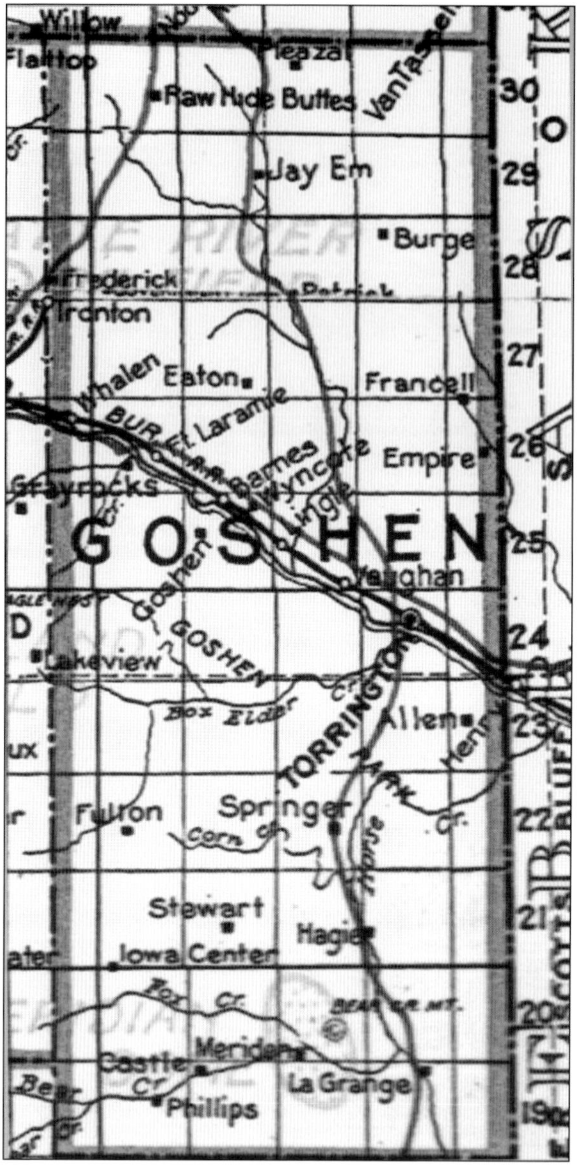

This map of Goshen County shows burgs and towns that were in existence around 1915. There are several that are no longer in existence, such as Burge, Francell, Empire, Allen, Stewart, Hagie, and Felton. The town of Empire was very interesting in the early days of the county. It was located along Sheep Creek and was started by two brothers who came from Nebraska. Their parents were born in North Carolina and were slaves. Radford and Joseph Spence came and homesteaded hoping for a better life. By 1912, the community had a post office, school, and church, but by 1920, it was a ghost town. (Homesteaders Museum.)

On the Cover: Surrounded by a bountiful harvest of pumpkins and squash are Lois (back), Eula (right), and baby Jay Knowlton around 1921. They were the children of William and Winnie Knowlton, who lived on their farm six miles east of Veteran. Winnie was a widow who homesteaded nearby with her son Bill. Their family also consisted of Richard and Betty, the youngest children (Homesteaders Museum.)

IMAGES
of America

GOSHEN COUNTY

Vickie Zimmer

ARCADIA
PUBLISHING

ISBN 978-0-7385-9302-9

Published by Arcadia Publishing
Charleston, South Carolina

Printed in the United States of America

Library of Congress Control Number: 2011936217

For all general information, please contact Arcadia Publishing:
Telephone 843-853-2070
Fax 843-853-0044
E-mail sales@arcadiapublishing.com
For customer service and orders:
Toll-Free 1-888-313-2665

Visit us on the Internet at www.arcadiapublishing.com

To all the pioneers, homesteaders, business people, families, and individuals who carved out the ranches, farms, towns, and city that today make Goshen County such a wonderful place to live.

Contents

ACKNOWLEDGMENTS

Without the nudge from the Goshen County Historical Society, I would never have thought of putting this book together. Thank you.

I would never have been able to compile the many treasured photographs that make up this book without the most amenable assistance from the following: the Torrington Homesteaders Museum and Dan Ringle, director; the Wyoming State Archives; the Wyoming Department of State Parks and Cultural Resources; Suzi Taylor and Cindy Brown, reference archivists; Velma Malone; Waldon Smith; Margie Raben Jones; Naomi Schaffer; Dudley Haines; and Bill Law. Thank you.

Without the knowledgeable assistance of Don Hodgson and Paul Puebla, who provided fountains of history, read and offered suggestions to the introduction, and gave me confidence to continue, I would never have been able to complete the text. Thank you.

Without the help of answering questions to provide me with local history and information, I would not have been able to complete all the captions. I cannot name all of you who helped, but know that I appreciate all I learned from you. Thank you.

Without the appreciation of history instilled in me by my parents, Russell and Ila Zimmer, I probably would not have been interested in working on or completing this project. Thank you.

Without the understanding, cooperation, and assistance provided by Coleen Balant and Arcadia Publishing, I would not have been able to get this volume published. Thank you.

Without the patience, cooperation, and understanding of time that was needed and stress involved in writing such a book provided by my spouse, Michael Bond, I would not have been able to finish this book. Thank you.

INTRODUCTION

What makes a place special? One could say history, people, resources, geography, weather, or culture. All of these answers would be correct, so what makes Goshen County unique?

Before the coming of wagon trains that followed the Oregon, Mormon, California, and Overland Trails, Indians and mountain men traversed the river waterways and explorers tried to find passes to take them further west. This was followed by the Butterfield Overland Mail Trail, which carried mail from Memphis, Tennessee, and St. Louis, Missouri, to San Francisco, California. The Cheyenne-Deadwood Stage Road was also developed, which took miners to the gold rush in South Dakota. These early pioneers left their history in the form of wagon ruts, place names, and historic sites.

Robert Stuart and a party of "Overland Astorians" were the first documented white men to camp in the area near present-day Torrington. They headed east about January 1, 1813, on their way to report to John Jacob Astor, owner of the fur-trading empire known as the American Fur Company. Other explorers passing along the North Platte River included Capt. Nathaniel J. Wyeth in 1832. Capt. Benjamin Louis Eulalie De Bonneville, along with 110 men, brought the first wagon train into the valley.

Originally part of Laramie County, Goshen County was created under Gov. Joseph Carey, who signed a legislative act on February 9, 1911. It was not officially organized until 1913. The county is a long rectangle—72 miles long and 31 miles wide, with Nebraska to the east, Laramie County to the south, Platte County to the west, and Niobrara County to the north. It was decided that Torrington would be the county seat.

There seems to be several ideas of how the name "Goshen" was applied to an area in the county and to the county itself. One idea is that it was originally Goshe's Hole, after an early French trapper named Goshe. Records from the expedition of John C. Fremont indicate that they camped near Goshe's Hole on July 14, 1842. Another version is that around 1846, the name referred to the rich, fertile lands and plentiful water that was the agricultural basis of the irrigated farming area. The name "Goshen Hole" first appeared on a map in 1888. Seth Ward, a post sutler at Fort Laramie, told early rancher John Hunton that the county was named for the biblical land of Goshen.

The first permanent settlement in the Goshen County area was Fort William, a trading post built in 1834 near the junction of the Laramie and North Platte Rivers. Fur traders Robert Campbell and William Sublette established and built the original wood stockade buildings that would later become known as Fort Laramie. The settlement had an important impact on travelers going west, since it was the major place to resupply, pick up mail, and rest. In 1849, Fort Laramie was purchased by the US government and operated as a military post, but it was abandoned in 1890.

People moved to the area initially to graze cattle, now known as ranching. The first permanent breeding herd, started by W.G. Bullock and B.B. Mills at Fort Laramie, eventually moved south to Chugwater Creek. Other pioneer ranchers in the area included John Hunton, Hiram B. Kelly, John Kessler, Charley Coffee, and Philip J. Yoder. A couple of the big ranches were called Union Cattle

Company and Swan Land and Cattle Company. Early ranching was mainly in the southern part of the county known as Bear Creek; it spread north of the North Platte River by the 1870s.

Ranching did not bring a large population of settlers, and as a result, homesteading acts were passed. The Homestead Act of 1862 offered the applicant 160 acres of undeveloped federal land to improve. Applicants had five years to complete the improvements, but only about 40 percent of them were able to complete the process and receive a deed to the property.

Trails through Goshen County were part of the highway for westward expansion. The Oregon, Mormon, and California Trails followed the flow of the North Platte River. Groups of emigrants began passing through southeast Wyoming in June 1842. Next came the Pony Express from April 1860 to November 1861, followed by the telegraph line, which was completed on October 24, 1861. The Cheyenne-Deadwood Stage Road came next; it was active from September 1876 to February 1887. Few people stayed very long, stopping only to rest a bit, wash clothes, and resupply at Fort Laramie. These trails passed diagonally through the county and left many historical sites. The northern part of the county was not settled as quickly as the southern part because of an early treaty with the Sioux Indians that confined settlers to south of the Platte River.

Starting in 1900, the Burlington Railroad helped populate the area. It entered Wyoming from Nebraska at Torrington and assisted in the development of several business opportunities along its routes, such as livestock, coal, and growing grains and sugar beets. Passenger service began in May, and George King was the first station agent.

Ashland B. Smith of the Lincoln Land Company of Nebraska surveyed Torrington's town site on April 21, 1900. In June, the land was sold to its residents for $1 by the president of the real estate extension department of the Chicago, Burlington & Quincy Railroad. William G. Curtis named Torrington for his Connecticut birthplace and his English ancestral home.

One scheme to help populate the area dealt with irrigation of the dry land. The Reclamation Act of 1902 funded irrigation projects for the arid lands of 20 western states. The act set aside money from sales of semi-arid public lands for the construction and maintenance of irrigation projects. The newly irrigated land would be sold, and money would be put into a revolving fund that supported more such projects. This led to the eventual damming of nearly every major western river. The North Platte River would provide the necessary water for irrigation in Goshen County.

The village of LaGrange on the banks of Horse Creek is the oldest in the county. In 1867, Kale LaGrange was a driver for a stage route between Denver, Colorado, and the Red Cloud and Spotted Tail Indian Agencies in what is now eastern Nebraska. In 1883, he arranged for water rights from Horse Creek and is thought to have plotted the town site in 1889 serviced by a mail route from Pine Bluffs.

Although still in the planning stage, irrigation was to be the element of success for the homesteaders. The Jewish Agricultural Society, formed in 1900 by the Baron de Hirsch Fund to promote farming among Jews in the United States, sponsored about 50 families by establishing a new Zion community in the Huntley area. These people came from New York and Pennsylvania, as well as some new emigrants from Europe. Six men filed on July 6, 1906, in Cheyenne for 160-acre homesteads located in what is now known as the Huntley area.

These settlers first built dugout shelters for dwellings. Water was a problem, as the nearest water was about a half-mile away in the Katzer Canal. Supplies were also a problem, as the nearest general store was in Mitchell, Nebraska. These men did not have horses, so they walked and carried their supplies of flour, sugar, beans, rice, and salt in a knapsack on their backs. It was a hard-shuffle life, but finally, in 1907 or 1908, the Jewish Agricultural Society sent $500 to each family. With this money, horses, wagons, some machinery, a cow, and tools were purchased. Eventually, Huntley had a post office, church, grocery store, and lumberyard. Also in 1908, another 40 or 45 families moved to Wyoming and established a school and synagogue, calling the community Allen.

Another community that was established around 1900 was Wyncote. It was located several miles west of Torrington on the Burlington Railroad route. The town residents were instrumental in building the Northside Ditch. Because the railroad was unable to secure a town site there, land to the east was donated for a town, and the Wyncote railroad section house was moved to the new site. It was called Lingle for promoter and financier Hiram D. Lingle.

When it came time to select a county seat for Goshen County, citizens from both Torrington and Lingle thought it should be in their town. Lingle residents felt their town was more centrally located. Finally, the state legislature said that whichever town could raise $57,000 to build a courthouse could have the county seat; Torrington won.

Jay Em's advent in the northern part of the county was also related to water. One of the last watering holes before reaching Lusk on the Texas Trail was claimed by Jim Moore in the 1860s. By 1869, Moore had the second largest cattle ranch in the Wyoming Territory with the brand J Rolling M, which gave the name of Jay Em to the small drainage creek. Moore died in 1875, but Silas Harris and his three sons took over the ranch, called the Jay Em Cattle Company. One of those sons, Lake, filed a homestead claim on Rawhide Creek in 1912 and started the small town of Jay Em. During the 1920s and 1930s, the town was a center for commerce. There are a few residents in Jay Em today.

Yoder was named after Jesse Yoder, who headed the Goshen Townsite Development Company. He wanted to build a town beside the Union Pacific Railroad, which passed several miles east of the Yoder ranch. This combined the two settlements of Springer and Lacy Corners. The town boasted real estate offices, a grocery, hardware and dry goods stores, and a bakery and cream station. In 1922, a schoolhouse was added, and a weekly newspaper was started. By 1925, between 500 and 600 people lived there, so the town built three drugstores, two barbershops, a hotel, a bank, several churches, a doctor's office, a community hall, a telephone office, a rooming house, and livery stable. Because of all the commerce, Yoder seemed to be in competition with Torrington for the business and trade center of the county. By 1970, the citizens numbered 101. Today, Yoder has an elementary, middle, and high school, a restaurant, a bar, and a post office.

Ex-servicemen returning from World War I were enticed to settle in the area by a second round of homesteading acts. Each veteran and family would receive an 80-acre irrigated farm to develop. Around 1920, this helped the town of Veteran grow, and it is where the town got its name.

Hawk Springs, located on the highway linking Torrington to Cheyenne, was legendarily named for "the gentle spring where the falcon stood." According to an article in the *Torrington Telegram* in 1946, Nelson H. "Nels" Sherard, who was one of the earliest settlers in the LaGrange area, said that the name came from a saloon keeper at the springs (now covered by Hawk Springs Reservoir) whose name was Black Hawk.

Dry-land farming continues today, with farmers growing wheat, dry beans, corn, sunflowers, and sugar beets. The Holly Sugar Company was one of five sugar processing factories in the state. In the early days, thinning and topping the growing beets was done by Mexicans, who migrated to the area in the early summer and left when the work was finished. Today, machines do that work, and Western Sugar Company has bought out the Holly Sugar Company. Dairying was another industry that helped Goshen County expand by using the milk to make cheese and butter.

Today, the population of Goshen County numbers 13,245. Farming and ranching is still the predominant livelihood other than education and government occupations. There are three high schools: Torrington, Lingle/Fort Laramie, and Southeast. Students also have the option of attending Eastern Wyoming College. Torrington hosts the Goshen County Library and one museum, Homesteaders. Between Lingle and Fort Laramie is another museum, the Western History Center. Many citizens are also involved with the Goshen Community Theater. Two groups promote economic development and community enhancement: Goshen County Economic Development Corporation and Goshen Chamber of Commerce. There are also seven banks. The Torrington Senior Friendship Center, with its branches, offers meals and programs to entertain and enlighten senior citizens. The Banner Health System offers hospital, clinic, and various therapies in the area. There are 21 churches and civic clubs, including Rotary International, Elks

Club, Moose Family Center, Travis Post No. 5 American Legion, Lions Club, 4-H, and many other organizations and groups.

For recreation, there are parks, trails, lakes, reservoirs, rivers, and state and federal historic sites. The area is growing, offers friendly, mostly crime-free communities, and is a good place to live and raise children.

One

Fort Laramie

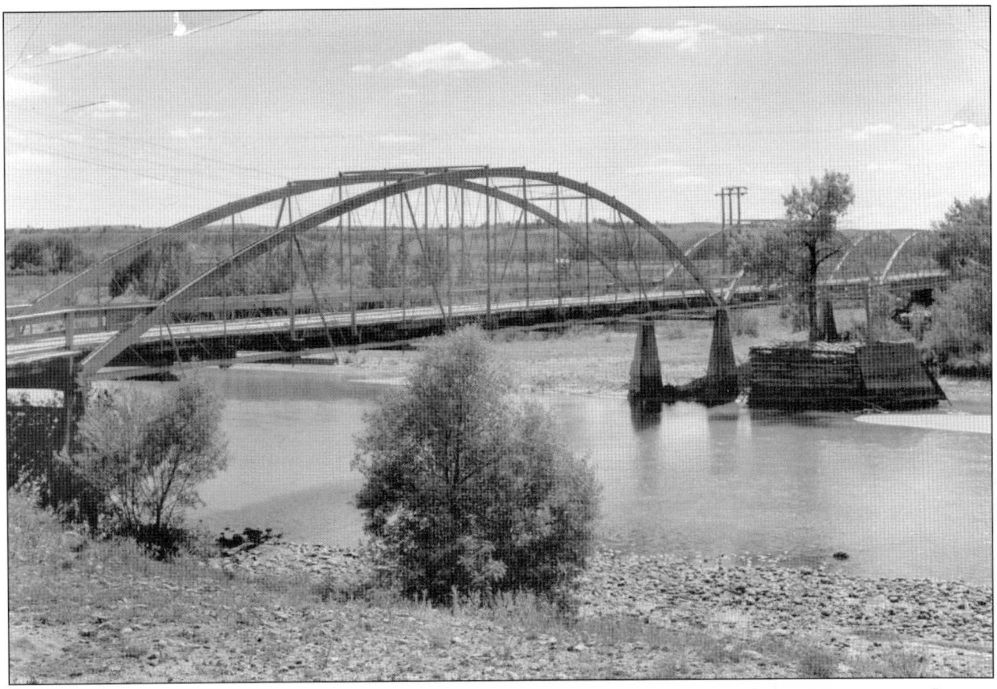

The Fort Laramie military bridge is the oldest existing bridge west of the Mississippi. It was constructed at a cost of $10,500 by King Iron Bridge and Manufacturing of Cleveland, Ohio, between July 1875 and February 1876. William R. Steele asked Secretary of War William W. Belknap for a bill requiring the military to build the bridge, and Pres. Ulysses S. Grant signed it. Originally, freighters and the Deadwood stage used the bridge. It remained in use until 1958 under the maintenance of Goshen County. In 1961, the US Park Service took over maintenance of the bridge. (Homesteaders Museum.)

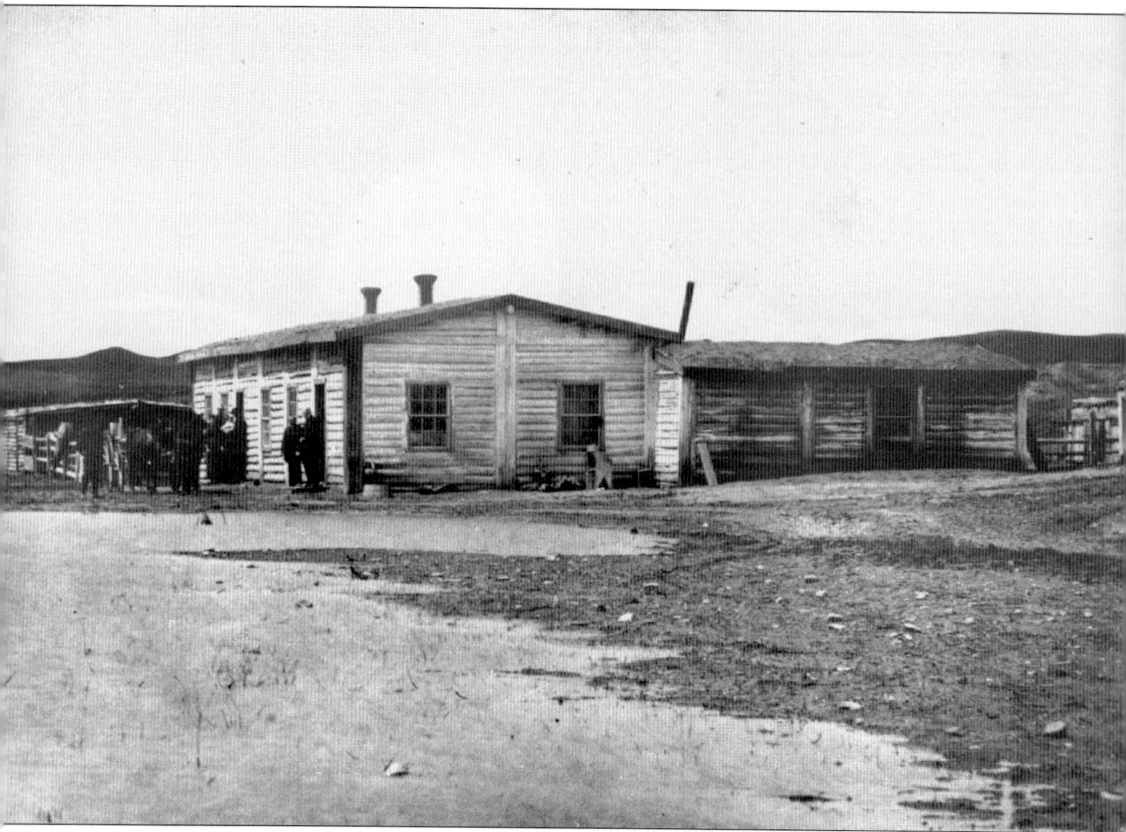

Post trader John S. Collins constructed these buildings in 1876. They were known as the Rustic Hotel, stables, corrals, and stage station. Headquartered at Fort Laramie, they were used on the Cheyenne–Black Hills stage route. They were in use around 1883, but the buildings burned down shortly after the fort was abandoned. (Wyoming State Archives, Department of State Parks and Cultural Resources.)

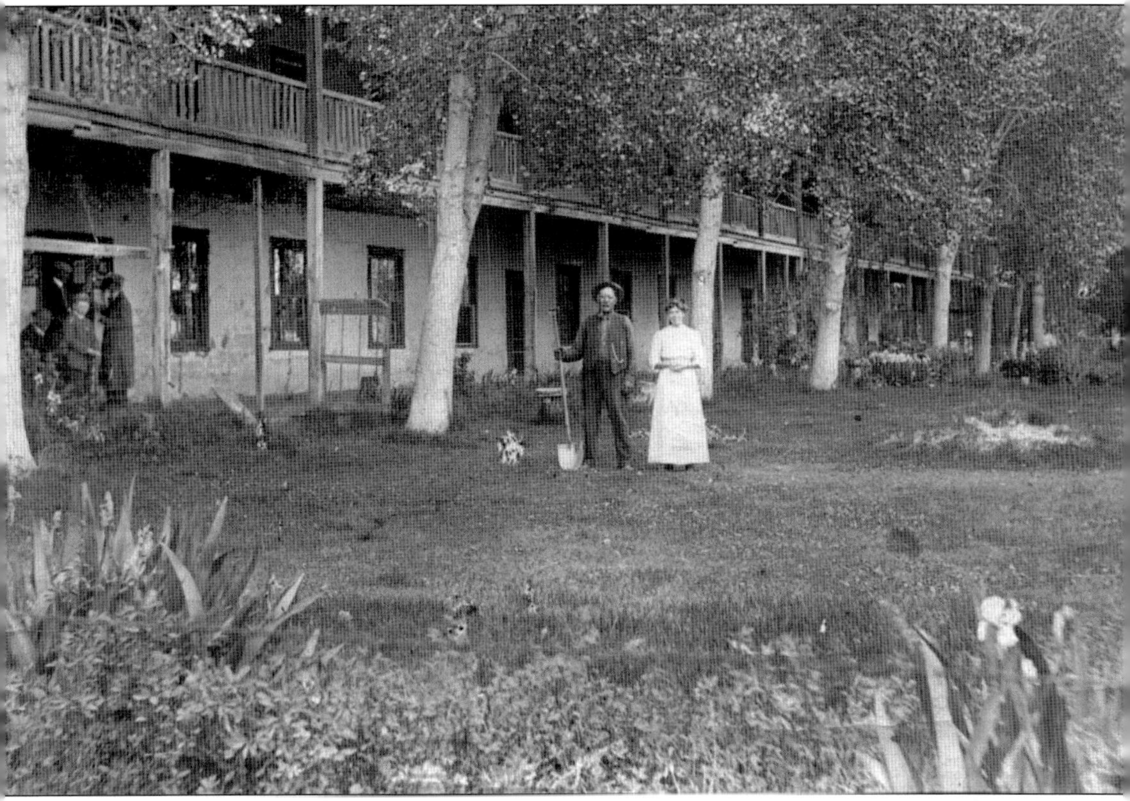

Joe and Mary Wilde, pictured here, purchased the cavalry barracks at Fort Laramie for $50 at the 1890 government auction. Completed in late 1874, it was the largest building at the fort, designed to provide quarters and other needed support facilities for two companies of soldiers. The veranda was not added until 1883. The entire second floor consisted of two large rooms, each room housing about 60 soldiers. The Wildes turned it into a store after acquiring a stockpile of goods from John Hunton and added a shoe shop, a 12-room hotel, a saloon, and a dance hall. Joe was a former freighter and quartermaster employee at the fort. The building became a social center for area ranchers and farmers. (Homesteaders Museum.)

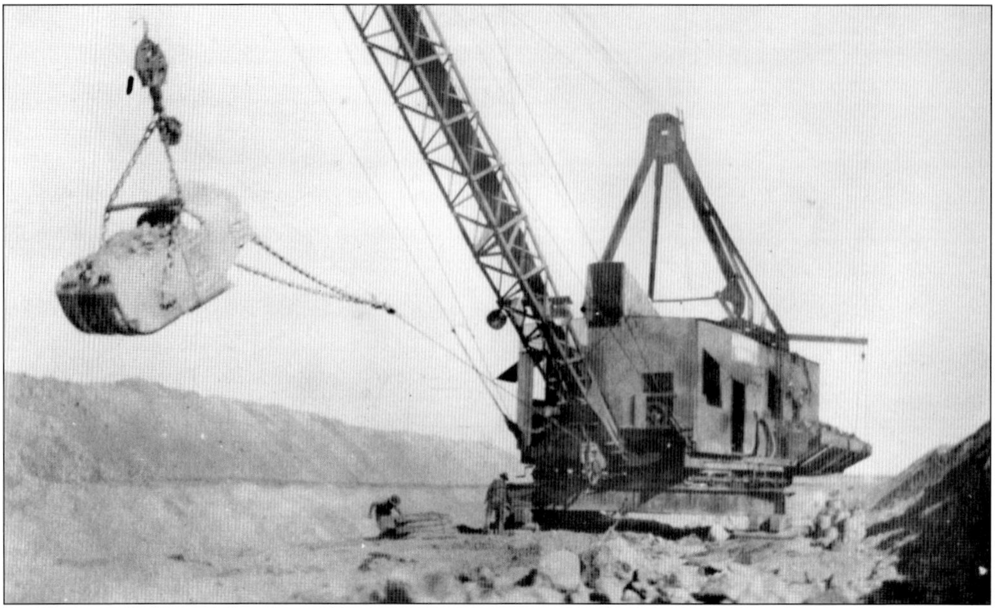

Two major irrigation ditches diverted water from the North Platte River across Goshen County. One canal runs north of the river, and one runs on the south. In 1918, this dragline was at the deepest cut of the Southside Canal, or the Fort Laramie Canal. This canal was the second one to be constructed, but it was delayed by World War I and its projected cost. Work was started after 1915 and was not completed until 1923. (Homesteaders Museum.)

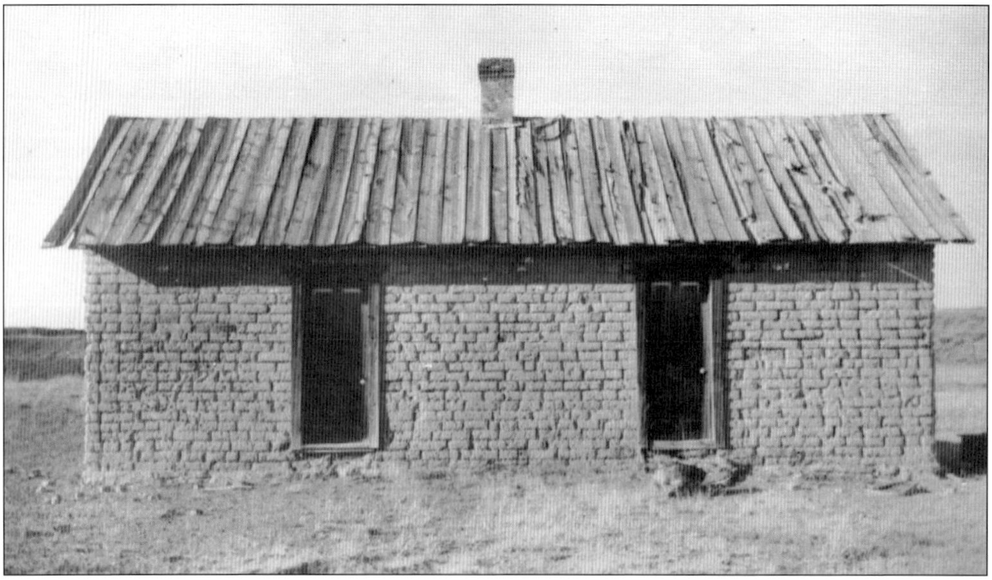

This adobe house is located right across the road from the entrance to the Fort Laramie National Historic Site. The house, which was owned by John and Blanche Hunton, had separate apartments with separate front doors—to be used as necessary when they were feuding. The exterior of the structure has since been stuccoed. Hunton was a fixture at the fort, having first arrived in 1867. He was a bullwhacker on freight trains, served as a clerk at the Sutler's Store, supplied the Army with wood, beef, and hay, and was the last post trader. He lived in the Burt House, which he purchased. (Homesteaders Museum.)

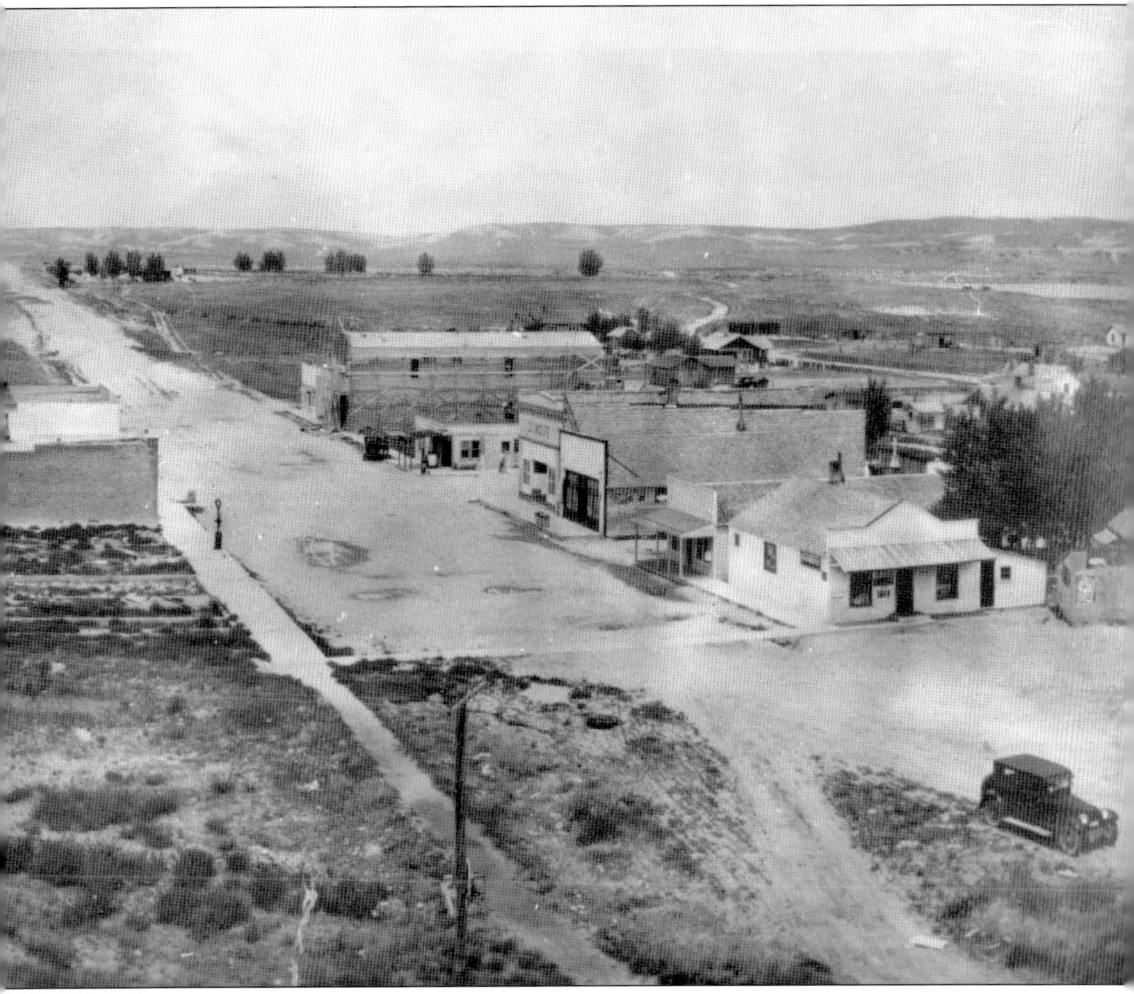

In the mid-1920s, the main street of Fort Laramie had several businesses, including the J.C. Wolfe General Mercantile Store, a butcher shop, the train depot, post office, Foote's Grocery Store, the Fort Laramie Saloon, and the Fort Laramie Hotel. The school was also located on the main street at that time. (Homesteaders Museum.)

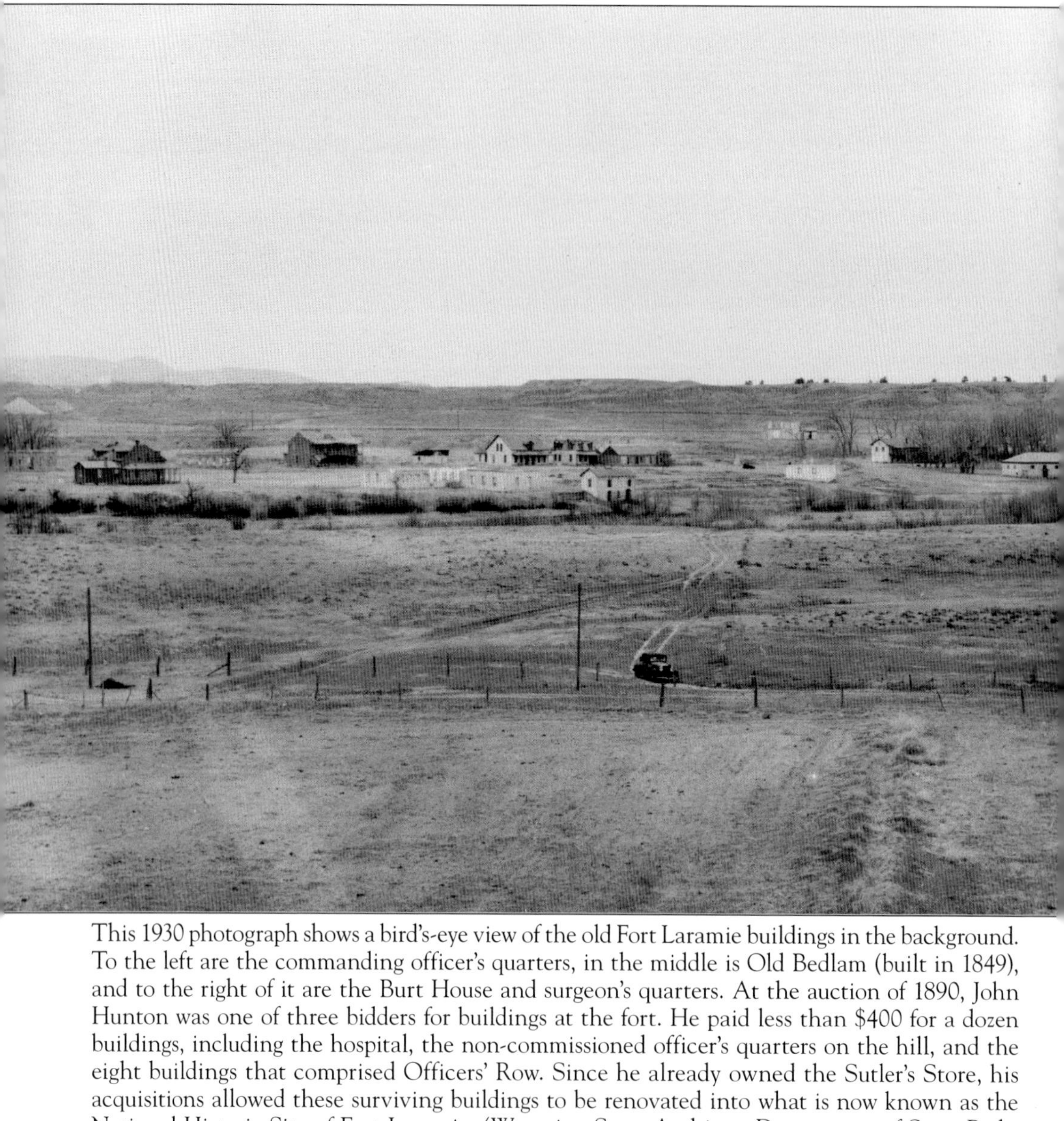

This 1930 photograph shows a bird's-eye view of the old Fort Laramie buildings in the background. To the left are the commanding officer's quarters, in the middle is Old Bedlam (built in 1849), and to the right of it are the Burt House and surgeon's quarters. At the auction of 1890, John Hunton was one of three bidders for buildings at the fort. He paid less than $400 for a dozen buildings, including the hospital, the non-commissioned officer's quarters on the hill, and the eight buildings that comprised Officers' Row. Since he already owned the Sutler's Store, his acquisitions allowed these surviving buildings to be renovated into what is now known as the National Historic Site of Fort Laramie. (Wyoming State Archives, Department of State Parks and Cultural Resources.)

Two

Bear Creek and LaGrange

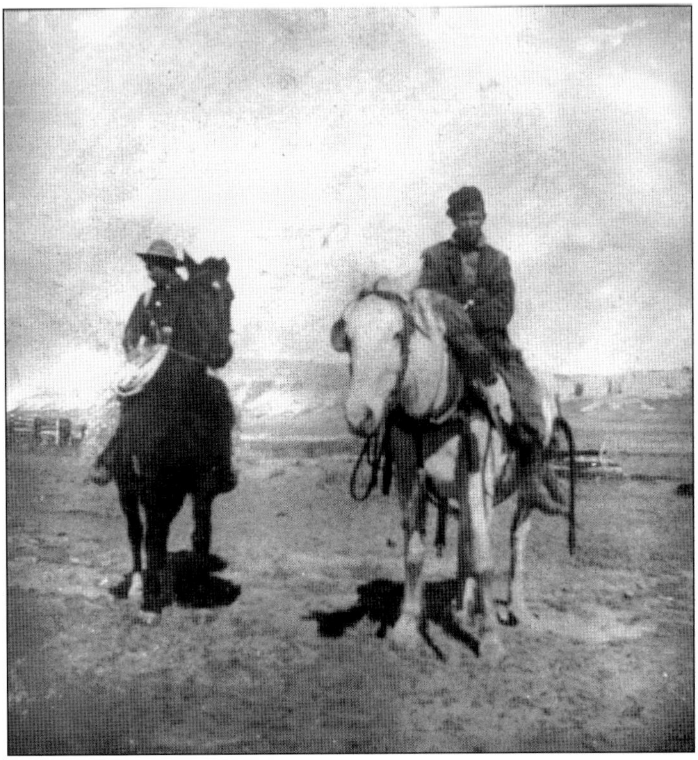

Otis N. Lovercheck and Arye Chamberlain were early homesteaders in the Bear Creek and LaGrange area. Lovercheck homesteaded the C.P. Ranch in 1904, having migrated there from southeast Nebraska. He married Nancy Gill, and they became the parents of four boys and two girls. He served as a Goshen County commissioner and was killed in a gas explosion on the ranch. He was the great-grandfather of Ron Lovercheck. Chamberlain was the great-uncle of Doug Chamberlain, a local realtor. (Homesteaders Museum.)

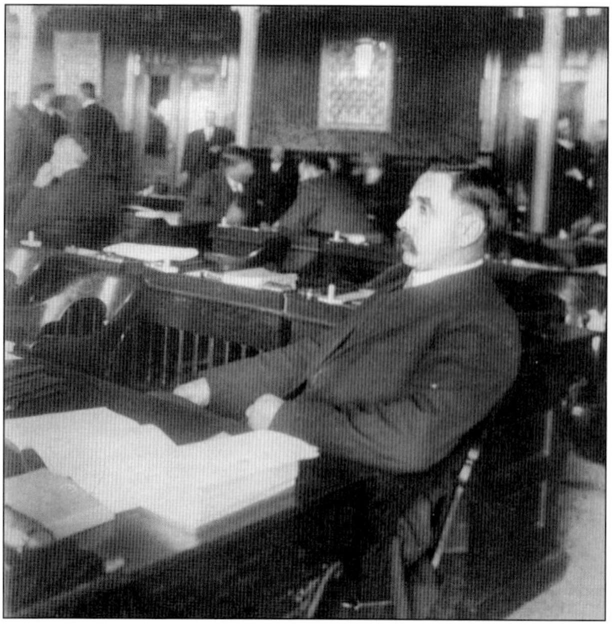

Frank "B.F." Yoder was Goshen County's first representative in the state legislature. He served two terms before he resigned to become the mayor of Torrington. He was the son of Phillip J. Yoder. His son, Oscar T., also served in the Wyoming Legislature from 1955 until 1966—six years as a representative and four years as a senator. (Oscar Yoder Collection, Homesteaders Museum.)

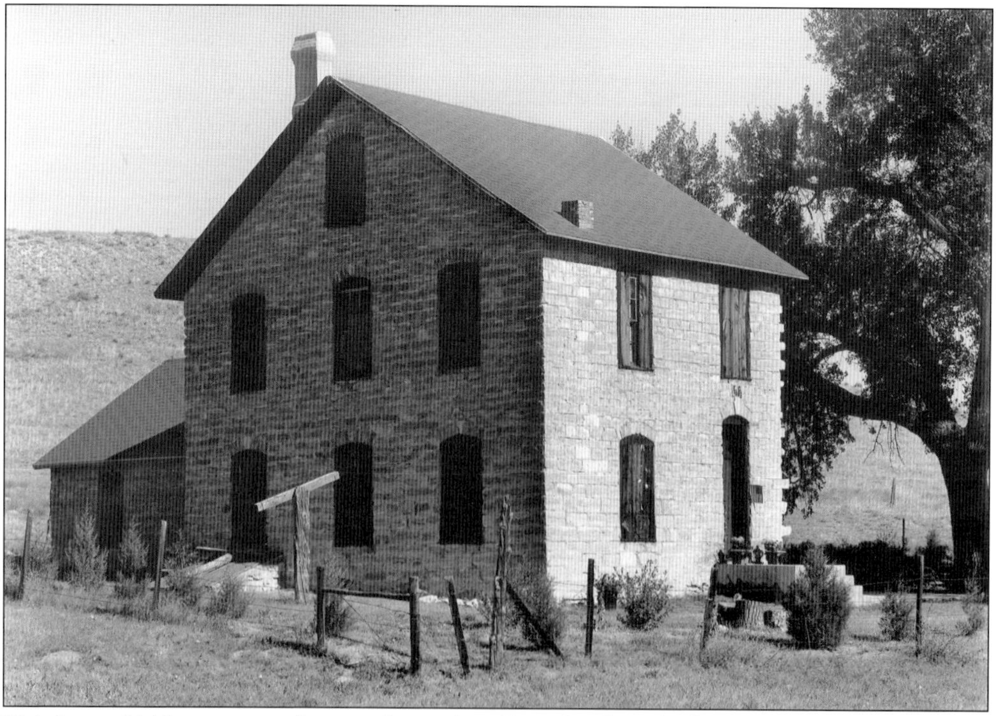

This large old 11-room stone house is located on Bear Creek and is known as the Griffin House. It was built in 1882 by Eric Gardner, an Englishman. The blocks for the house were cut from sandstone cliffs south of the ranch. The staircase was imported from England. Each room was equipped with stovepipe outlets for heat. M.B. "Mark" Bouton, who started the VB cattle brand, originally owned the land on which the house sits. James Harvey Griffin and his brother Curt purchased the ranch in 1890. Their cattle brands were BU-, BU, and VB. The house is currently owned by Dudley Haines of Torrington. (Dudley Haines.)

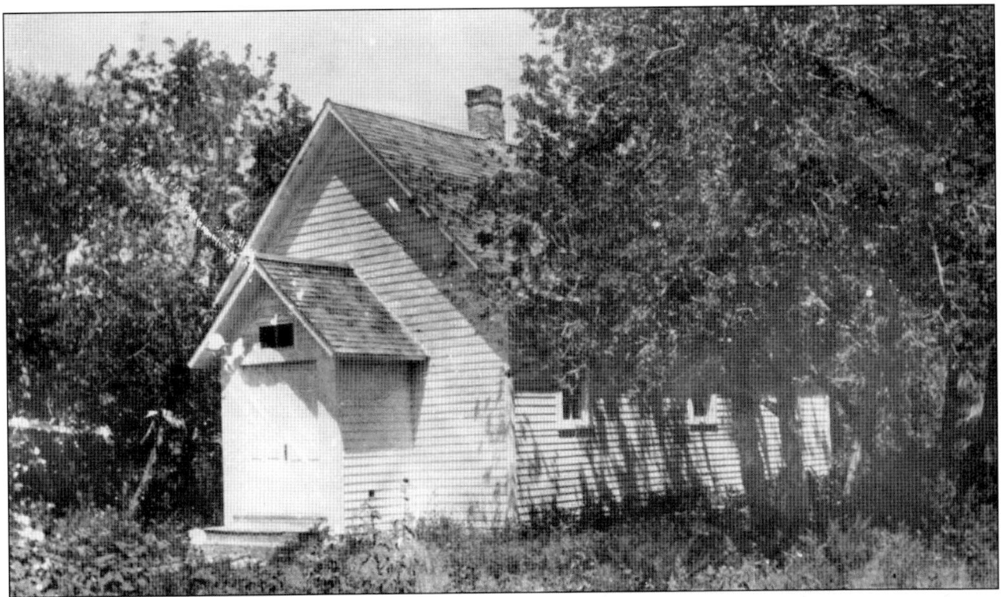

A minister named E.P. Hughes initiated this Bear Creek church, which was built in 1897. For $2.90, the articles of incorporation of the Methodist Episcopal church were recorded in Cheyenne on October 19, 1897. Material for the building came from Chugwater. The church held intermittent services but was also a community house for social occasions and local talent programs. Early on, a group of women formed the Ladies Aid Society. In the 1950s, the name changed to the Women's Club, whose mission over the years has been to help people in the neighborhood as well as to reach out to needs of others around the world. (Homesteaders Museum.)

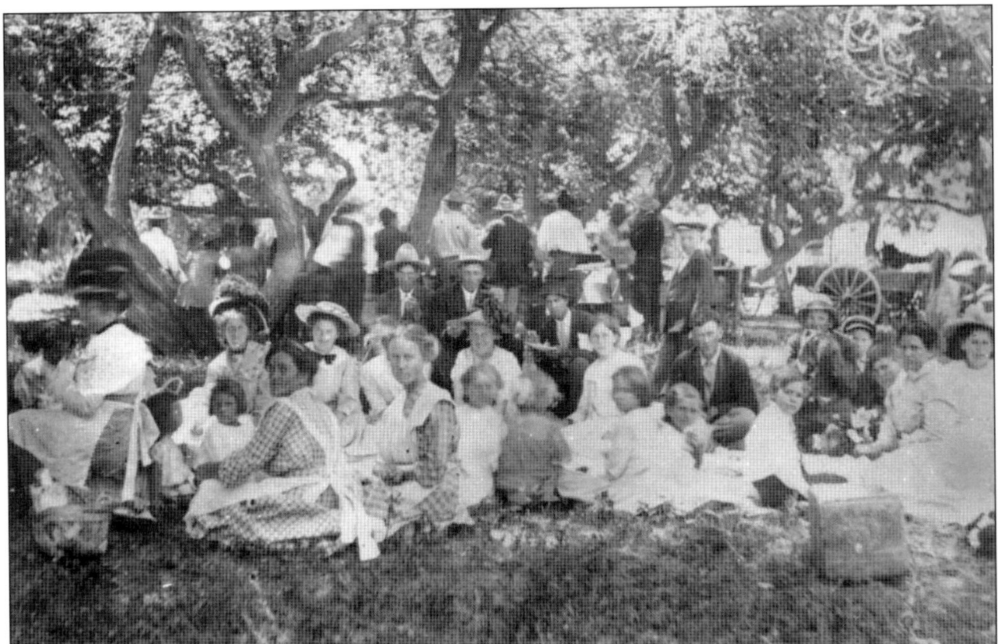

Picnics were very popular in the early days as a way for neighbors and friends to get together. This Iowa Center group celebrated July 4, 1911, by picnicking at the home of Frank Yoder. (Homesteaders Museum.)

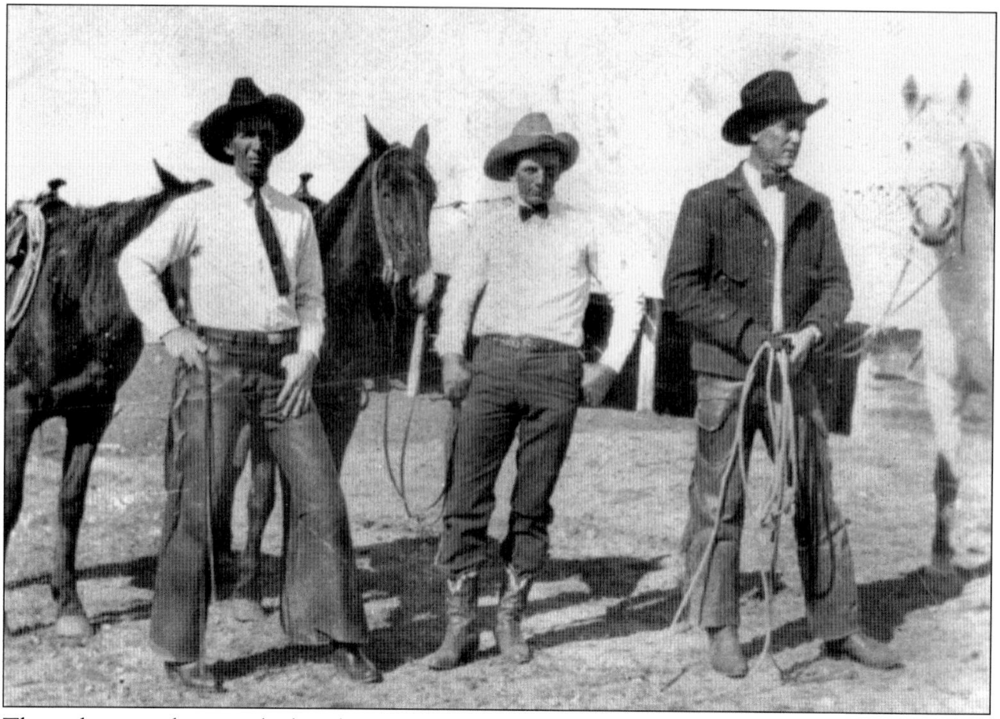

These three cowboys worked in the Bear Creek area and were part of the Griffin brothers' outfit. Notice the differences in their hats and ties. (Homesteaders Museum.)

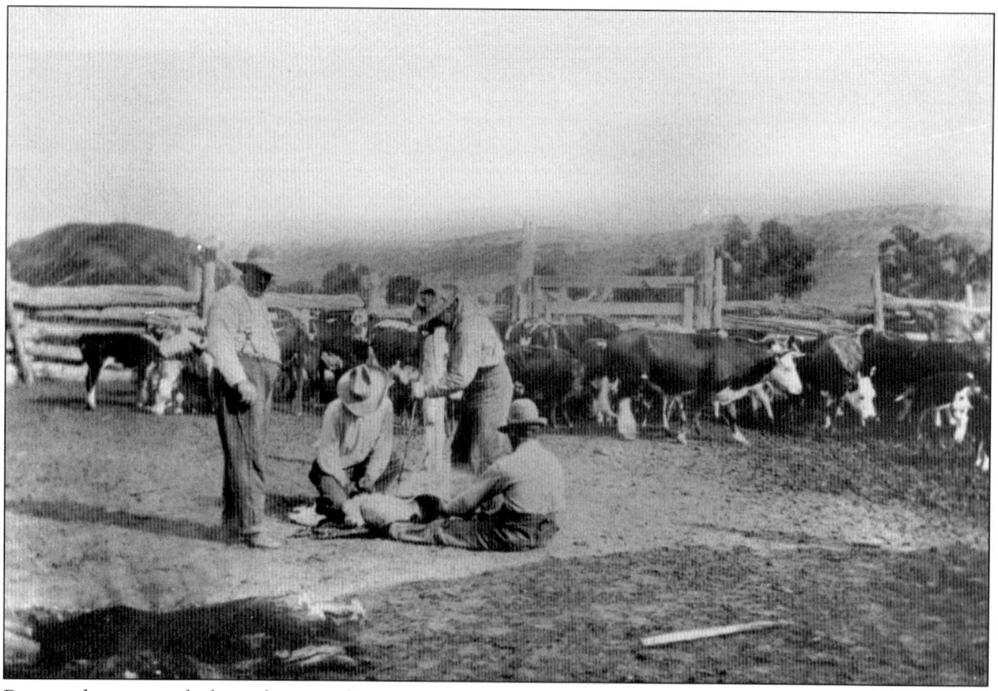

Pictured is an early branding at the Griffin brothers' VB Ranch. Curt is supervising while Jim handles the branding iron. The VB cattle brand originally belonged to its former owner, M.B. "Mark" Bouton, whose wife, Virginia, gave her initials to the ranch's name. (Homesteaders Museum.)

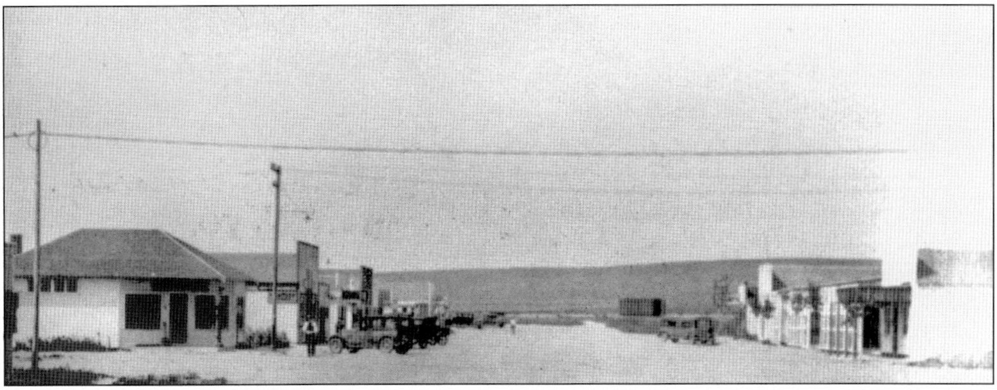

Pictured in 1930 is the west side of Main Street in LaGrange. (Cletis Arnold Collection, Homesteaders Museum.)

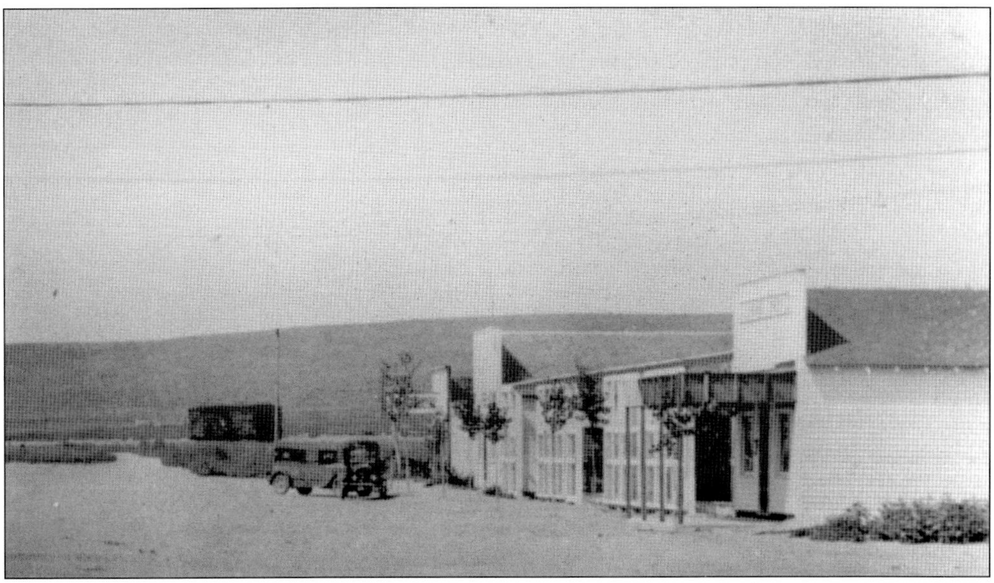

This c. 1930 photograph shows the east side of Main Street. (Homesteaders Museum.)

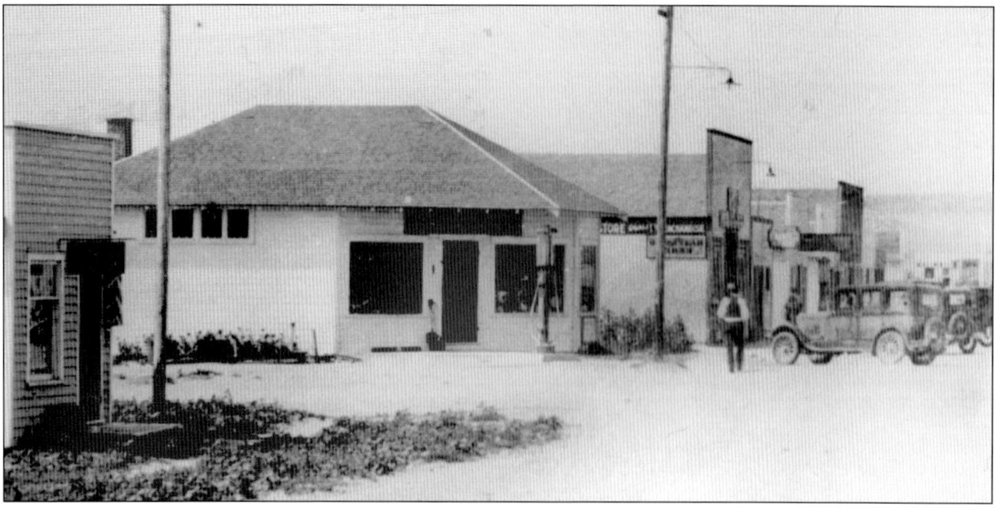

Pete Carlstrum and Bill Harrison of Pine Bluffs built the filling station on Main Street when the railroad came through. They sold it to Dan Donahue, who then sold it to K.G. Tremain. George Wendt bought it on January 17, 1936. Wendt delivered gas and diesel and also sold Conoco products and International/Case machinery. He sold out in the mid-1960s, and his son Glen had an appliance dealership in the building. It later housed the LaGrange library and the city hall. (Cletis Arnold Collection, Homesteaders Museum.)

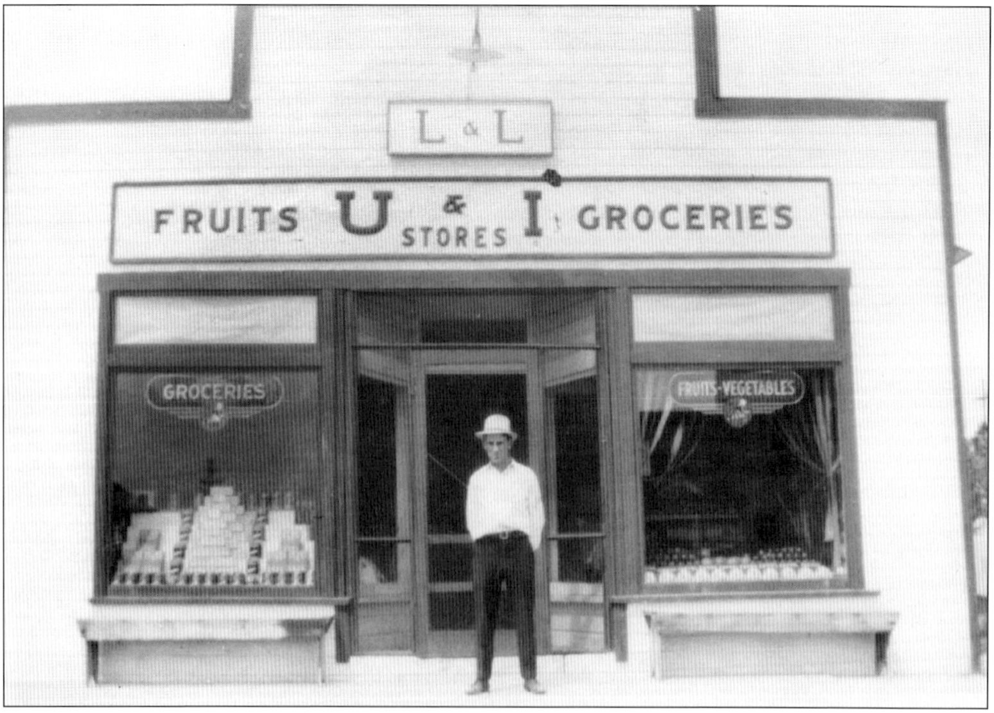

Lloyd Craton is pictured standing in front of this grocery store that he and his wife, Lila, operated during the 1930s. The top sign, which reads "L&L," stood for their first names. They had purchased the building from its original owner, John Zurbreigen. At least six other owners have operated some type of store in the building since then. The U&I Store was an earlier company name. (Homesteaders Museum.)

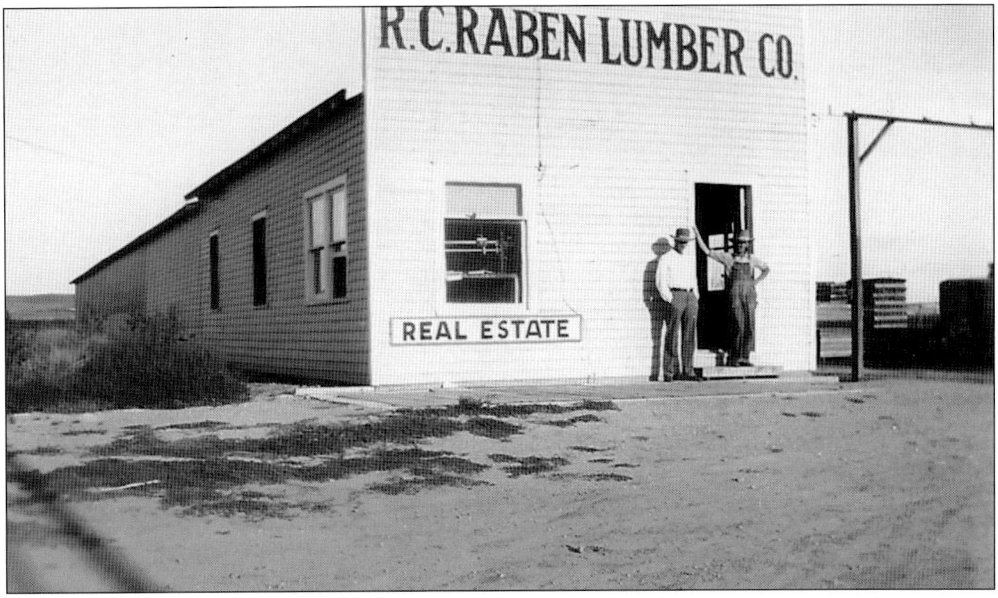

When the Union Pacific Railroad extended its line toward LaGrange, Roy Raben and his boyhood friend Earl "Monty" Montgomery started a lumberyard. This photograph shows Wells Raben and Montgomery in front of the lumberyard building, which also sold real estate. Raben opened another lumberyard in the 1930s in Gering, Nebraska, which Montgomery managed. They also had yards in Huntley, Veteran, and Yoder. Eventually, they changed the name to R&M Lumber and opened a yard in Torrington. (Margie Raben Jones.)

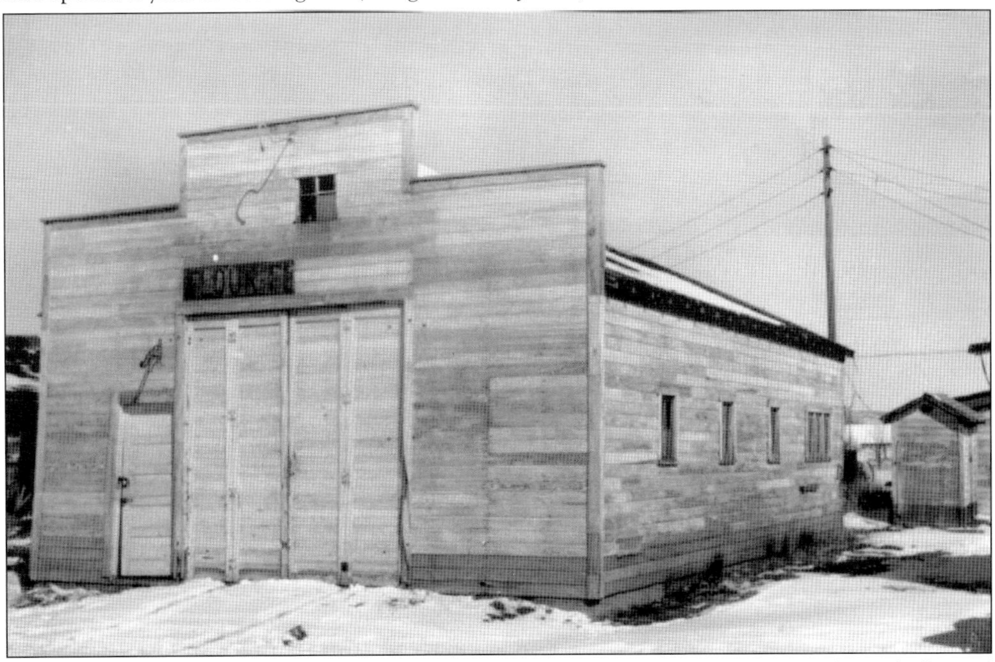

This building has been used as both a business and a residence. It was used as a dance hall, pool hall, and movie house in the early days. Floyd Sanders owned it around 1929, when it was used as a garage. Beginning in the late 1940s, Ruth and Bud Talbert lived in the building. It is now owned by the Frontier School of the Bible and is used for its offices. (Homesteaders Museum.)

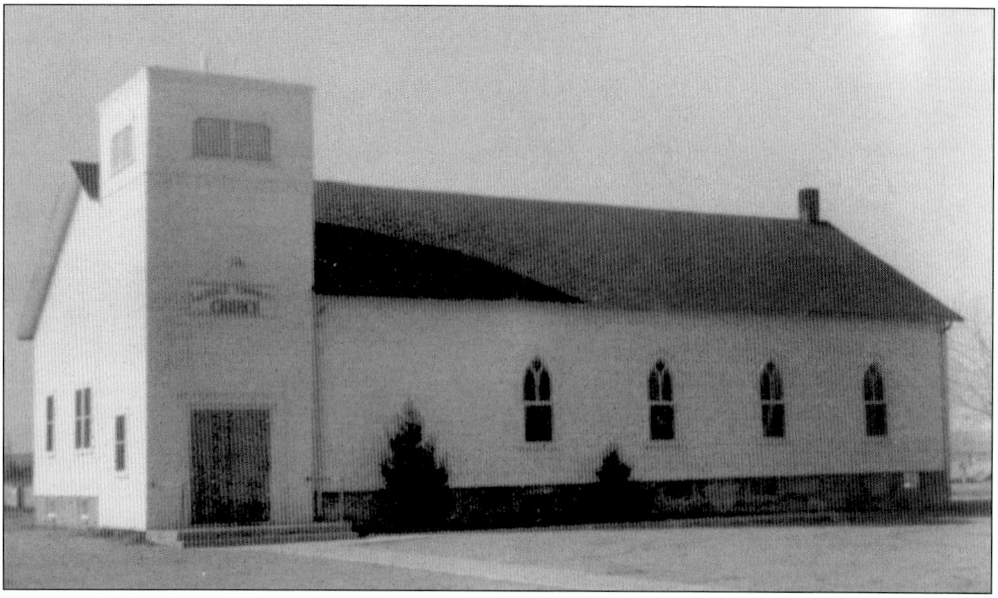

Construction began in 1919 for a building that would serve as a church and community center. Community members received a loan from the Presbyterian Church and locals gave money and provided labor to build the first edifice. The one room was over a basement. Articles of incorporation for the LaGrange Community Church were filed on September 27, 1921. In 1953, an addition was built and the basement was finished. At one time, there were around 200 members. There have been at least 21 pastors to serve over the years. (Homesteaders Museum.)

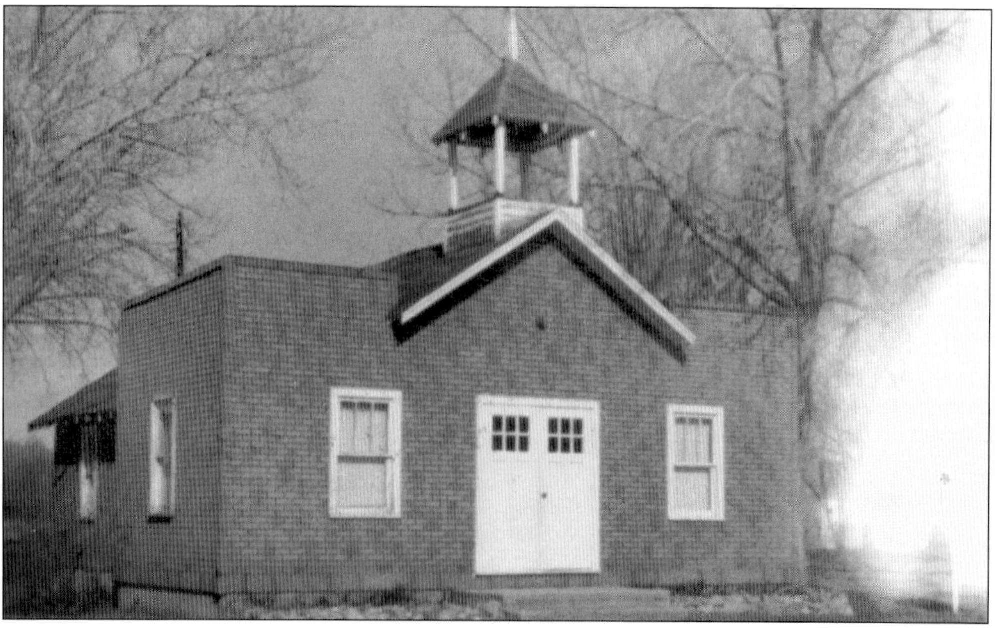

In 1928, the Reverend Glen A. Porterfield began the church that eventually became the LaGrange Holiness Chapel. Meetings were held in the high school. Rev. M.L. Hegwood saw the need for a church home, so he helped built the Little Log Church. In 1943, Rev. R.G. Hamilton remodeled and enlarged the building. Another remodel occurred when Rev. Philip Kline was the pastor from 1975 until 1979. (Homesteaders Museum.)

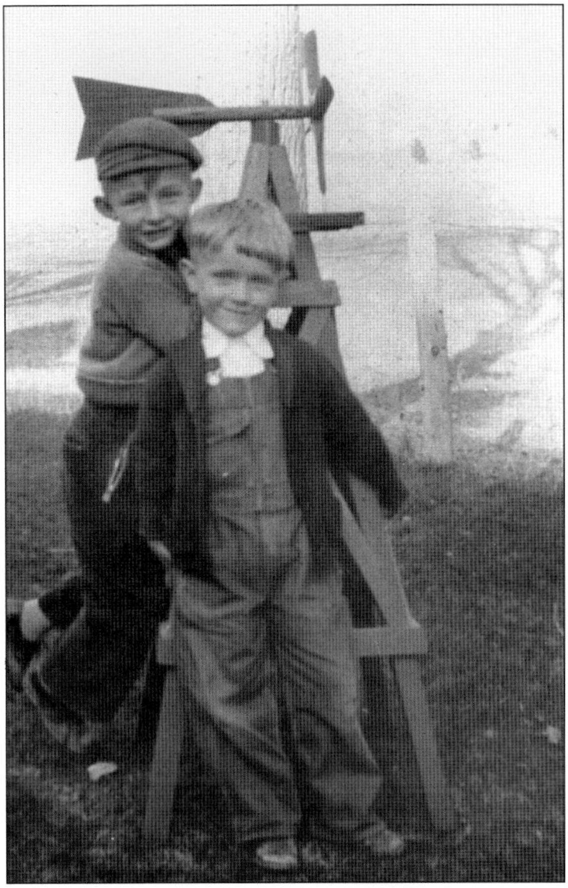

This 1937 photograph is of Bob Finch (left) and Donald Yoder, who were best friends and often played together. Their mothers, who were both teachers, and families often socialized. Bob Finch was the son of Walter and June Finch and owned a civil engineering firm in Denver, Colorado. Donald Yoder was the son of Oscar and Vivian Yoder and was an electrical engineer working in Wilmington, North Carolina. Both men are now deceased. (Oscar Yoder Collection, Homesteaders Museum.)

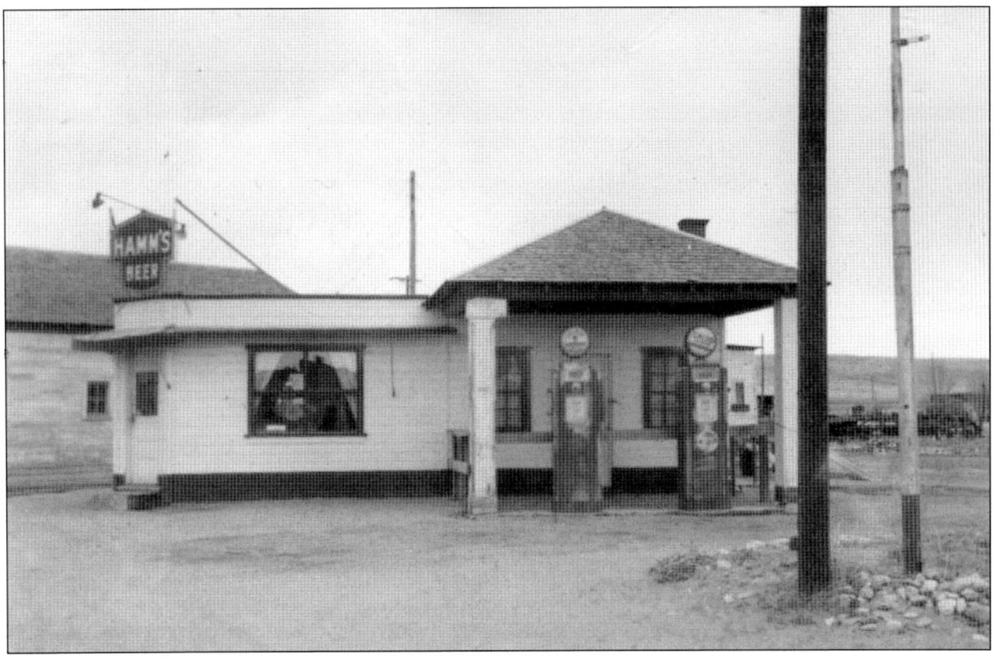

Carl Sawyer owned this early LaGrange gas station with products provided by Standard Oil. At one time, Cletis Arnold also had a barbershop in part of it. A section of the building has been moved to another site. (Homesteaders Museum.)

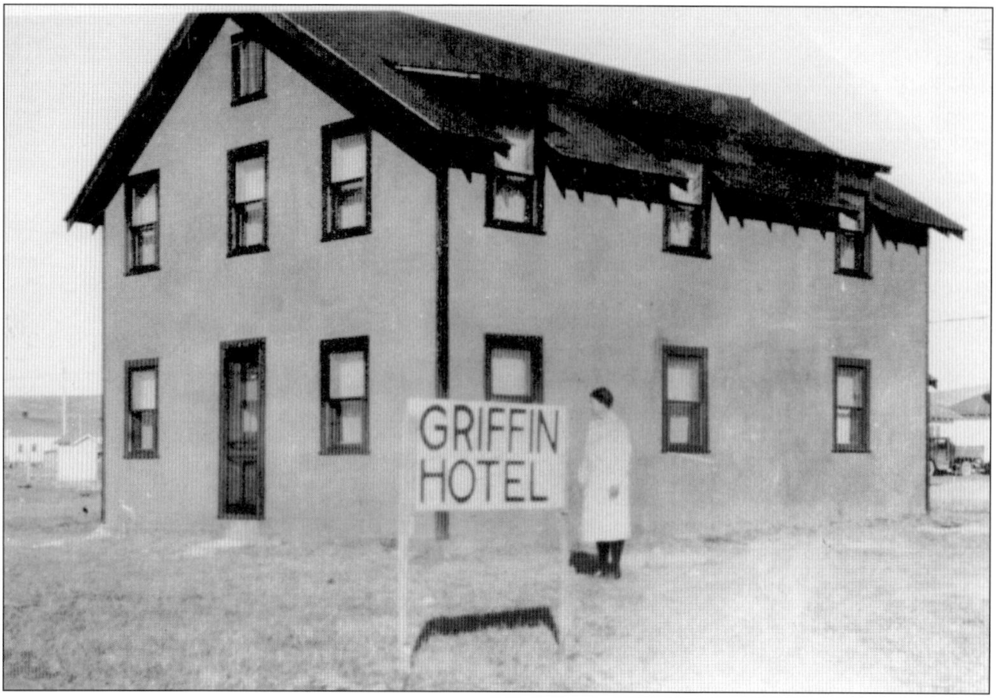

Olive Johnson Rodeman bought this hotel in 1948 and operated it for 14 years. In 1962, she sold it to her daughter Audry, but she bought it back five years later. She sold it again to Harvey Thomas. (Homesteaders Museum.)

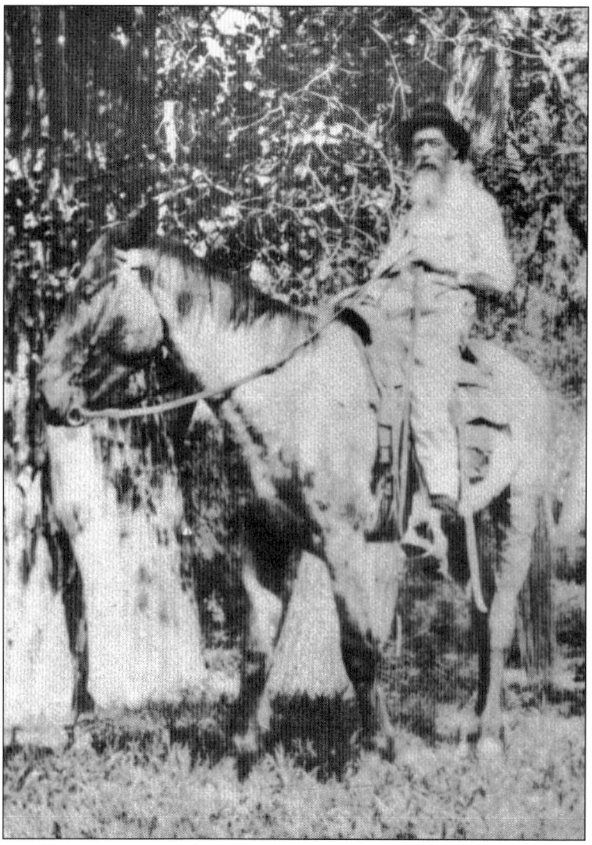

L.L. "Military Jack" Fulton, pictured here in 1900, was an early pioneer in Goshen County. He established a ranch along the breaks of southwest Yoder, where he allowed his Kentucky Thoroughbred horses to run wild on the pastures. He became obsessed with the idea that some military man had driven off the herd, so he began hunting for him. On January 17, 1929, Military Jack appeared before Judge F.E. Johnston on a sanity charge and was sentenced to the state institution in Lander. The complaint said that he was too insane and unruly and needed to be confined. He had been at the county farm when this occurred. (Homesteaders Museum.)

Three

Hawk Springs

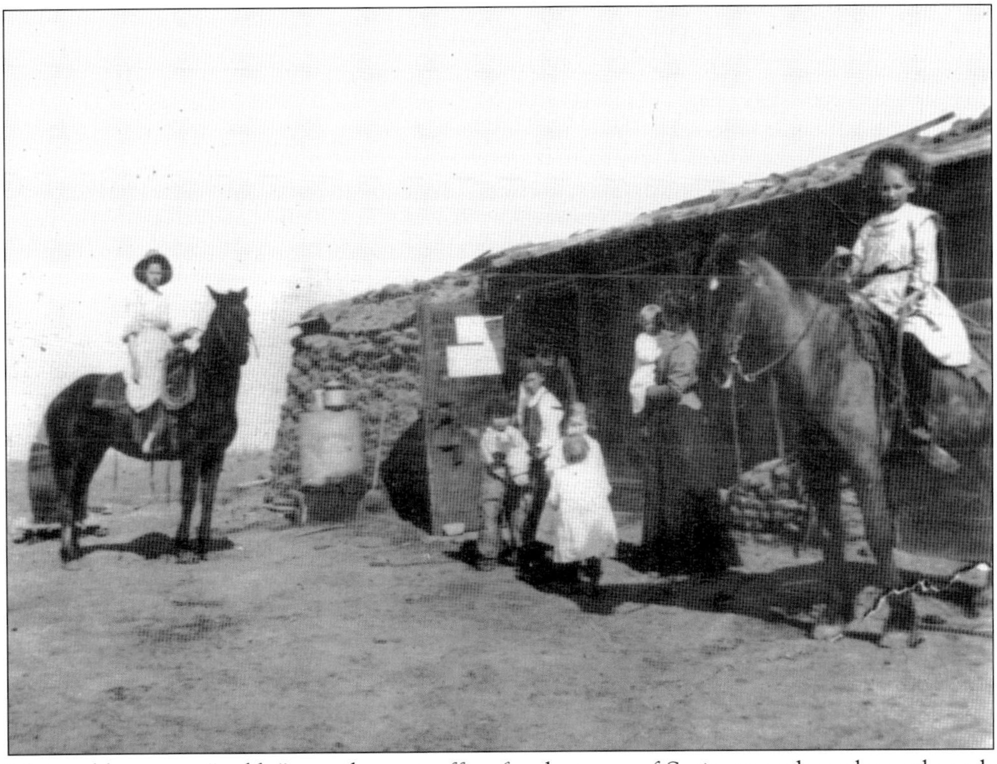

This sod house, or "soddy," was the post office for the town of Springer and was located north of the Springer Reservoir. It was an overnight stop for travelers. Blanche Smith, later Blanche Hughes, is shown on the horse on the left. The children in front of the door include Drum Smith, Mack Smith, and two Fields sisters. Waldon Smith stands in the doorway. To the right of the children are Lizzie Smith, later Lizzie Hewitt, and her daughter Mary. Helen Smith, later Helen Marlatt, is on the horse on the right. (Waldon Smith.)

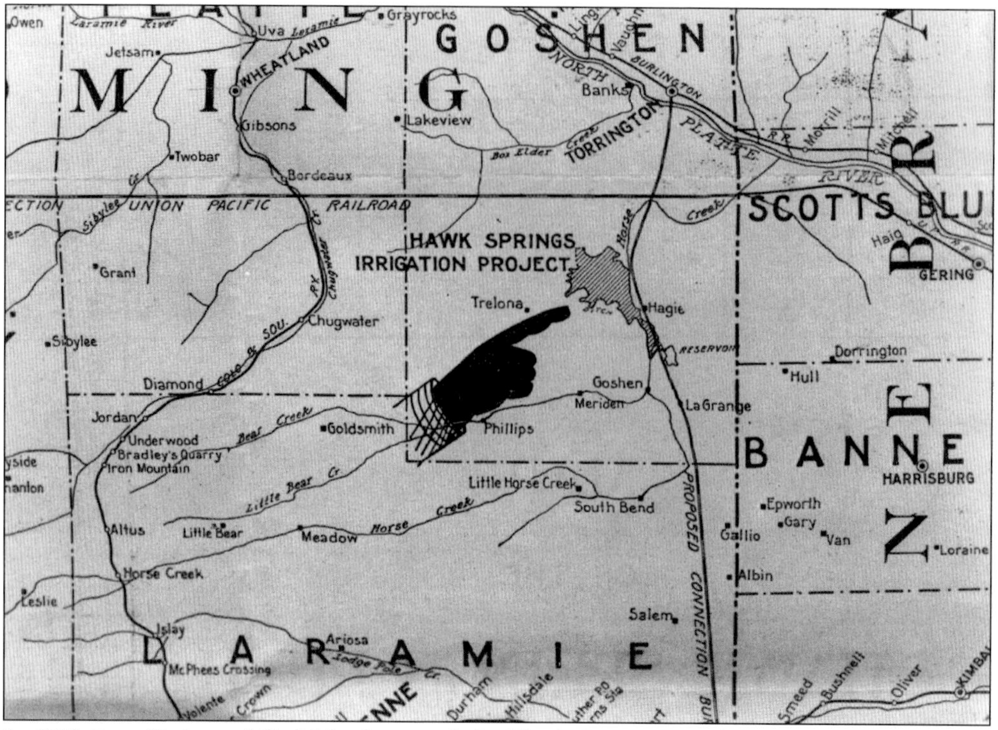

In 1910, Jesse Yoder and Earl Marsh started the Hawk Springs Development Company, which later became the Horse Creek Conservation Development. The purpose of the company was to irrigate the farmlands to the north and northwest. The photograph below was part of the Hawk Springs irrigation promotional booklet, printed in 1917. This irrigation system was started in 1903. The map, which was also part of the booklet, shows the location of the spring-fed reservoir that would feed the irrigation system. (Both, Homesteaders Museum.)

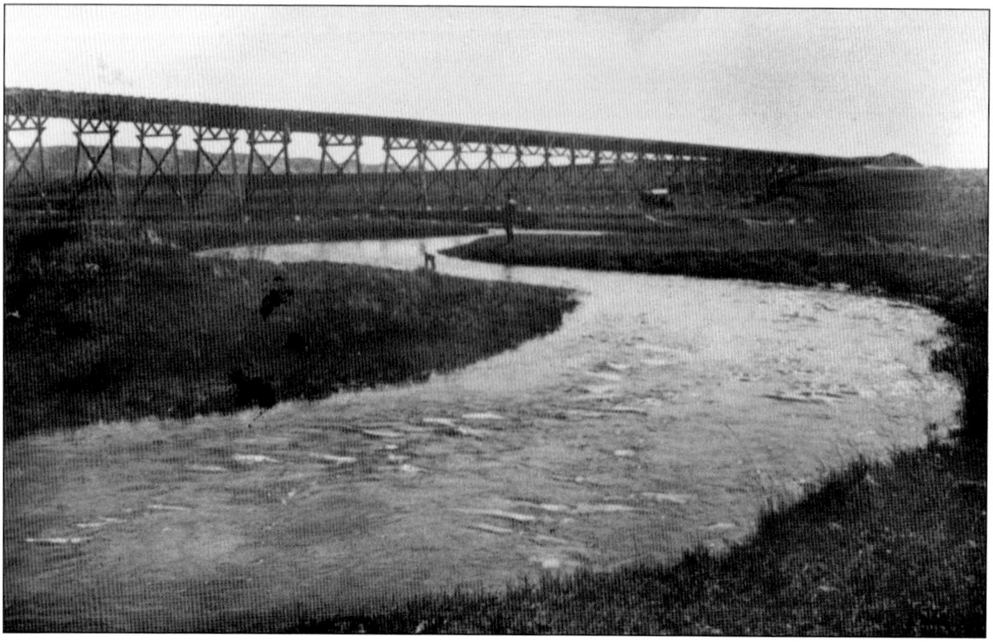

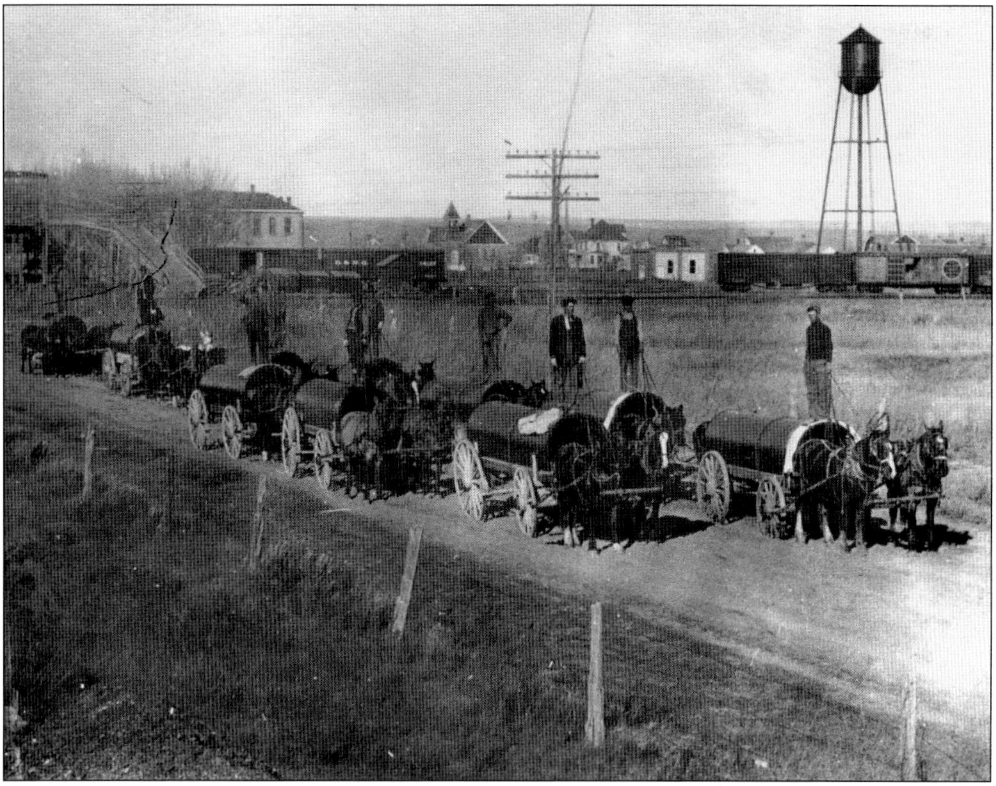

Approximately 10 wagons were loaded in Mitchell, Nebraska, to haul pipe sections for the Hawk Springs Reservoir dam in October 1914. Each pipe section was 12 feet long, 3 feet high, and weighed 4,800 pounds. (Homesteaders Museum.)

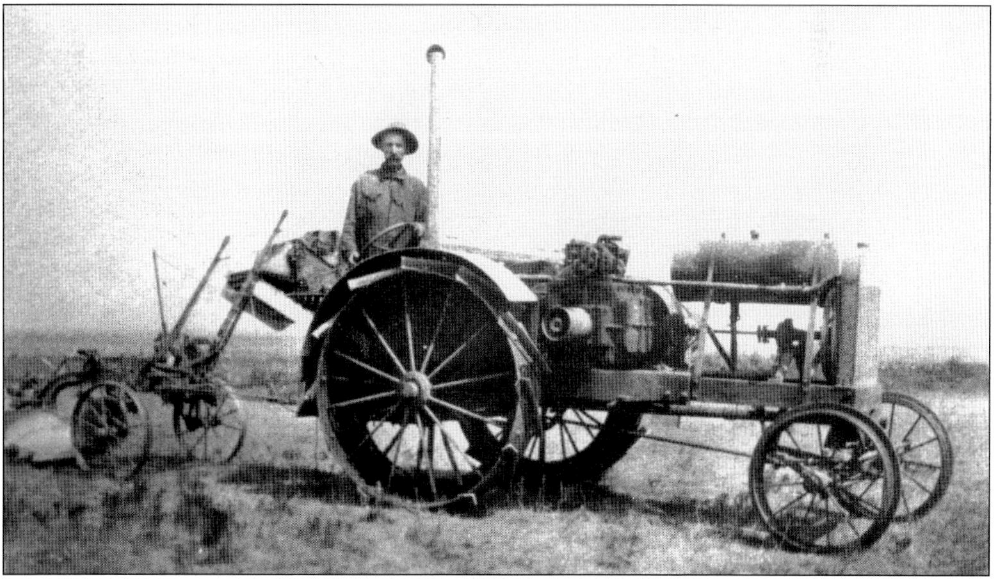

Ed Schwab is pictured around 1930 on this early—possibly Farmall—tractor, which was the first one in Hawk Springs. Schwab and his wife, Mary, lived a half-mile north of Hawk Springs and raised beets, hay, cattle, hogs, and chickens. (Wilbur Shannon Collection, Homesteaders Museum.)

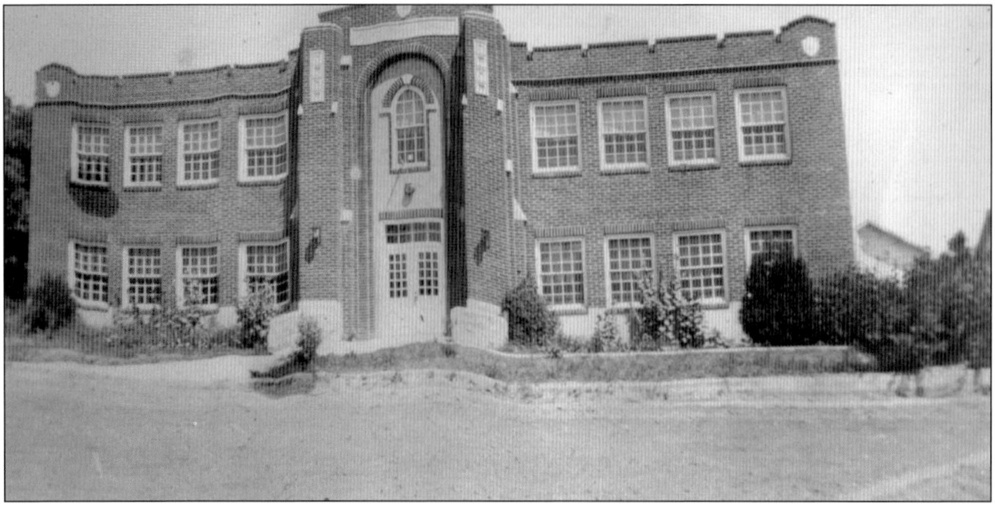

The first school in the Hawk Springs area was the Hagie School, which was used from 1916 until 1917. The second school was the Cooper School for up to grade 10, and it was used from 1917 until 1927. The two-story redbrick Hawk Springs High School was built in 1928 and included a small gymnasium. The building committee consisted of C.D. Davis, W.G. Vance, and Ed Schwab. An addition in 1951 included a larger gym. The building was last used as a school in 1966. After being abandoned by the consolidation of the school districts in Goshen County, the building was purchased by Lon David, who tore off the front of the building. The next owner, Lamb Construction Company, remodeled the building into a shop and then sold it to Frank Weyrich. The current owner is Doug Howe, who uses it for a shop. (Homesteaders Museum.)

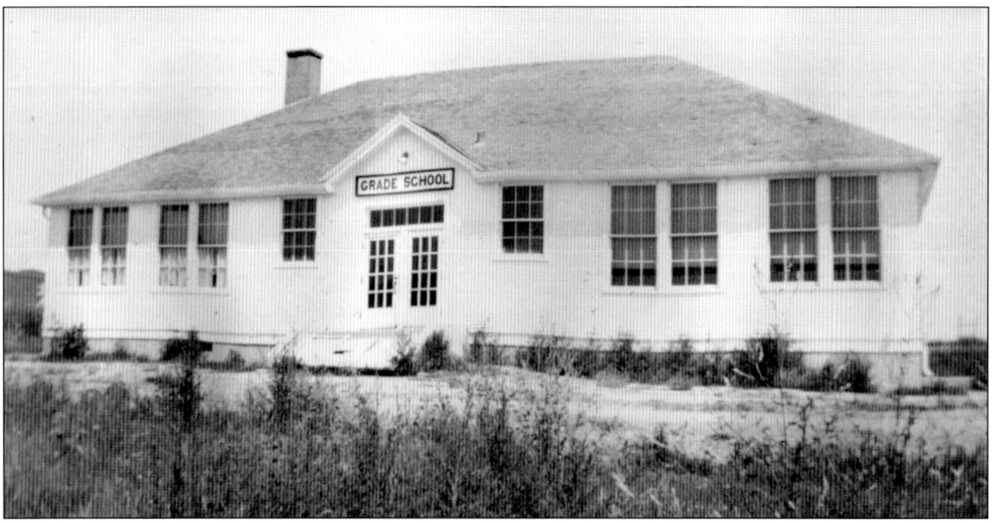

The Hawk Springs Grade School was built in 1939 through funding from the Wyoming New Deal programs. Public schools built under these programs had the advantage of funding as well as expertise from nationally recognized architects. Grades one through six were educated here until 1965, when all the students went to the high school building. When Goshen County School District No. 1 was reorganized, the school was abandoned in 1966 and sold to the Hawk Springs Community. The remodeled building now serves as a community center. (Homesteaders Museum.)

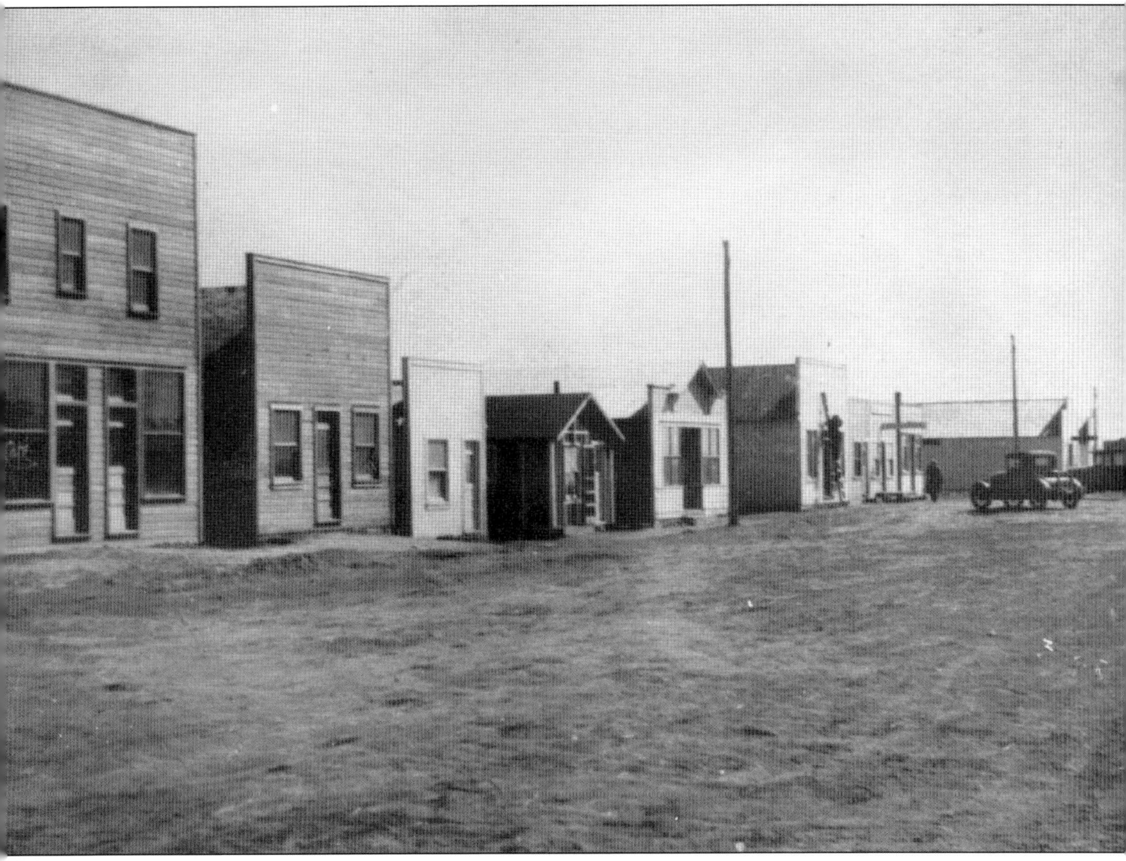

This 1929 photograph of the Hawk Springs Railroad Street includes a portion of the 28 businesses that were established there. From left to right, the first building housed the Hawk Springs Hotel and café, owned by W.L. Worley; the second building was the Hawk Springs Meat Market, owned by P.L. Mapes from 1928 until 1935, and since 1940 it has been home to the post office; the third building was Luana Busskohl's Clothing Store until 1947, when Arnold Hageman opened his soil conservation office there, and he sold it in 1949 to Ruth Hirsch; the fourth building housed the Bartran Café, which was run for a short time by a lady from Lyman, Nebraska; and the Rice-Kilpatrick Drugstore, known as the Nyal Store, was the fifth building. After them, there were the G.P. Blunt Billiard Parlor, Hammerlun Grocery, Raines Café, and Kelly Hardware. (Homesteaders Museum.)

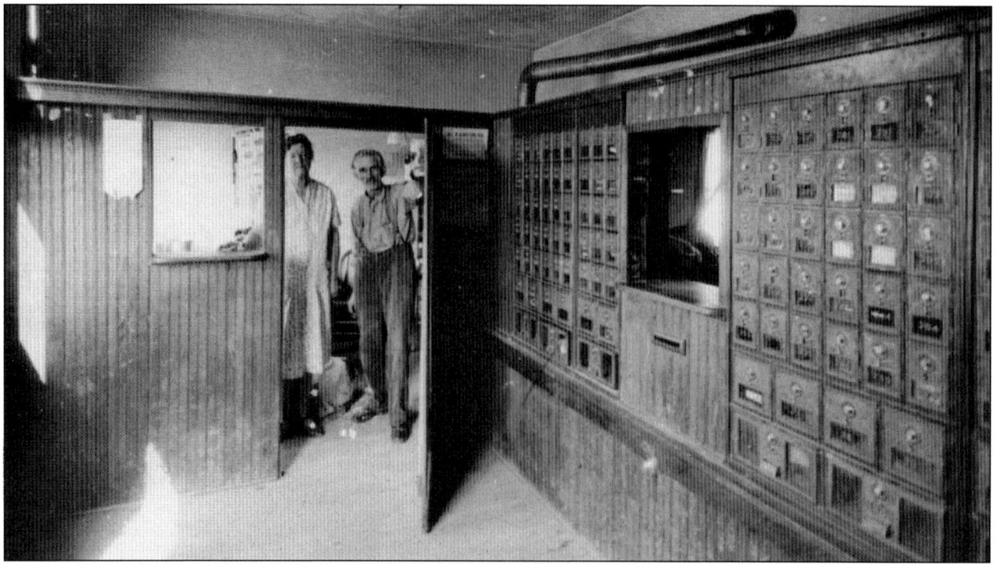

The first post office in the Hawk Springs area was located at the Hagie farm, which was a half-mile from town. It moved to the Vance farm and, finally, the McMillan farm, where it did business in a railroad boxcar. A modern structure was built in 1928; in it, Hattie and George McMillan, pictured here, continued the duties of mail delivery until 1940. The post office was then moved uptown, where it is currently located. (Homesteaders Museum.)

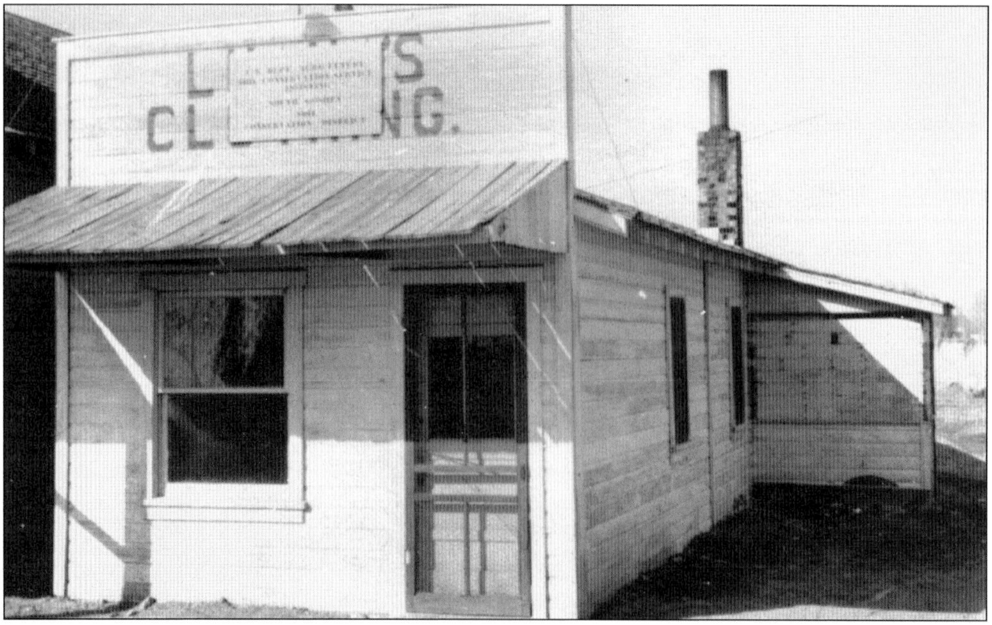

Originally the Bloedorn Lumber Company yard office, this building housed a clothing store and barbershop combination for many years. From 1928 until 1935, Minnie Johnson and her husband, Nick, owned the store, selling ladies and children's clothing and work clothes for men. Nick was the barber. They decided to open a grocery store in the hotel, so they moved out of the building, but the clothing side was taken over by Minnie's sister Luana Busskohl, who stayed until 1940. Arnold Hageman moved his soil conservation business into the building and operated it for many years. (Homesteaders Museum.)

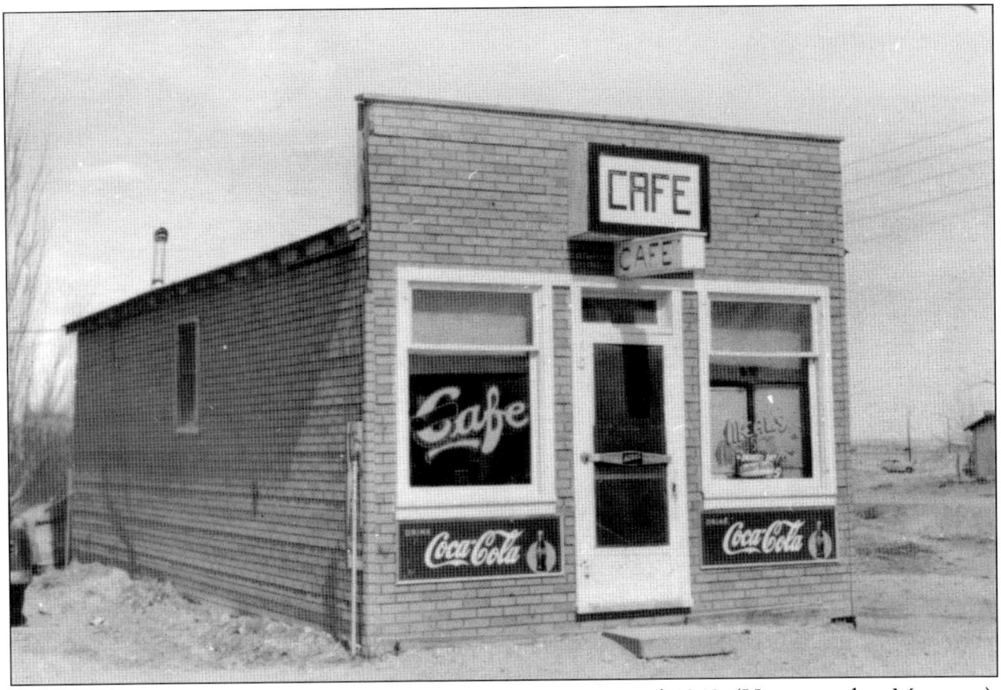

Bill's O-Deal Café was an eating establishment from 1928 until 1949. (Homesteaders Museum.)

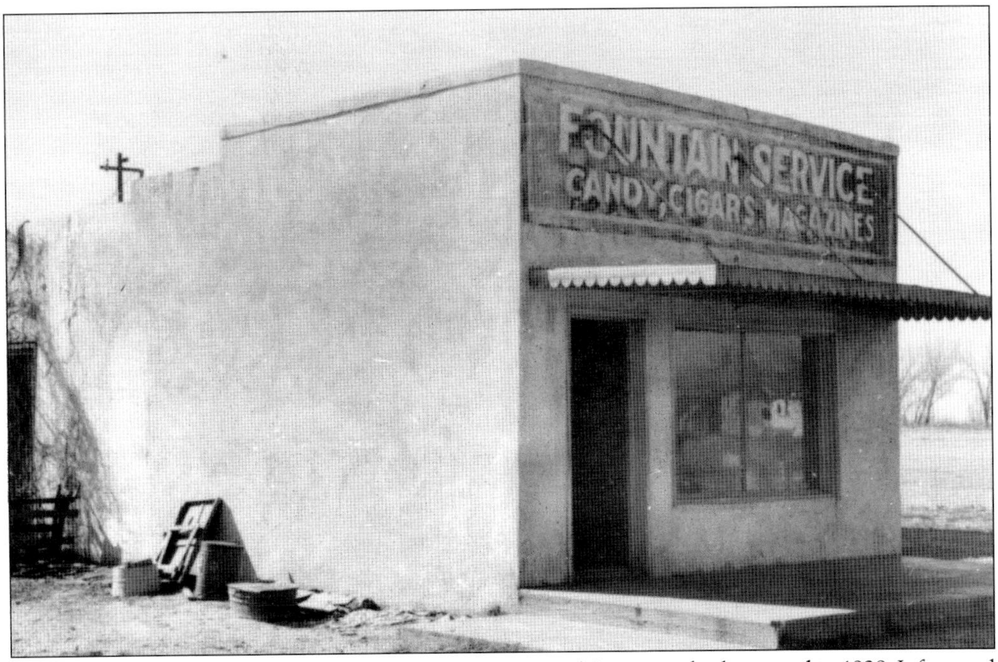

In use for 30 years was the George H. Schwab Fountain and Service, which opened in 1928. It featured a full-service soda fountain where customers often enjoyed ice cream sundaes. The drugstore also had candy, cigars, magazines, drugs, and patent medicines. Over the years, Schwab had collections of apothecary jars, guns, and arrowheads along the walls of his store. (Homesteaders Museum.)

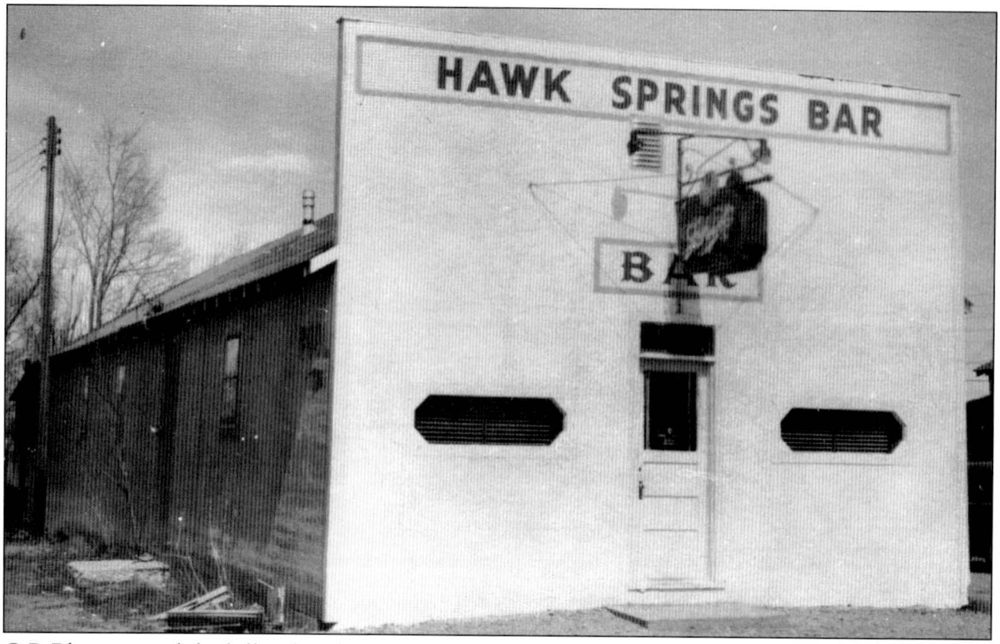

G.P. Blunt owned the billiard parlor in Hawk Springs from 1928 until 1945, when Victor Schlager took over. Earl Hubbs moved Bill's O-Deal Café to the back of the building in 1949 and ran the business for two years. From 1951 until 1955, Carl Gregory was the owner, followed by Brock Ashburn for one year. In 1957, Bob Garrison bought the business, and Ed Kunesch purchased it the following year. He ran the bar and café until 1970, when one of the walls caught on fire and the building burned down. (Homesteaders Museum.)

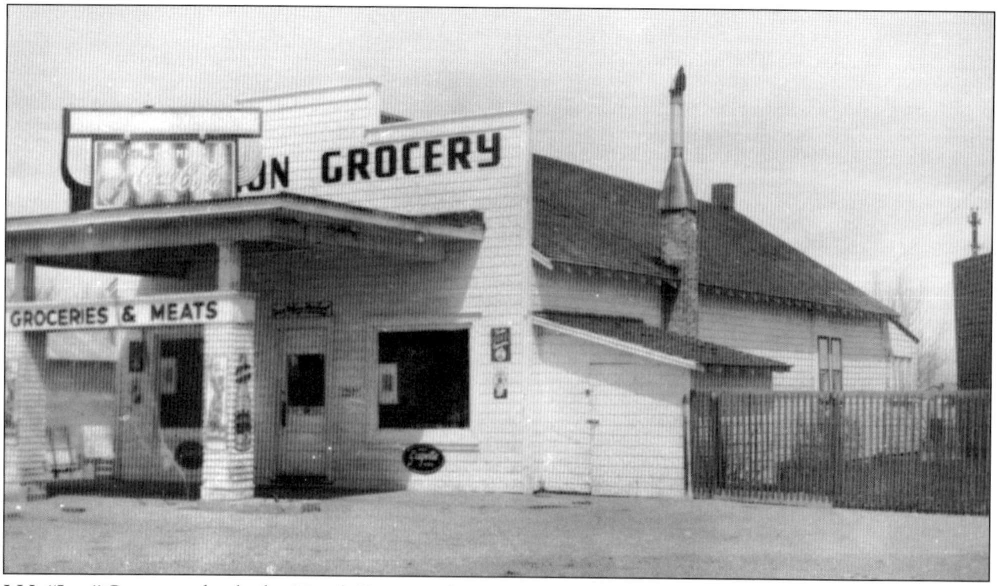

J.H. "Jess" Swanson built the Hawk Springs Grocery Store in 1928. The store was the local grocery and meat store as well as a provider of dry goods and gasoline. Bernice and Wilbur Shannon purchased the store in 1945 and ran the business until 1967. Paul Arnold changed the business to the Little Maverick Café from 1972 until 1973, and Stanley Reynoldson ran the café for a short time after that. (Homesteaders Museum.)

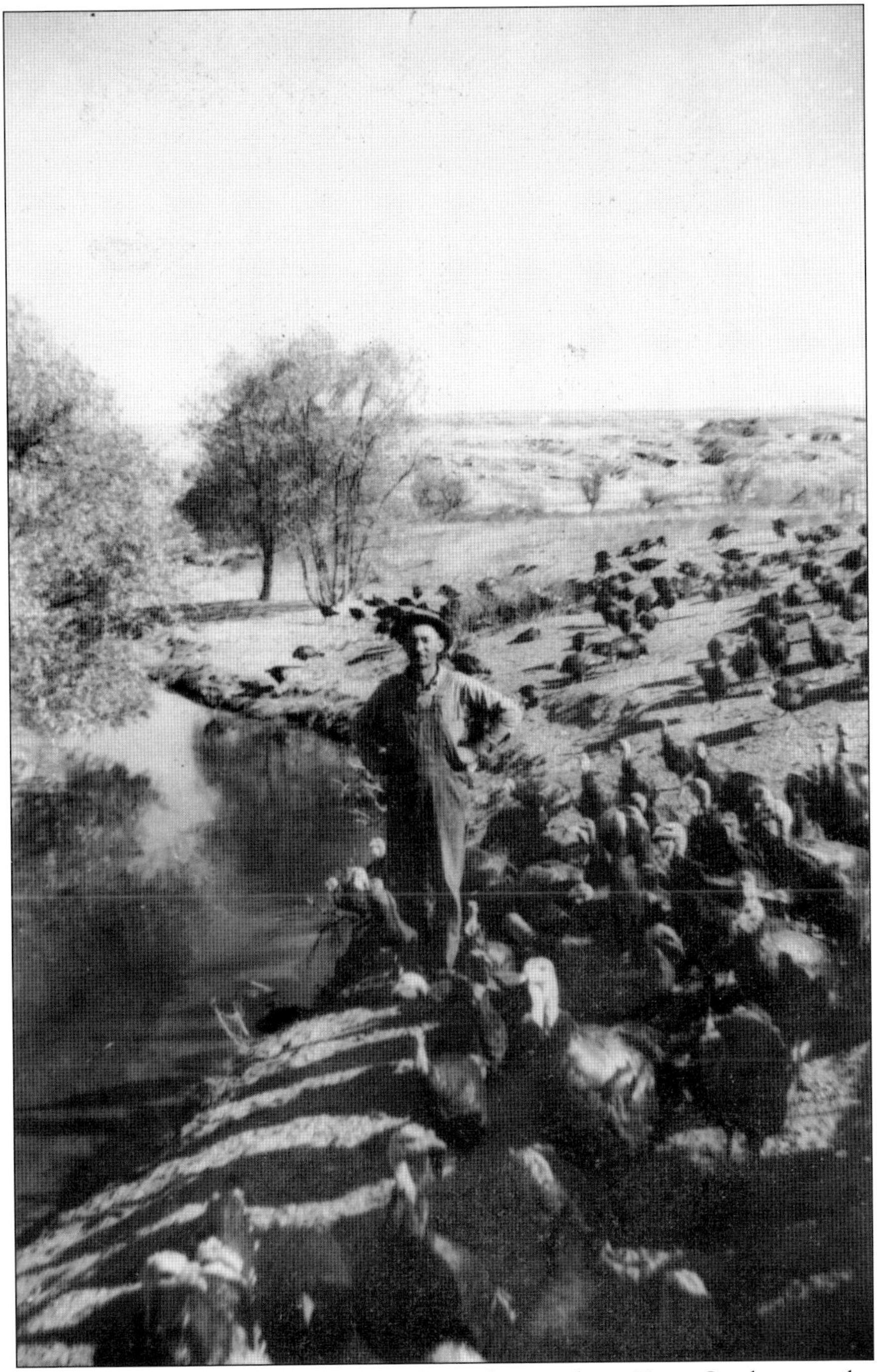

Conrad Kaufman is pictured around 1943 at his turkey ranch on Horse Creek, two miles south and two miles east of Hawk Springs. At one time, he had 20,000 birds in a year and sold them to a turkey processing plant in Alliance. Later, he sold them to a Swanson's plant in Omaha, where the meat was used by the military. Swanson's would send a truck to the ranch to pick them up. Kaufman and his son Howard operated a very successful cattle ranch where buyers would come to see the animals in their large sale barn. (Ila Zimmer.)

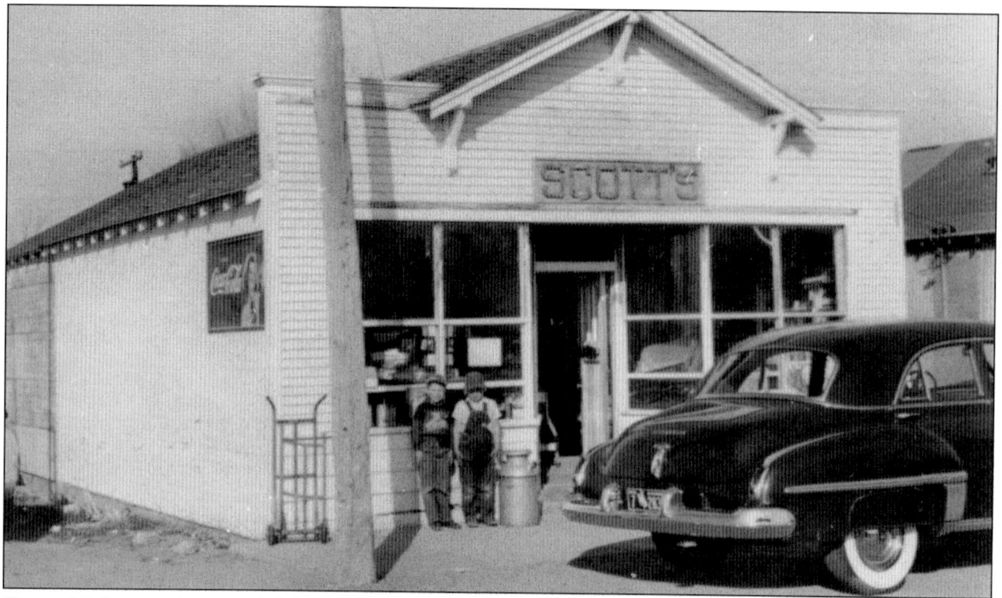

Harry Kirkpatrick owned the Nyal Drugs, Sundries, and Fountain Service in this building from 1928 until 1939. It was built by Harry Arnold. Kirkpatrick sold it to Mary and Tim Scott, who ran it as a grocery store and lived in the back part of the building. Ruth Howery remembers eating the best lemon ice cream there, which she purchased for 5¢. In 1974, the store was sold to Joe and Mary Chapman, who continued to run the grocery store until 1978, when part of the building burned and the store was closed. (Homesteaders Museum.)

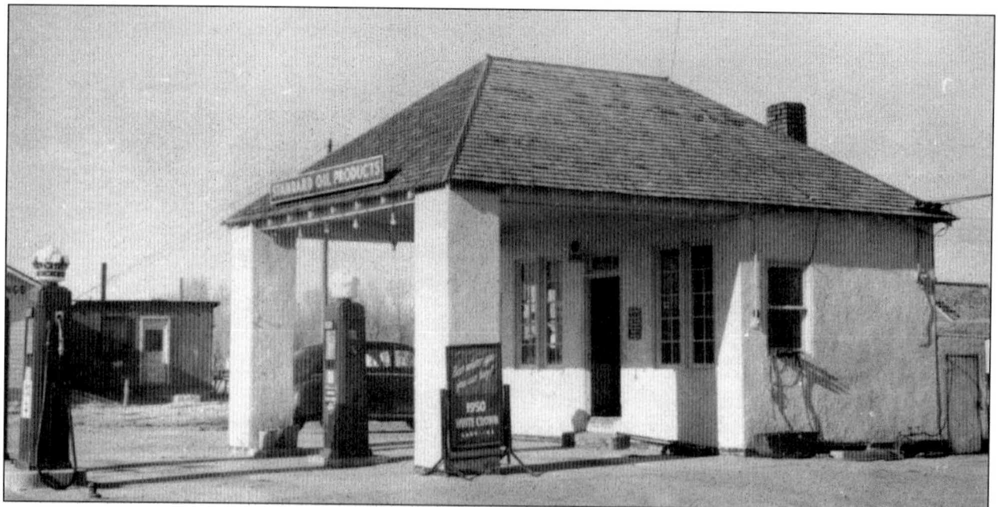

The Standard oil station sold gasoline, oil, and tires and was the first business of this kind in Hawk Springs, operating from 1928 until 1933 under the ownership of W.L. Killebrew. Darrell Hacker took over as agent in 1933 and had Albert Harris as his manager. When Hacker was in the service during World War II, Aubrey C. McBrien took over the operation. Hacker returned and operated the station until 1949, when he took over the family farm. His brother Perry moved to Hawk Springs and became the agent for one year until 1950. He built the bulk plant that served the station during that time. Perry and Aubrey also delivered fuel to the area farmers. Dick Wesch ran the station from 1955 until 1958, and McBrien retired in 1976. Operation of the two businesses ceased when the bulk plant was closed and torn down in 2003. (Homesteaders Museum.)

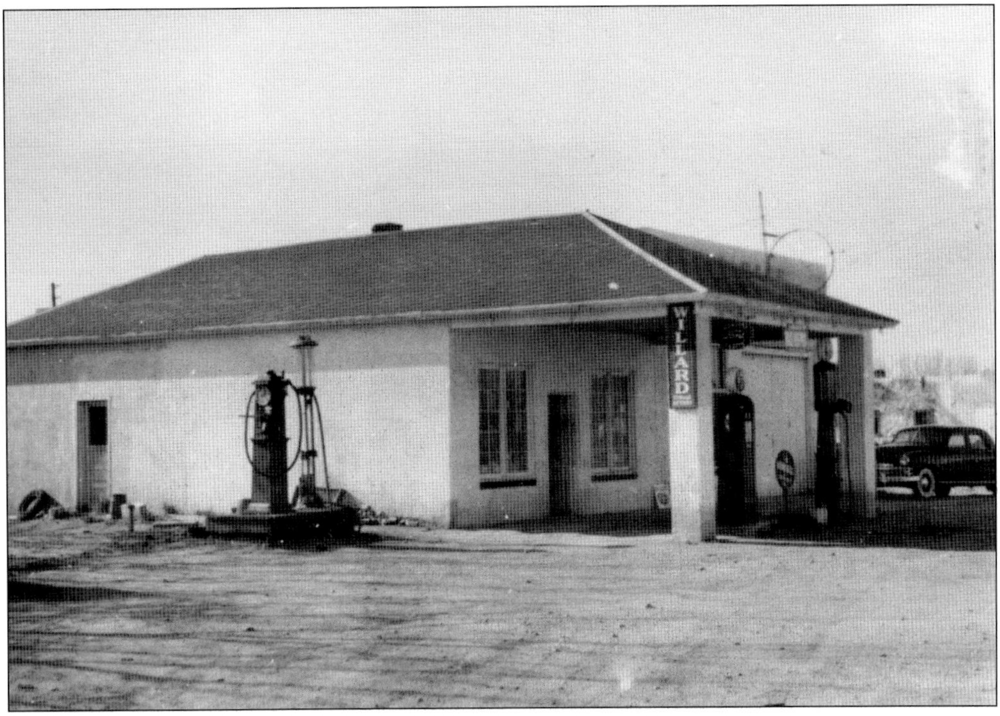

L.E. Blunt owned this hardware store, which sold Standard Oil gasoline, from 1928 until 1955. Other owners of the business were Hank Handly (1955–1959), Claton Coen (1959–1970), Walter Gregory (1970–1982), Bob Baker (1982–1988), and Tom Toedter and Dean Wilson (1988–1989). The last establishment provided gasoline, diesel, hardware products, welding, auto service, and repair. After this business closed, the building was turned back to Baker in 1990. Chuck Wilson leased the building from Baker in 1994. Since 1997, it has been the office of Bronco Drilling. (Homesteaders Museum.)

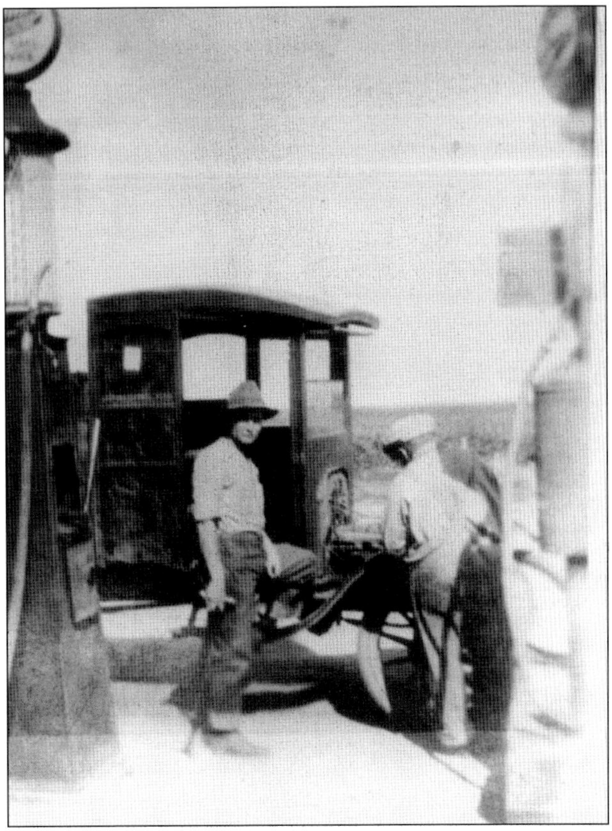

Pictured is the first truck in Hawk Springs. Notice the homemade cab. (Wilbur Shannon Collection, Homesteaders Museum.)

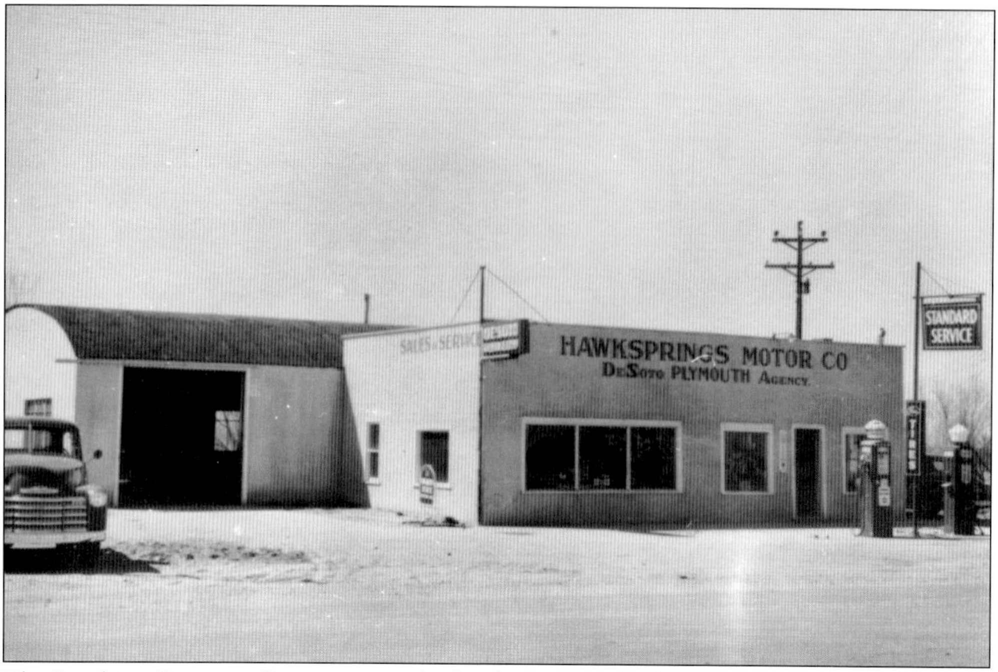

The Sunshine Creamery Company was the first business in this building, operated by J.H. Smith beginning in 1928. Advertisements said its transactions dealt with the creamery and poultry. From 1938 until 1946, a gas station and café operated by Frank Kuebler was housed in the building. Selling DeSoto and Plymouth cars from 1946 until 1958 was the Hawk Springs Motor Company, owned by John Stephenson. As an added attraction, after buying a car, one could also get gasoline there through the Standard Oil service. Ken Baker, a mechanic at the motor company, took over the business from 1958 until 1989. Currently, the Hawk Springs Horse Creek Conservation and Ditch Company occupy the building. (Homesteaders Museum.)

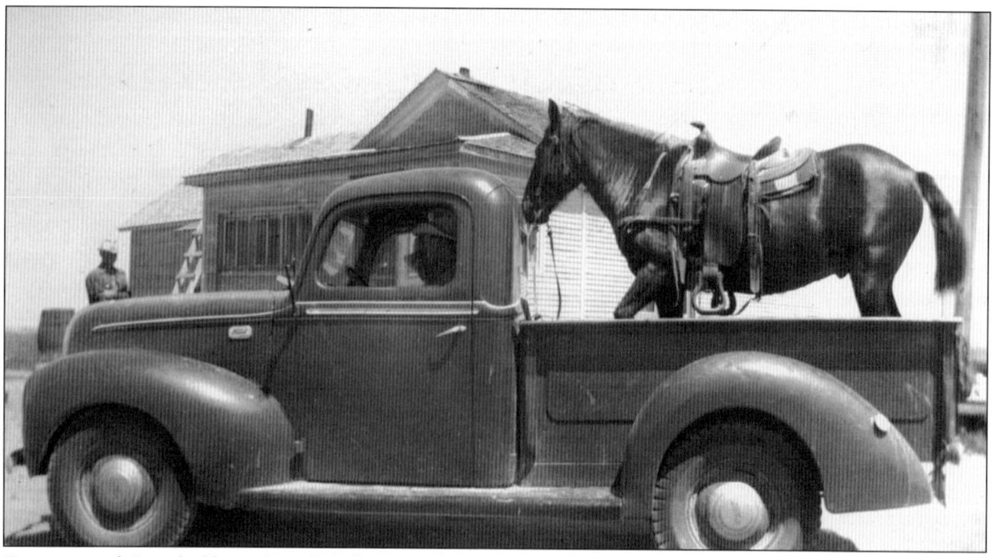

Drummond Smith (driver) and Arley Smith are taking Shortie, the horse, for a ride in the back of their 1941 Ford. The photograph shows how animals were transported before the invention of trailers. (Waldon Smith.)

Four

VETERAN

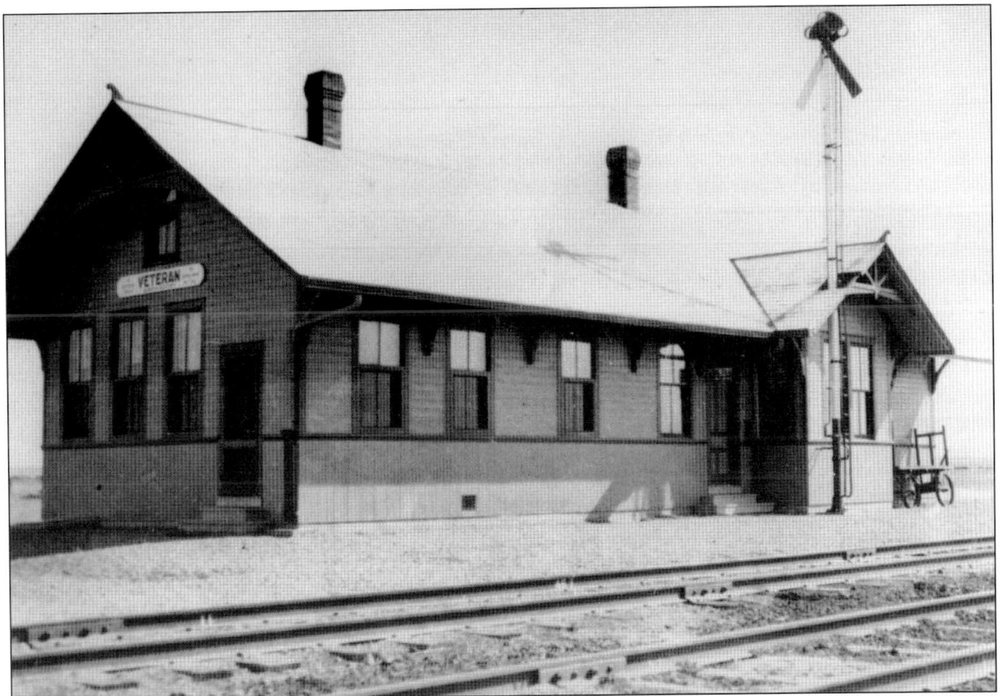

The Veteran depot was established in January 1922. The Union Pacific Railroad line had been extended from Haig, Nebraska, to Cottier, Wyoming, which made it pass through Veteran. The days they worked on the railroad were very cold. It was said that the steel rails would sing as they were pushed off the cars into place. The depot was a necessary part of the farming business for transportation of goods and animals. The Veteran farmers raised wheat and other grains, but often their main income came from milk cows and chickens. Milk was separated into cream and milk. The foam was fed to the cats, which were necessary to keep down the mice, and part of the milk was fed to calves. When the cream cans were full, or about once or twice per week, they were taken to the depot to be shipped to creameries in eastern Nebraska. (Homesteaders Museum.)

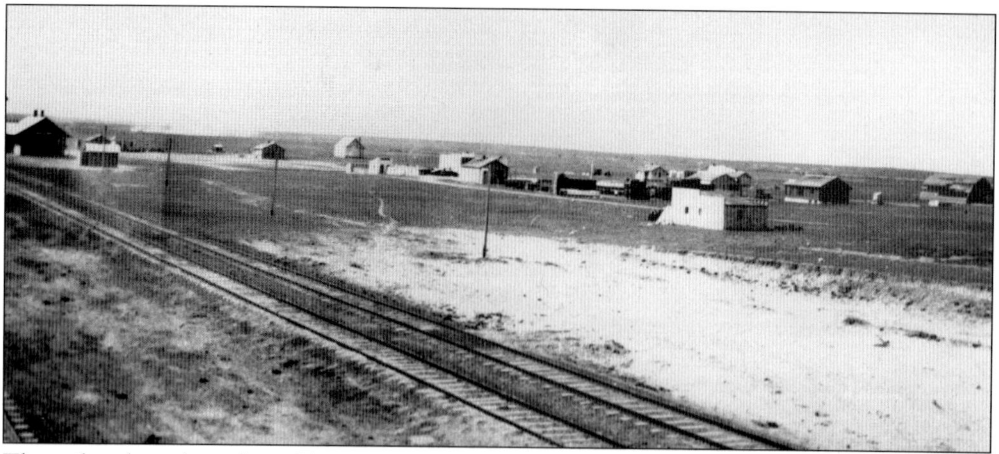

The railroad was brought to Veteran in 1921, but by then, the town had already begun to grow. Mail delivery was a very important part of those early communities, and Virgil Myers went daily to Yoder to pick up the mail and deliver it to the homesteaders. Businesses in Veteran included two grocery stores, a hardware store, a garage and filling station, a lumberyard, and a drugstore. In those early days, the town had not yet installed a sewer or water system, and there was no electricity. (Homesteaders Museum.)

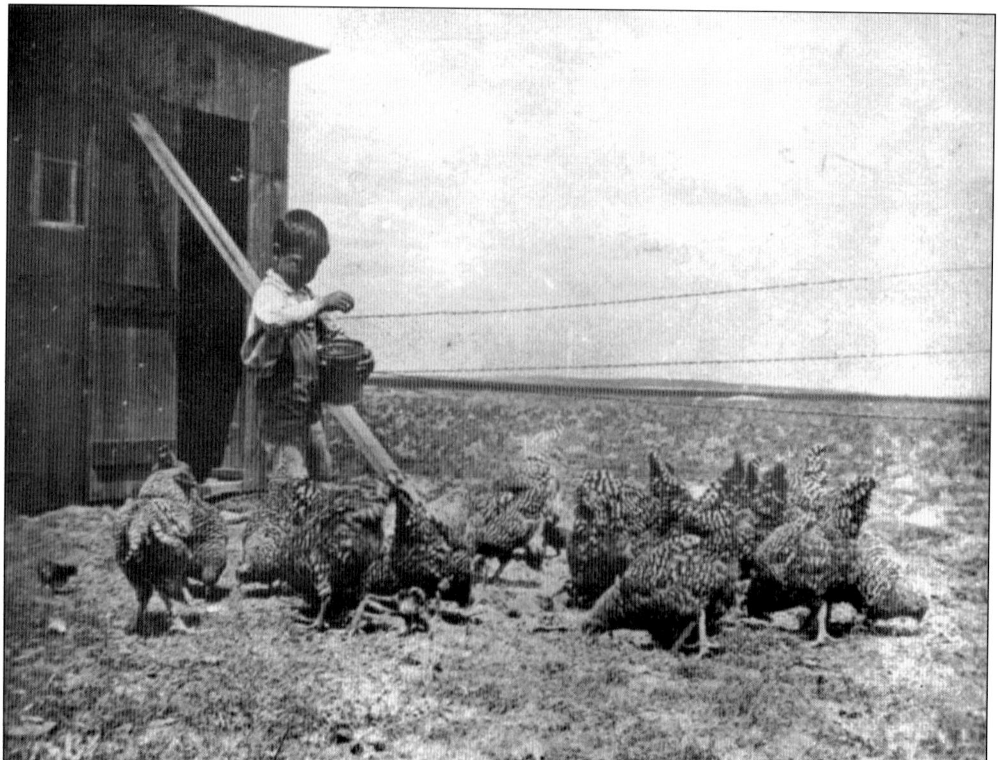

Pictured in 1912, Vernon "Bill" Jones is feeding the chickens on the farm of his stepfather, William J. Knowlton. Vernon Jones's father, Linn Jones, had died in Ohio of typhoid fever in 1907. His mother, Winnie Luada Blair Jones, traveled first to Loveland, Colorado, and then to Torrington, where she homesteaded near Cottier. She married William Jay Knowlton in 1911. (Homesteaders Museum.)

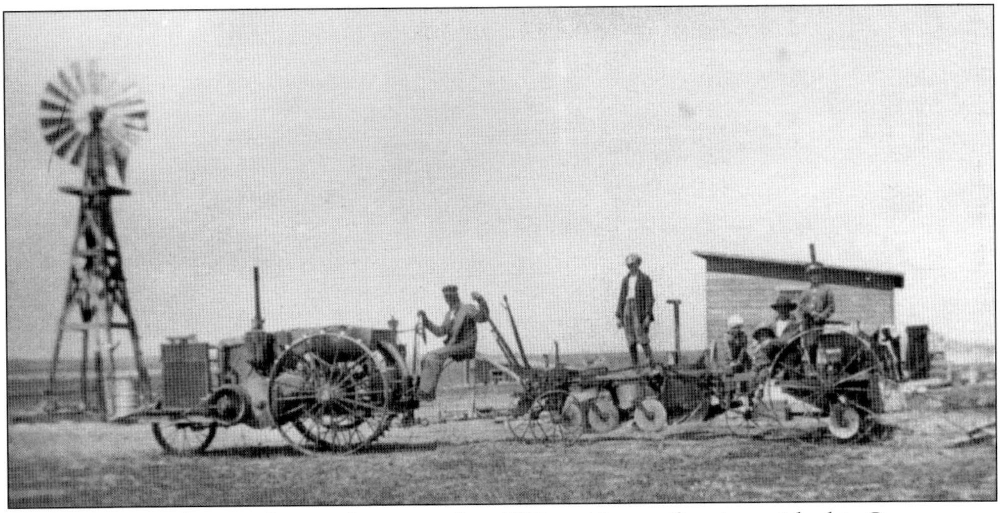

William J. Knowlton took out a homestead in 1919 and began farming with this Case tractor. Knowlton was originally from Iola, Kansas, and studied engineering at the college there. After taking out his homestead, he also worked as a ditch rider on the North Canal until the Fort Laramie Canal was finished. In the background is Knowlton's homestead house. These houses were built in Yoder on skids and then moved by being pulled with horses. These houses were 12 feet by 10 feet and were meant for the bachelor farmers. (Homesteaders Museum.)

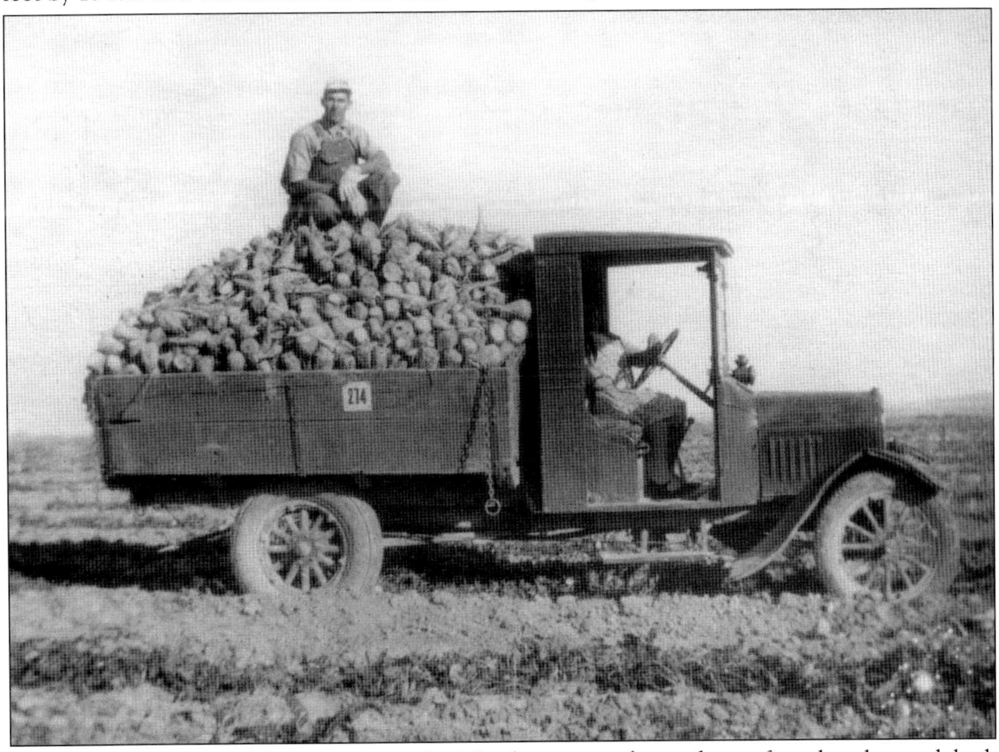

Harvesting beets was a labor-intensive job. After beets were dug and transferred to the truck bed, they were taken to a local dump, where they were weighed before being transported to the sugar factory in Torrington. Shown here with a loaded truck is Weimer Denney, and driving is his wife, Maxene. These beets were grown on the William J. Knowlton farm. (Homesteaders Museum.)

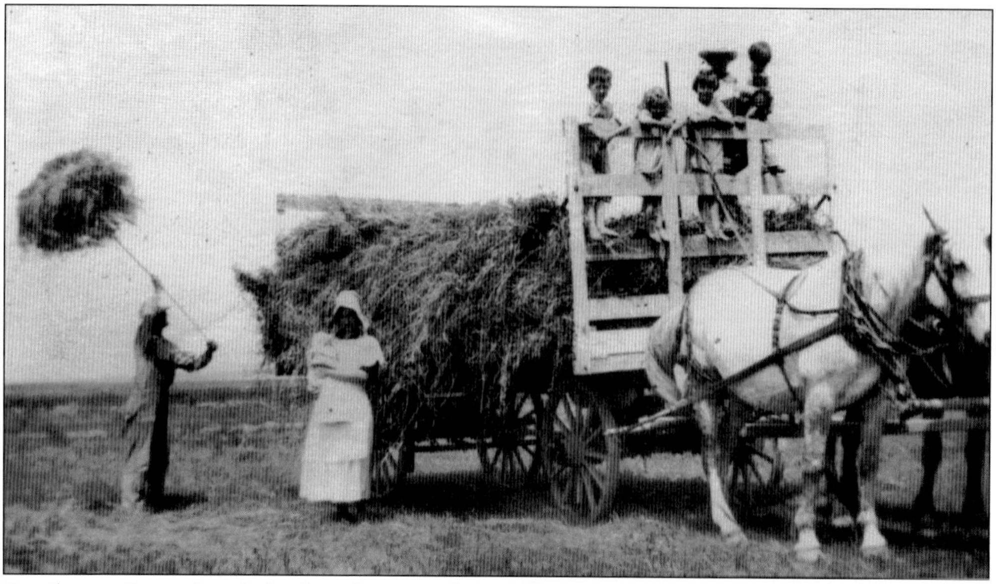

Family members often helped in farming chores. Here, aunt Blanche Blair (next to wagon) is helping to supervise the five Knowlton children on the hay wagon as their father, William, forks hay onto the load. (Homesteaders Museum.)

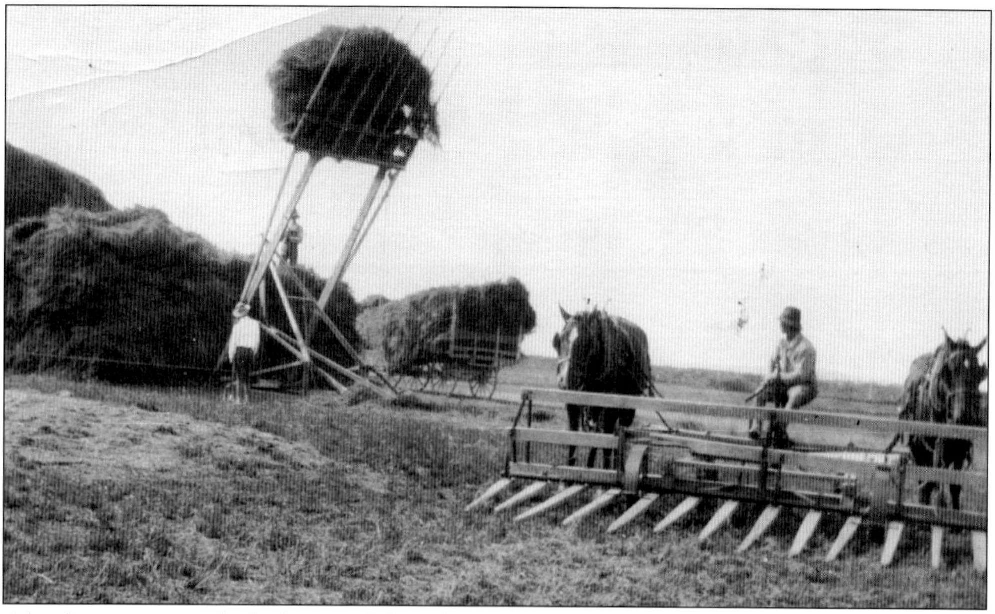

After hay was cut and raked, it was left to dry for a few days. When dry, the hay was placed with pitchforks onto a hayrack and then taken to where the hay was to be stacked for the winter. Hay stackers were usually homemade affairs and used a central pole rigged so that it could rotate on its base. By means of pulleys and a single tree attached to a one-horse hookup, the loading fork could be raised. As it was raised, it would rotate over the haystack. When tripped, the hay would drop onto the stack. Men on top of the stack would arrange the hay in such a way so as to shed water, making the hay cure rather than rot. The horse was then backed up and the fork was pulled back with the tripping rope and reloaded for the operation to be continued. This is the way hay was put up before bales were used. (Homesteaders Museum.)

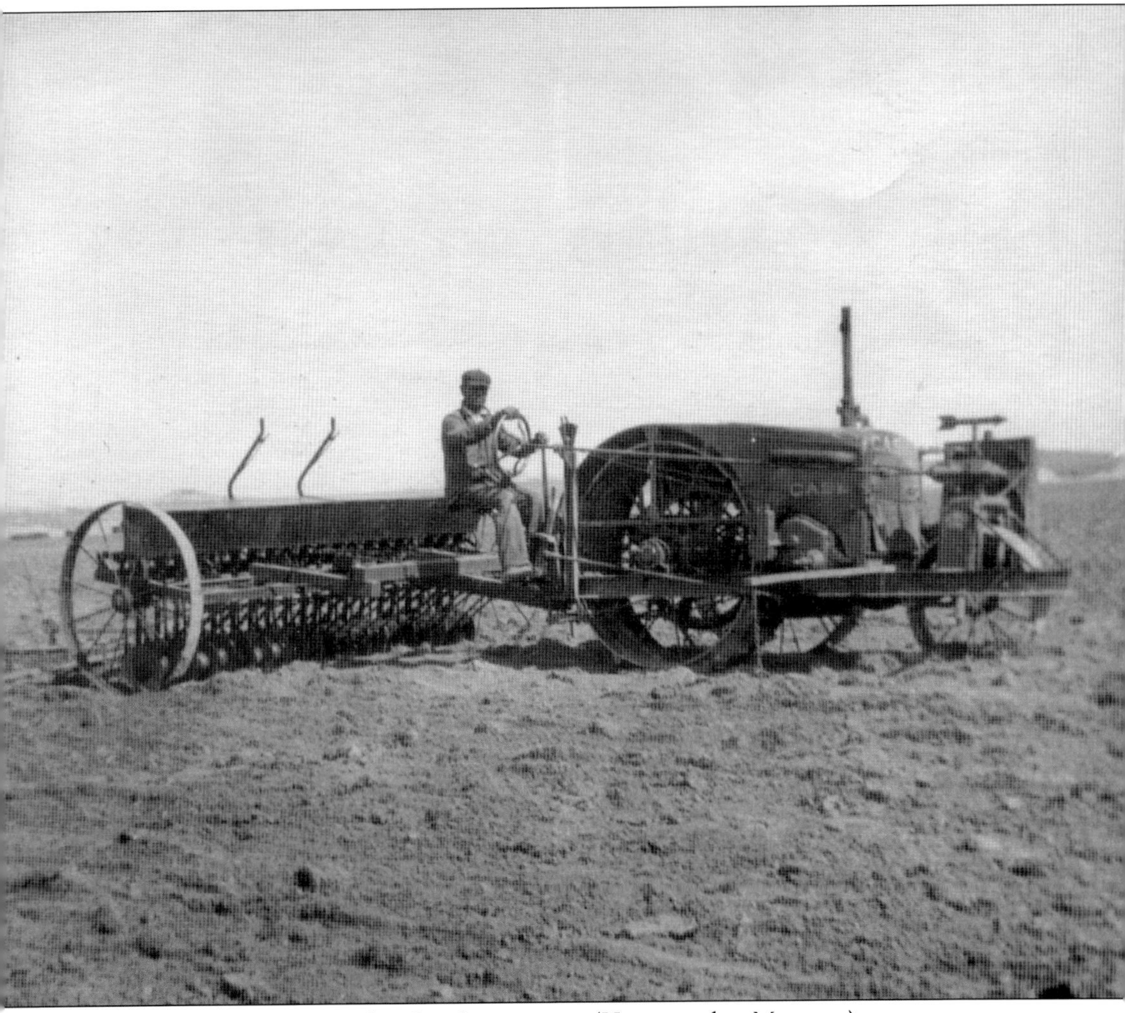

William J. Knowlton is pictured on his Case tractor. (Homesteaders Museum.)

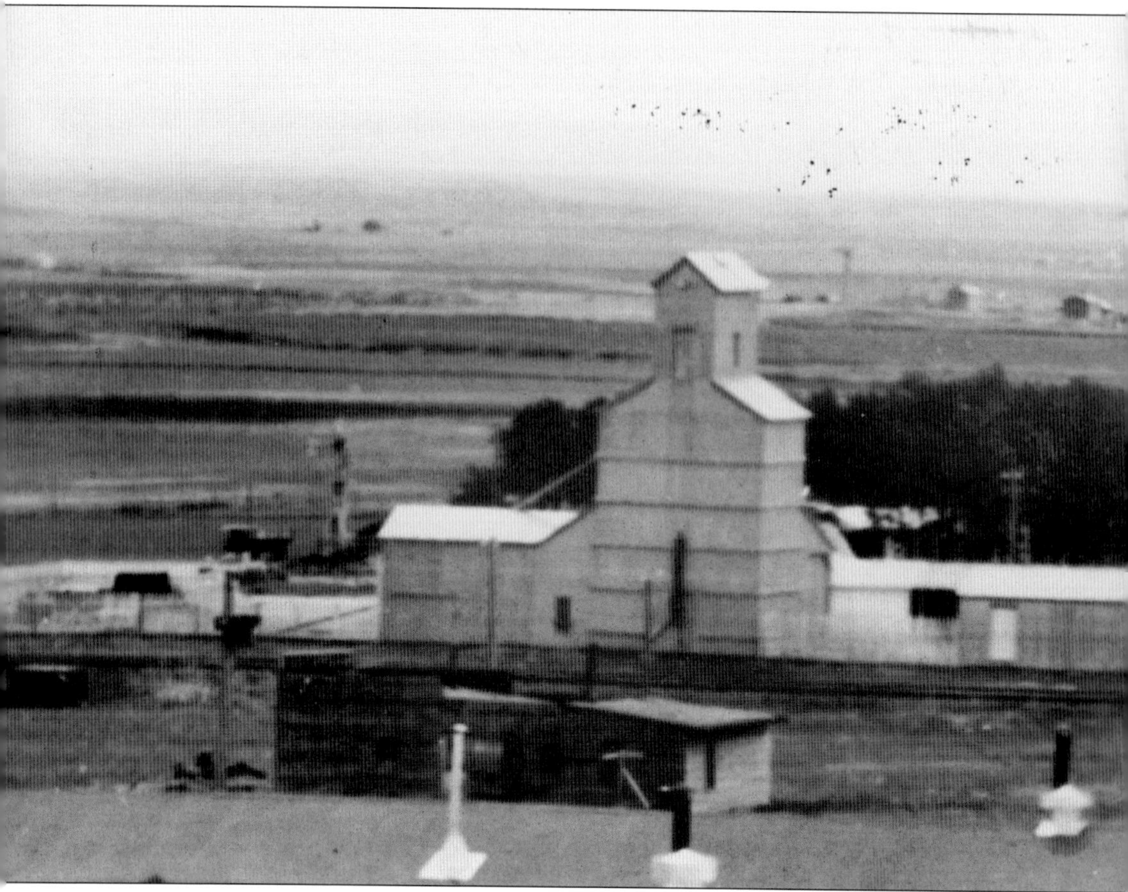

Early wheat harvest was accomplished when neighboring farmers would gather to harvest one man's crop and then go to another farm to continue the process. In 1916, Lingle had an elevator built to collect and store grain before it was ready to be put on train cars. Not until 1921 did most farmers have trucks to take their wheat to the elevators. The wheat farmers realized that the cost of hauling to Lingle was not profitable, so in 1923, an elevator was built in Veteran. Oscar Guth was co-owner and manager and Robert Cottier was part owner of the Veteran elevator. They also sold hardware and lumber and delivered coal, gas, and tractor fuel to the farmers. (Homesteaders Museum.)

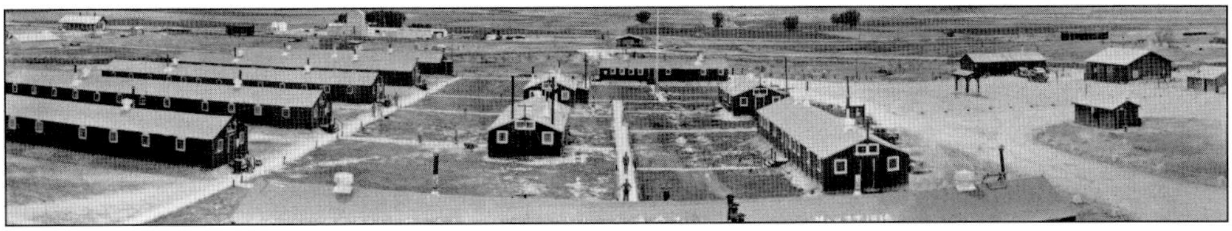

Veteran was host to a Civilian Conservation Corps (CCC) camp and then to a World War II relocation camp for prisoners of war. Men who were at the CCC camp hauled and dynamited the canal planned for irrigation in the Veteran area. It was then empty for two years. Pictured is the camp as it looked like in 1944. Italian prisoners were entrenched at the camp and worked the sugar beet fields while local men were engaged in the war. A few Latvian POWs were also housed here. It had a swimming pool that the prisoners as well as the local town people enjoyed. (Wyoming State Archives, Department of State Parks and Cultural Resources.)

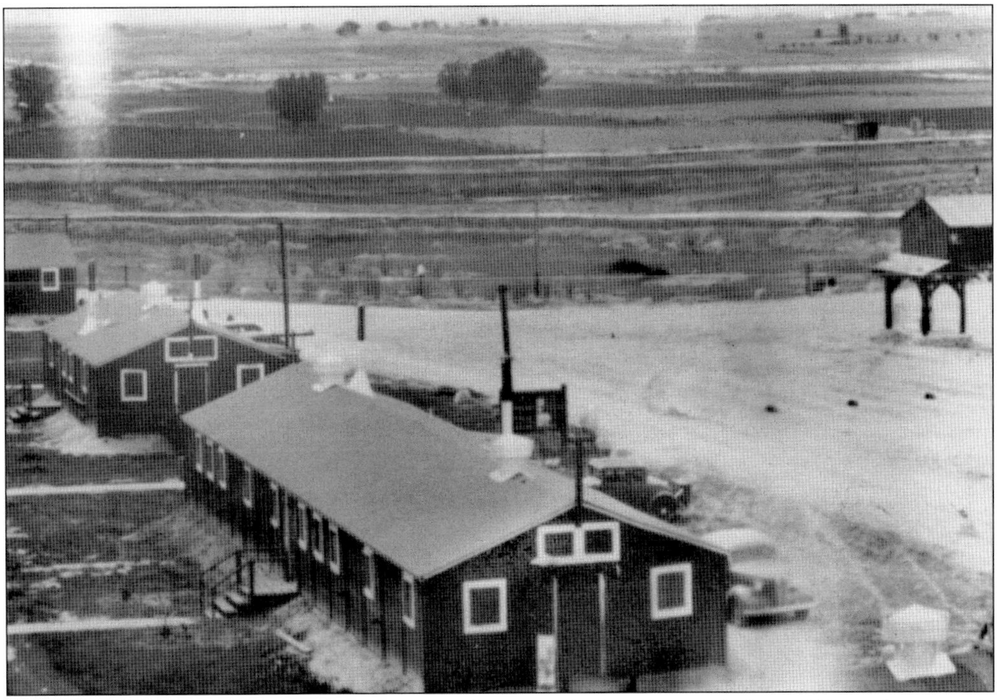

Two companies of the Civilian Conservation Corps worked at Guersey Lake—844 on the east side of the reservoir and 1855 on the west side. The men had been working on improving the aesthetic beauty of the park and building campgrounds. Some time in October 1937, the companies' work jurisdiction was taken over by the Bureau of Reclamation, and enrollees started "rip-rapping" the Fort Laramie canal banks under the direction of the Goshen County Irrigation District. A second camp was set up in Veteran. With this move to Veteran, the boys were able to attend high school. The Veteran camp was altered in 1943 to house 250 Italian prisoners of war. These men served their time providing farm labor, primarily in the beet harvest. (Homesteaders Museum.)

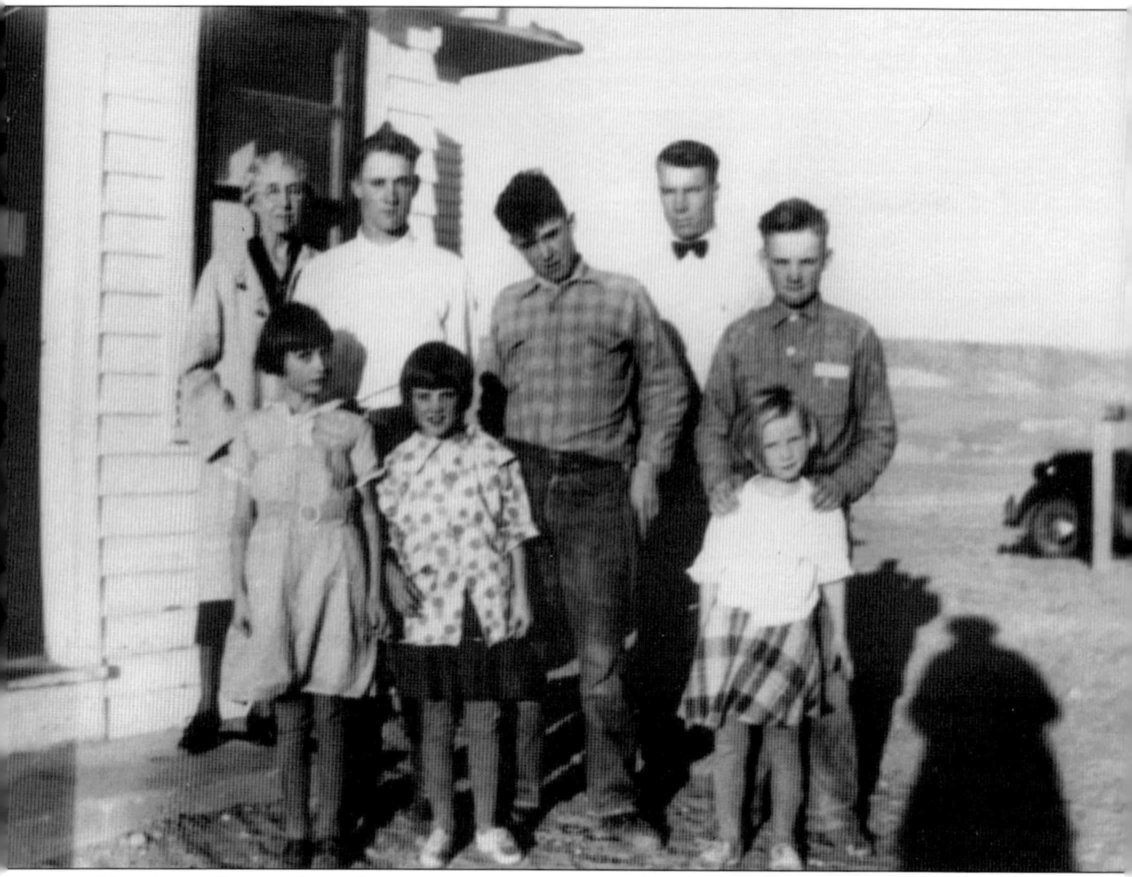

The Spoon Buttes School was in operation in 1939. Superintendent of Schools Ada Holdeman (back, left) was visiting the school. Students in attendance are, from left to right, (first row) Ruth Lay, Bessie Lay, and Joy Ann Lay; (second row) Bill Lay, Randal "Mike" Lay, teacher Carl Otto, and Ora "Doc" Lay. (Wyoming State Archives, Department of State Parks and Cultural Resources.)

Five

HUNTLEY

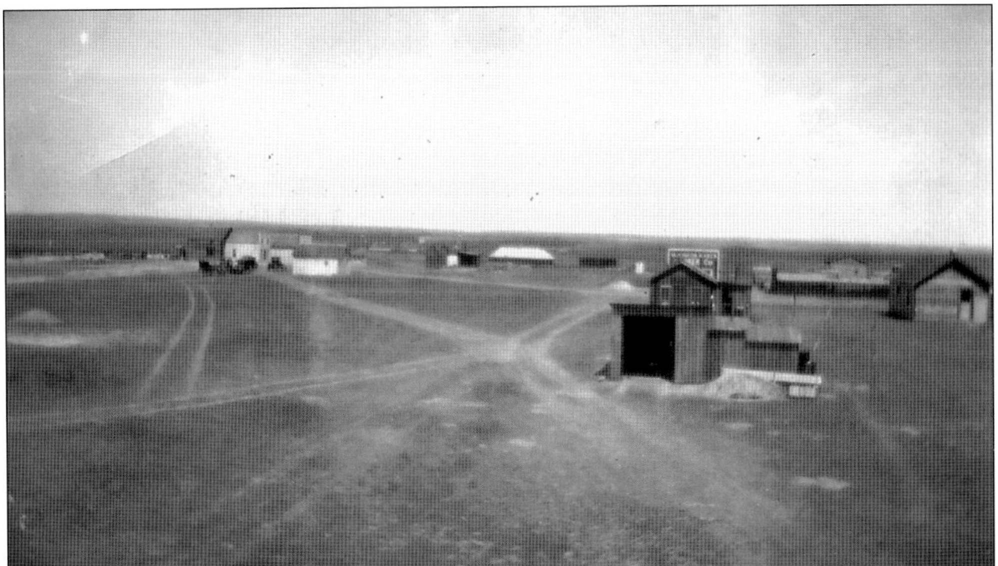

In 1923, Huntley was developing as a town. The buildings, from left to right, include a store and barbershop, Bassford Auto Shop, a residence, the Union Pacific Railroad Station, McKinnon-Raben Lumber Company, and the eventual location of Bussell Blacksmith Shop. In the foreground is a house where O.W. Bassford lived during World War I. The last residents of the building were Dessa and Buck Marlatt. (Margie Raben Jones.)

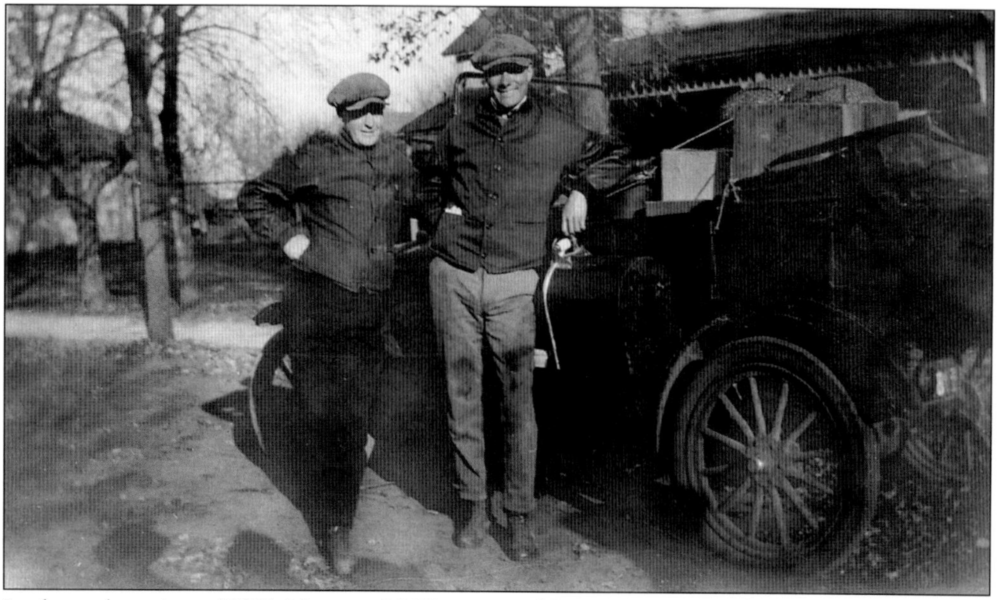

In the early spring of 1921, Norman McKinnon and his cousin Roy Raben left Armour, South Dakota, in Raben's Ford touring car to go to the homestead area of Huntley, Wyoming, which had been opened to World War I veterans. They built the first lumberyard, and Roy bought out Norman's interest in the late 1920s. (Margie Raben Jones.)

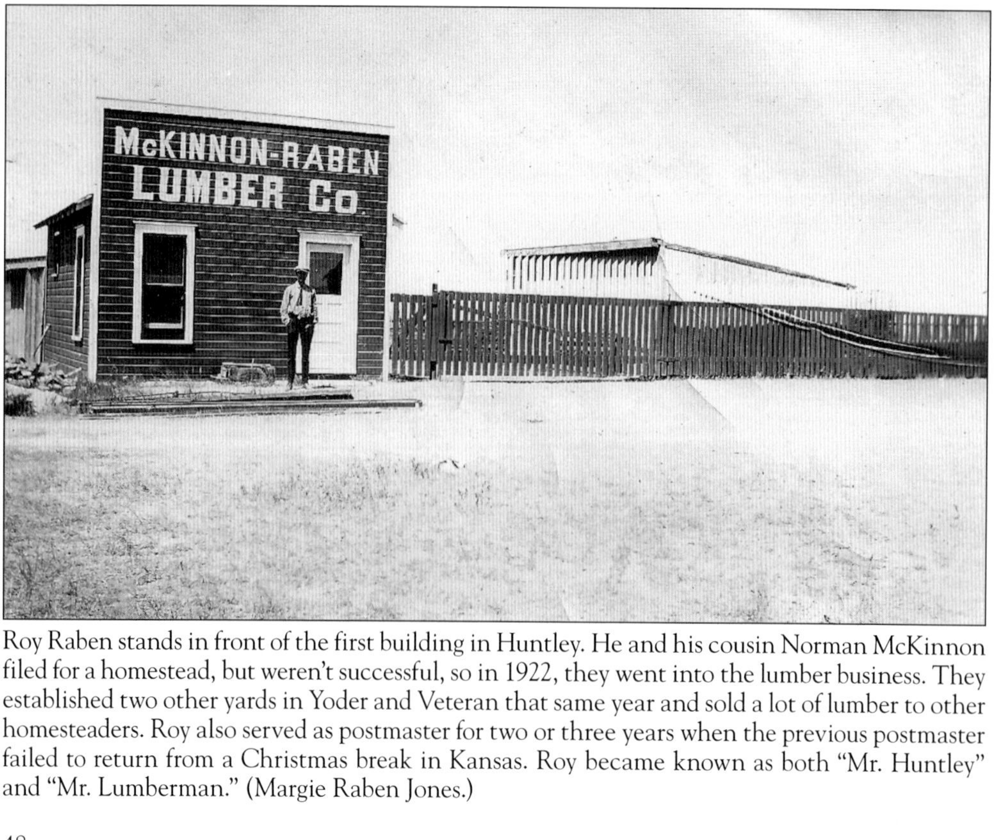

Roy Raben stands in front of the first building in Huntley. He and his cousin Norman McKinnon filed for a homestead, but weren't successful, so in 1922, they went into the lumber business. They established two other yards in Yoder and Veteran that same year and sold a lot of lumber to other homesteaders. Roy also served as postmaster for two or three years when the previous postmaster failed to return from a Christmas break in Kansas. Roy became known as both "Mr. Huntley" and "Mr. Lumberman." (Margie Raben Jones.)

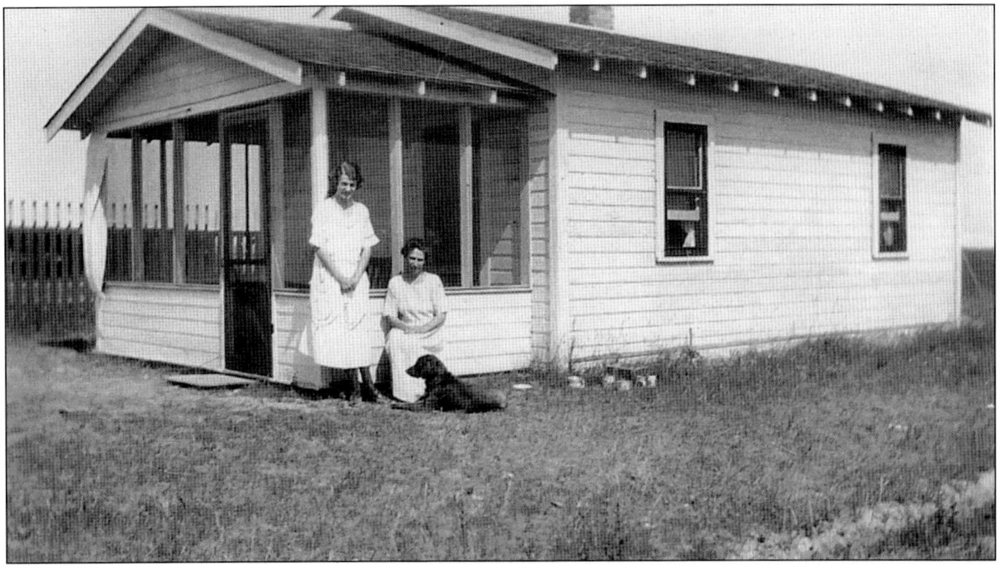

Elma and her mother, Minnie Raben, are outside the first home built in Huntley around 1924. Minnie was a widow and moved to Huntley to homestead with her daughter. The dog, Tuffy, belonged to Roy Raben. (Margie Raben Jones.)

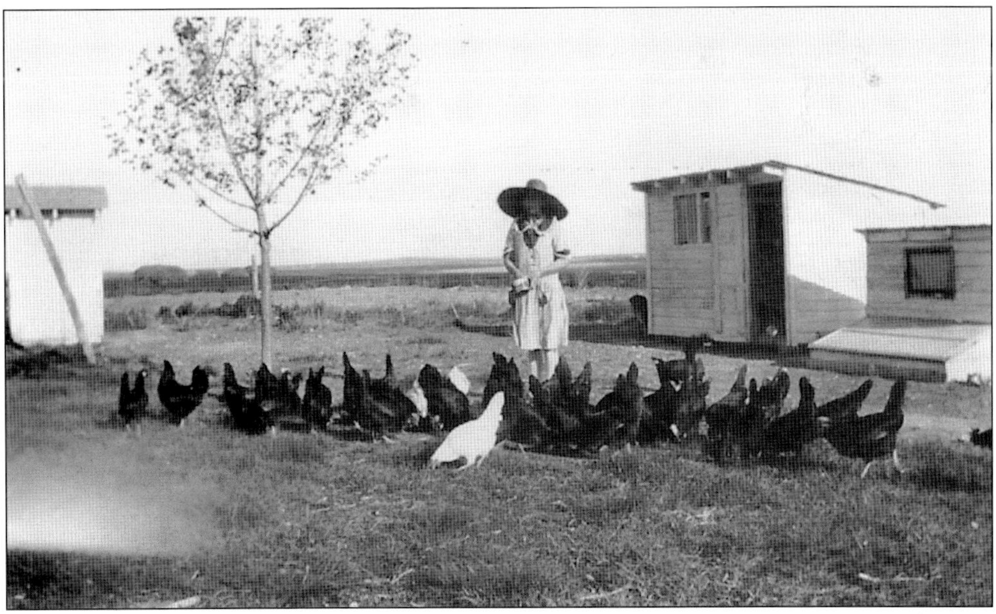

Minnie Raben, mother of Roy, Elma, and Wells "Pat," filed for her homestead in the Huntley area in 1925. She proved up on it in 1930, having chosen only women to sign for her. The chicken coop behind her was moved from Roy's homestead shack. Minnie had a vegetable garden, fruit trees, and flowers on her farm. She hired men to do the farming for her. (Margie Raben Jones.)

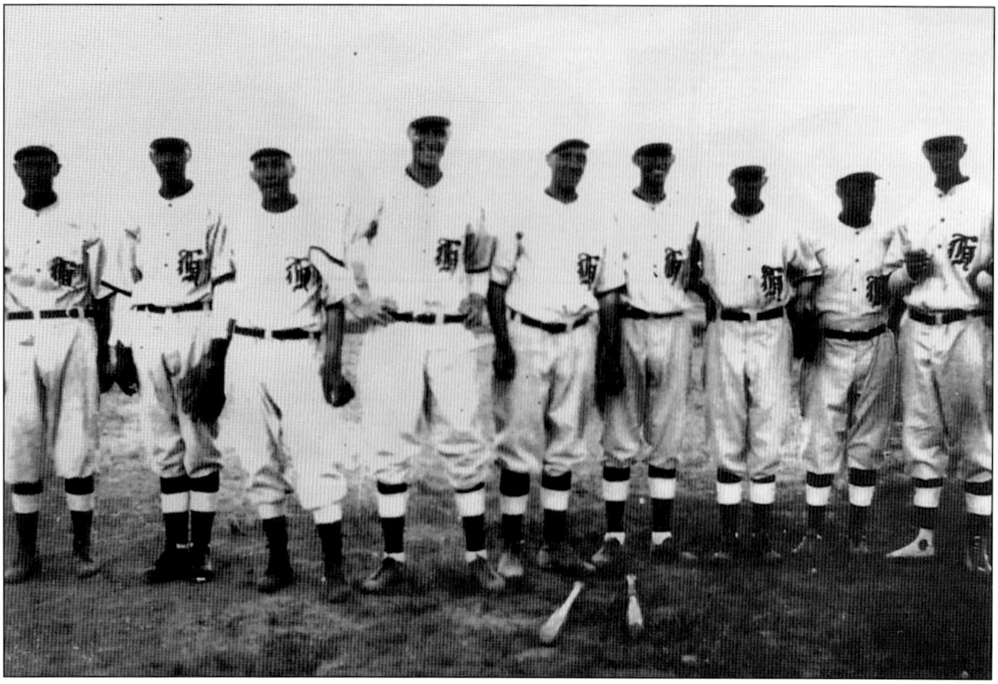

Along with Yoder, Huntley had a baseball team in 1926. From left to right are Rus Bower, Lou Drake, Ed Jepson, Roy Raben, Lou Otis, Charles Schulke, Charles Drake, Bill Hemrich, and Pat Raben. (Margie Raben Jones.)

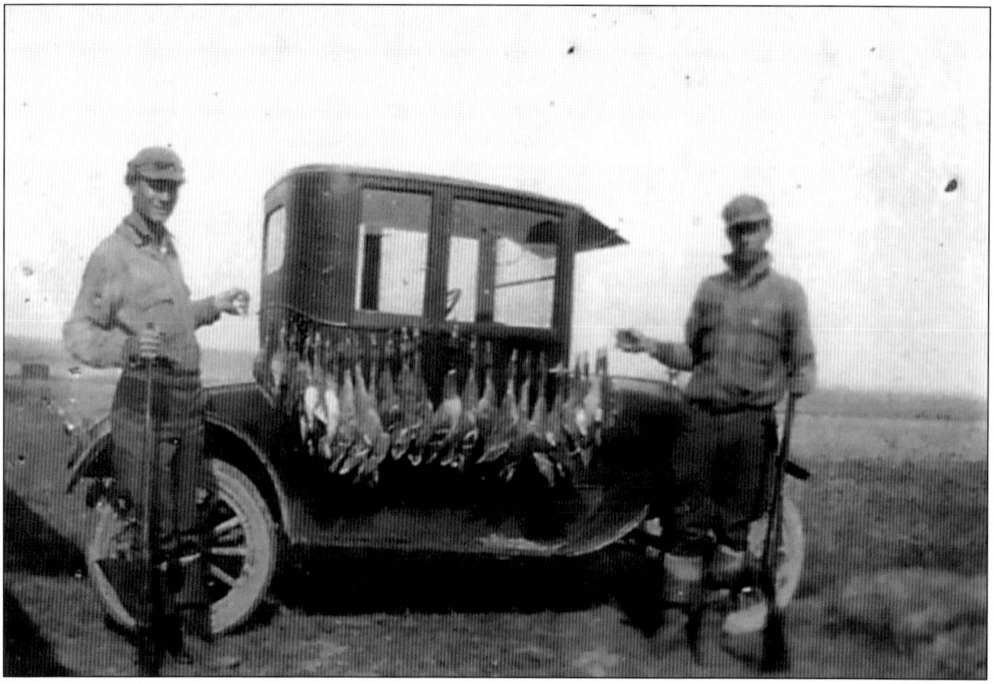

Roy (left) and his brother Wells O. "Pat" Raben were early entrepreneurs in the village of Huntley, Wyoming. In their leisure time, they liked to hunt ducks and geese. They are pictured in front of a Model T car. (Margie Raben Jones.)

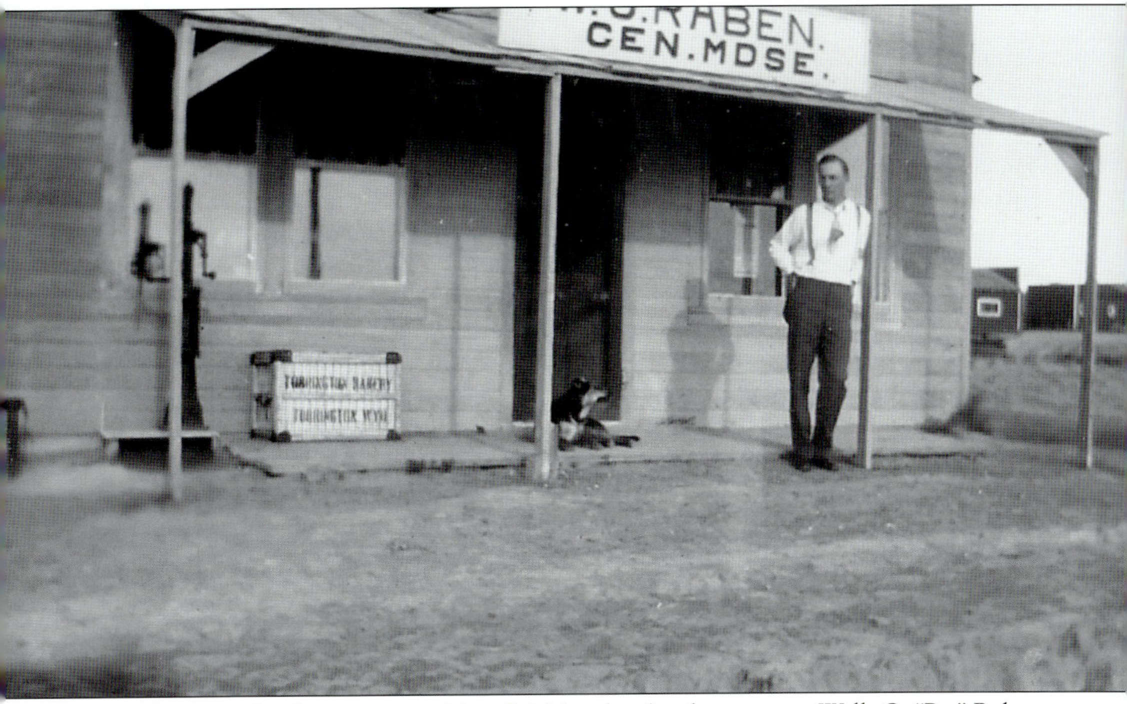

After working in a hardware store in Morrill, Nebraska, for about a year, Wells O. "Pat" Raben returned to Huntley in 1926 and bought the general merchandise store and a farm originally owned by one of the early Jewish settlers. He hired others to do the farming but fed cattle in the winter. He eventually changed it into a grocery store with gasoline pumps around 1927. Adding on to his enterprise, he moved a Conoco bulk plant from another jobber who had closed and installed it north of the railroad tracks and west of the road into Torrington to store fuel he had for the store. He also sold to the farmers for their machinery. In the late 1940s, he began having annual elk dinners to thank the farm customers for their business. (Margie Raben Jones.)

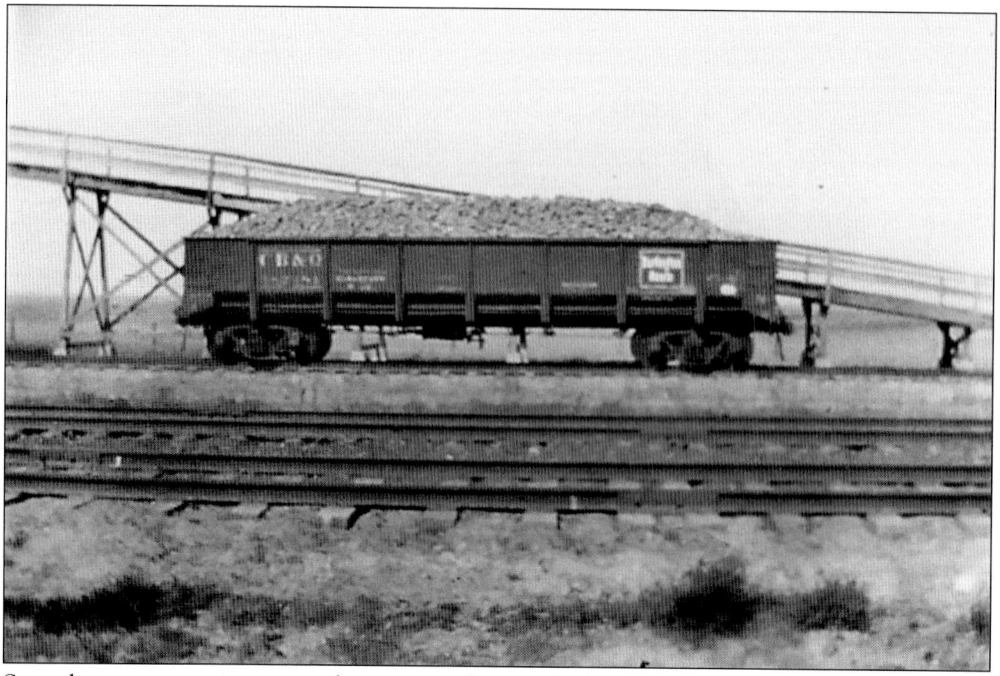

Sugar beets were an important farm commodity in Goshen County, especially after the Holly Sugar Corporation factory was built in Torrington. In 1928, the beets were shipped on railroad cars. The beets and tare, or dirt, were weighed on scales at the R.C. Raben lumberyard before journeying to the factory. (Margie Raben Jones.)

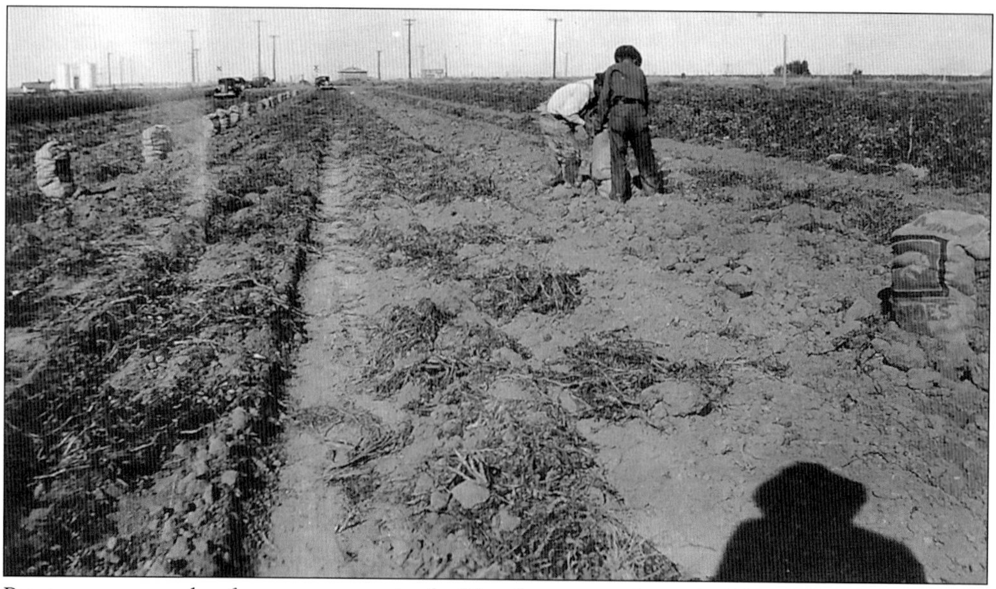

Potatoes were another farm crop grown in the Huntley area in the early 1920s. All of these farming methods were very work intensive. This photograph, taken on the Roy Raben farm looking north, shows the two gasoline tanks belonging to Wells O. "Pat" Raben in the upper left corner. Roy built a potato cellar to store the potatoes near his sheep pens. (Margie Raben Jones.)

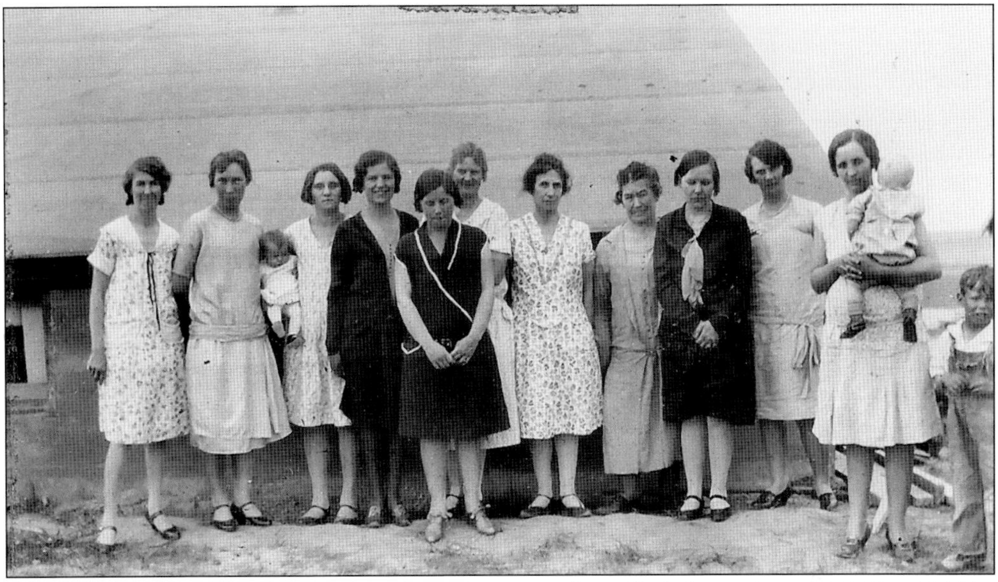

Good fellowship was the heart of a group of women who called themselves the 4 G's—Gibble, Gabb, Gobble and Git—and would meet together for lunch. Pictured in May 1929 from left to right are Marie Fuller, Mae Etzel, Leta Peters and baby, Peggy June, unidentified, Ruth Zerbigan, Minon Cully, Minnie Raben, Etta Powell, Jane Jepson, Ester Terry with baby, and Tommy Terry. Probably some of these women were also part of another group called the Ladies Auxiliary, which was involved with the Community Hall. The hall was used for dances, meetings, and school events but was eventually closed in the late 1930s because the dances got too rowdy, with too much drinking and too many fights. (Margie Raben Jones.)

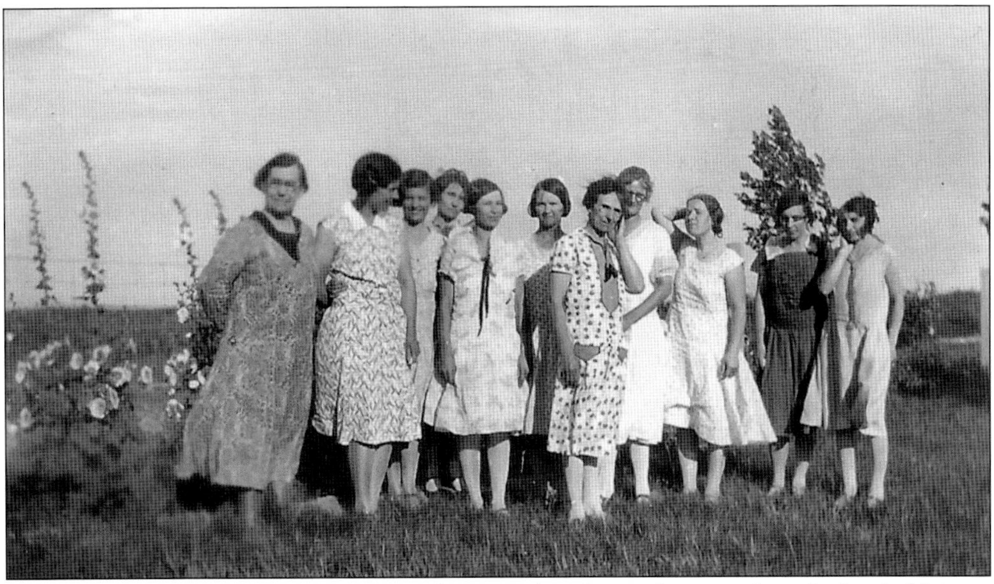

The wind has blown in Goshen County for many decades, and women have had to hold down both their dresses and hair on such days. This group of Huntley friends met on a windy day in 1929 at the homestead of Minnie Raben. They are, from left to right, Etta Powell, Laura Jepson, Helen Rouse, Mary Jones, Fern Morford, Florence Jepson, Minnie Raben, Minon Cully, Ruth Zerbriger, Lois Otis, and Leta Peters. (Margie Raben Jones.)

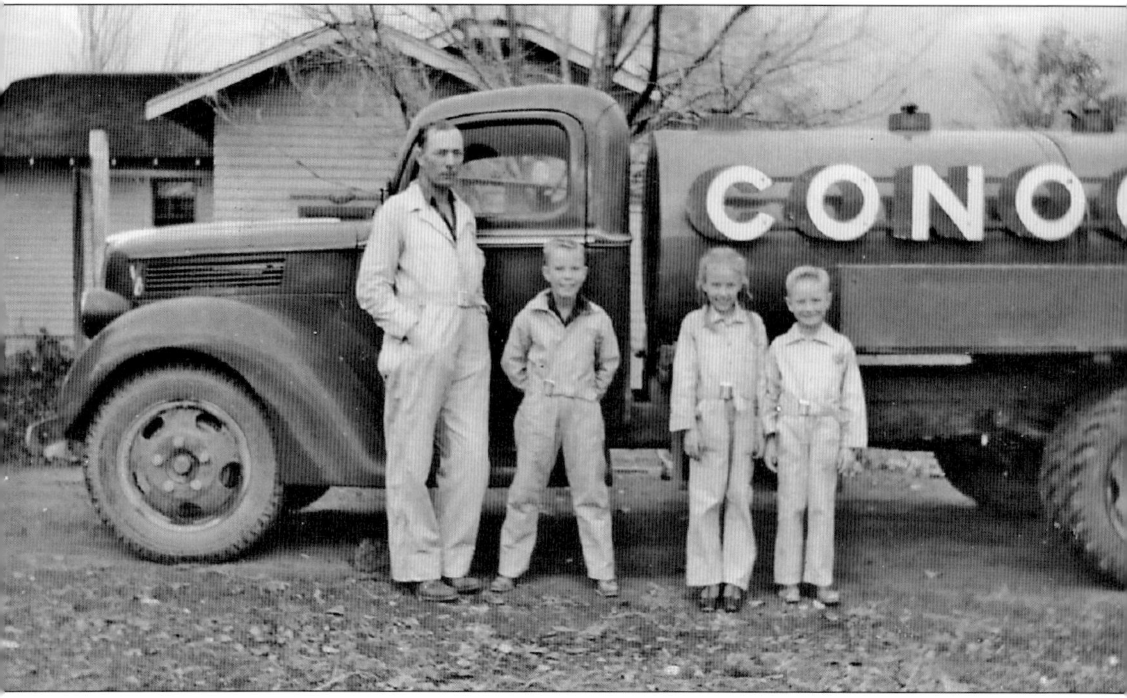

The popularity of Conoco motor oil and other products, which were sold to farmers by Wells O. "Pat" Raben as a side project, well surpassed his estimation. He was aided by Conoco marketers and eventually added four more storage tanks, a warehouse, and a pump house to this oil jobbing business. His annual sales reached nearly a half-million gallons. In 1941, he started delivering fuel, and he was sometimes aided by his children (from left to right) Bud, Margie and Dayton, whose coveralls had the business insignia on the back. Here he is at the home of his parents, Pat and Lyndal, north of town, which is now owned by Jo Meininger. (Margie Raben Jones.)

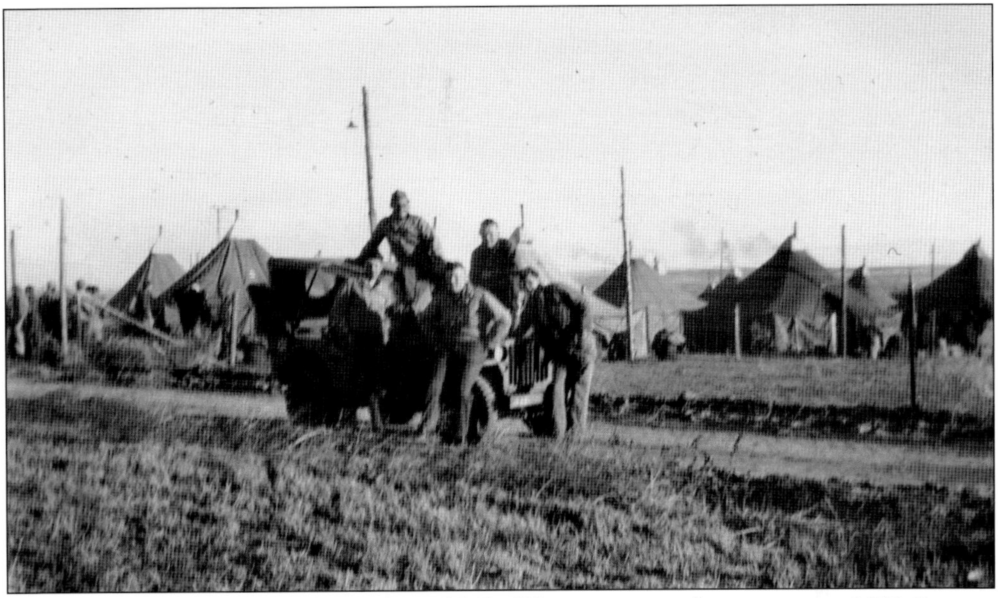

From about 1943 to 1945, the farm of Harold "Red" Lippincott was home to around 300 German prisoners of war who lived four to a tent. The guardhouse was turned into a labor house after they left, and it is still being used on the farm. Neighboring farmers would come to get the POWs to help with their farm work, and it was understood the prisoners would be fed dinner. At the end of the war, these Germans returned to their home country, but a few returned to this area and became successful farmers. (Homesteaders Museum.)

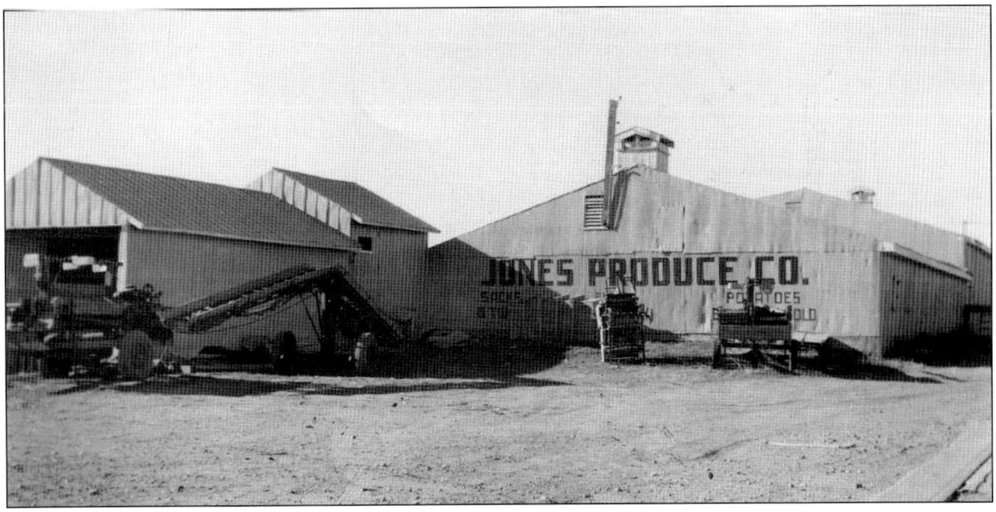

Jones Produce Company was located on the north side of the railroad tracks in Huntley. It was used by Charley Jones and other farmers as a collection point for potatoes. The potatoes were washed, bagged, and shipped in train cars in the 1940s and early 1950s. Elmer Harpstreith also stored potatoes in this building. In the Huntley area, potatoes were a common crop, along with sugar beets, barley, oats, and alfalfa. Farmers also raised lambs. They were brought in on train cars from the Red Desert area (Rawlins and Rock Springs). When they arrived, they were unloaded and herded to each farm. When fat, they were again loaded into double-deck train cars and taken to Omaha for sale. When triple-deck stock trucks came in use, some of the lambs were taken to Chicago for sale. (Homesteaders Museum.)

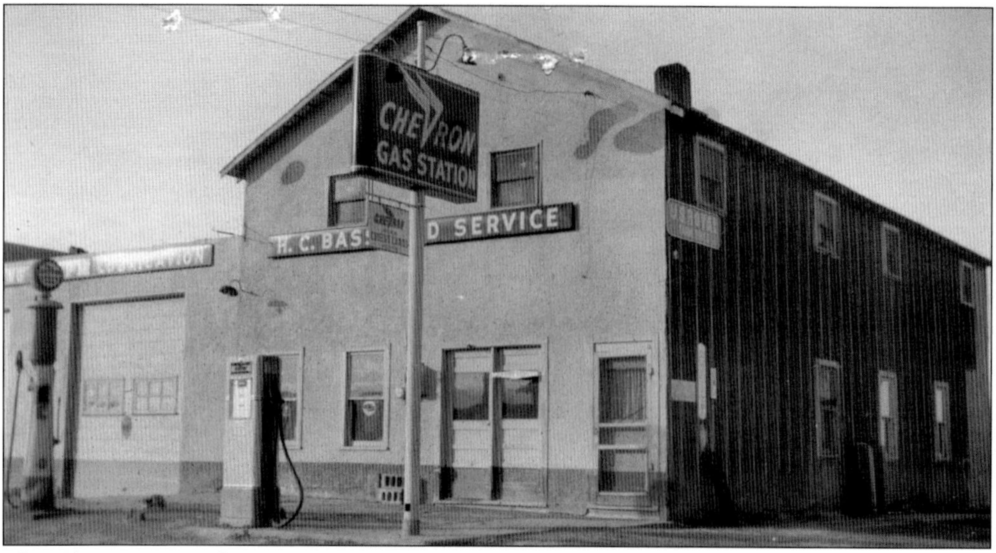

This Chevron gas and service station was owned and operated in the early 1940s by R.C. Bassford, who also offered auto repair. The couple lived upstairs in the building. Around 1944, Bassford closed the business, and in 1960, Vern Lackey had an auto repair shop here. Later, Jim O'Keefe bought the building for a personal garage. Raben's had bulk Conoco gas across the street and also sold household staple groceries, including meat. (Margie Raben Jones.)

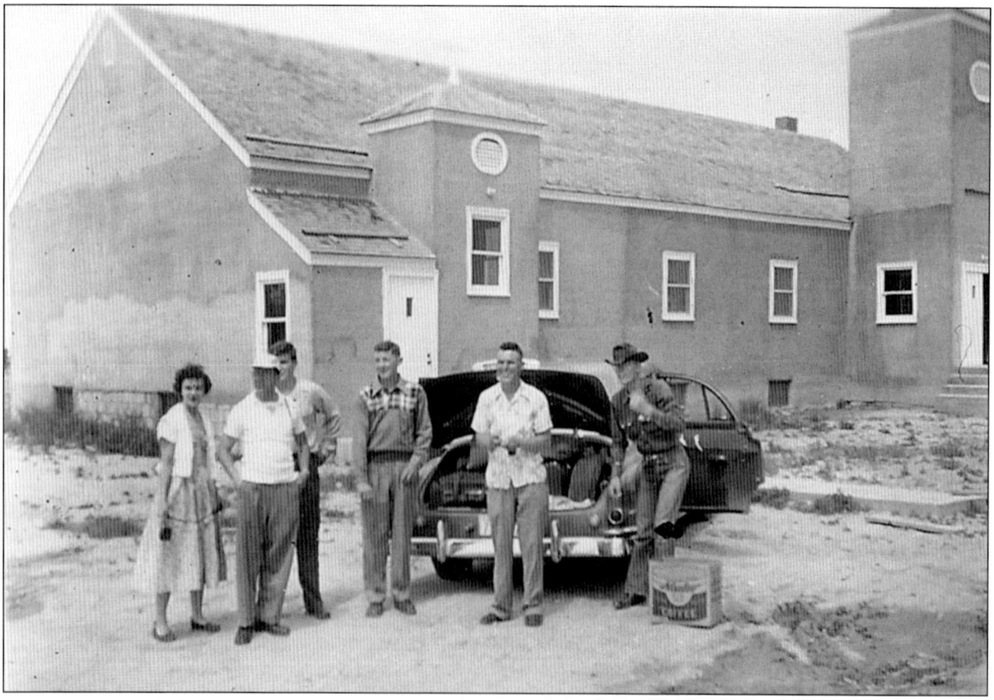

Pictured around 1949 packing the car to go off to church camp in front of the Huntley Community Presbyterian Church are, from left to right, Sylvia Degi, Rev. Joe Degi, Lonnie Eschiliman, Gerald Bassford, Gale Ludwig, and Bud Raben. One half of this church building had originally been part of the Community Hall and was purchased some time after World War II. (Margie Raben Jones.)

Six

COTTIER AND YODER

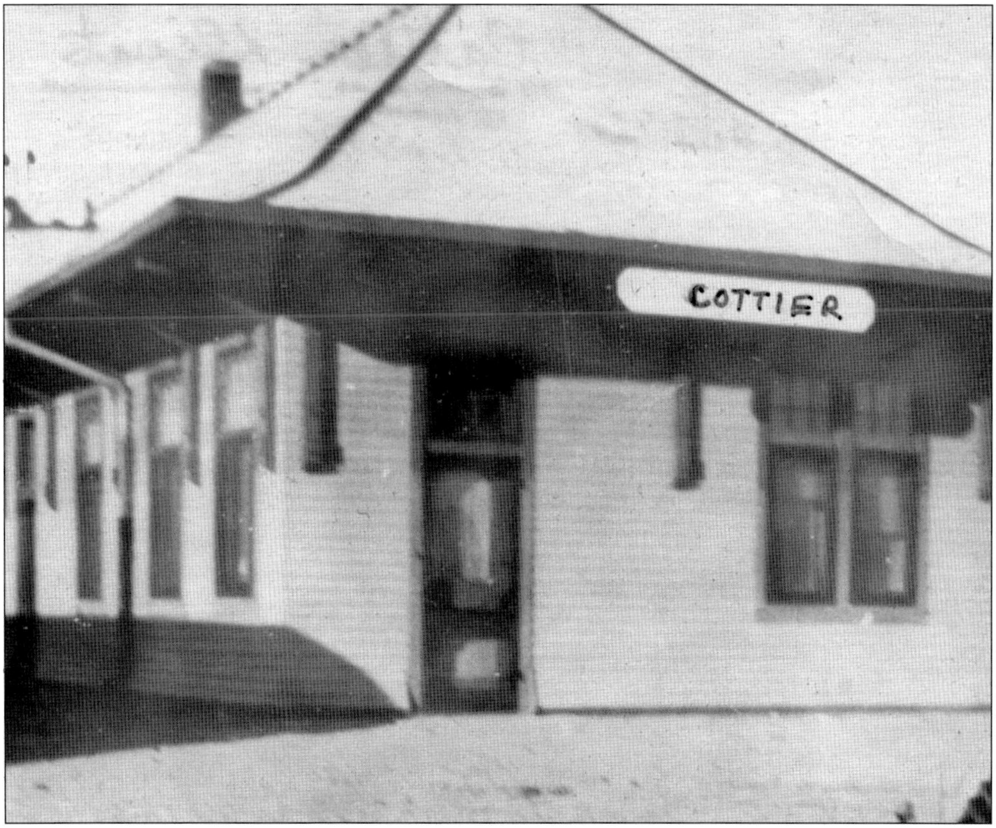

This Union Pacific Railroad depot was established at the end of the railroad line. Robert Cottier told the *Torrington Telegram* in late December 1921 that he would establish a town at this site and name it after himself. The town was surveyed in February 1922 with a grid pattern of streets named after fruit, such as Grape, Plum, Orange, Peach, and Lime. (Mrs. Bill Pursley Collection, Homesteaders Museum.)

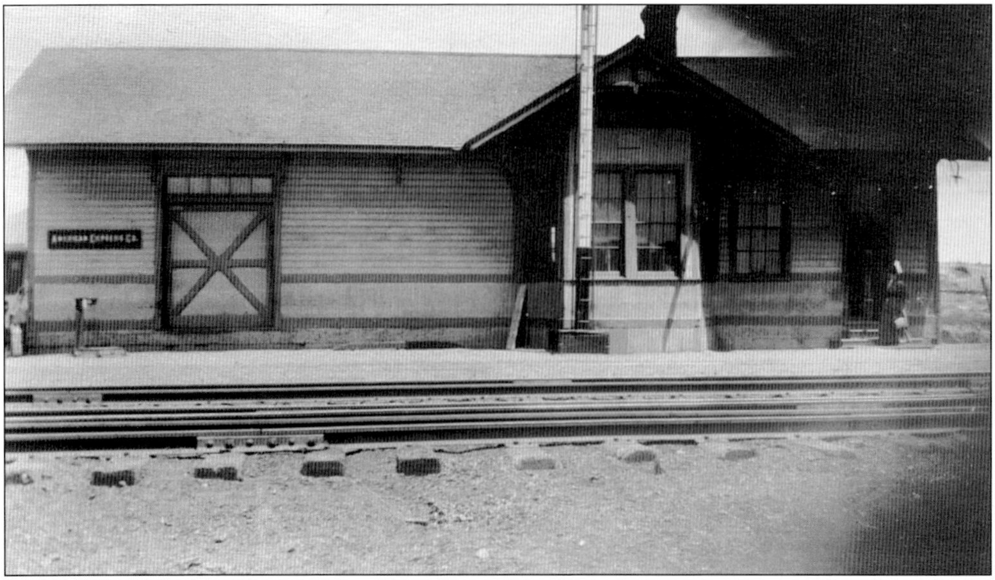

On November 25, 1921, a work train from the Utah Construction Company came to Yoder to begin work on a Union Pacific railroad track to connect Yoder with the outside world—or at least to Gering, Nebraska. By December 15, trains started running, and regular passenger service was established by May 1, 1922. Most of the train routes that were established in Goshen County became part of the North Platte cut-off. (Homesteaders Museum.)

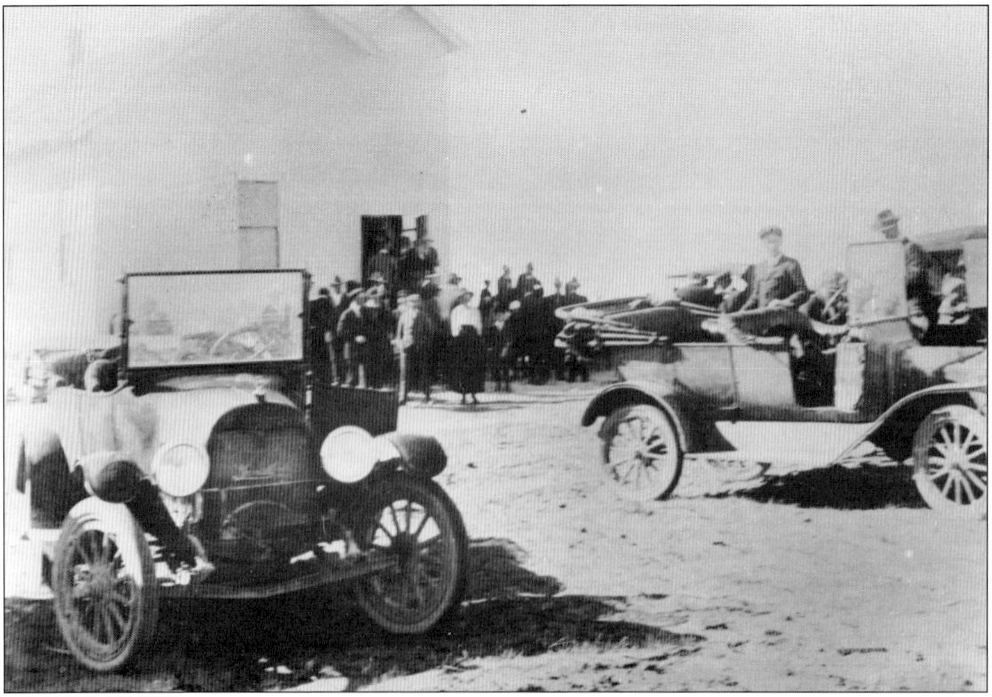

Built in 1917, the Yoder Community Church was originally situated one mile south and two and a half miles west of Yoder but was moved into town later. Church services had first been held in the pool hall and then moved to the city hall before the new church was built. Fords from 1919 are pictured parked outside. (Homesteaders Museum.)

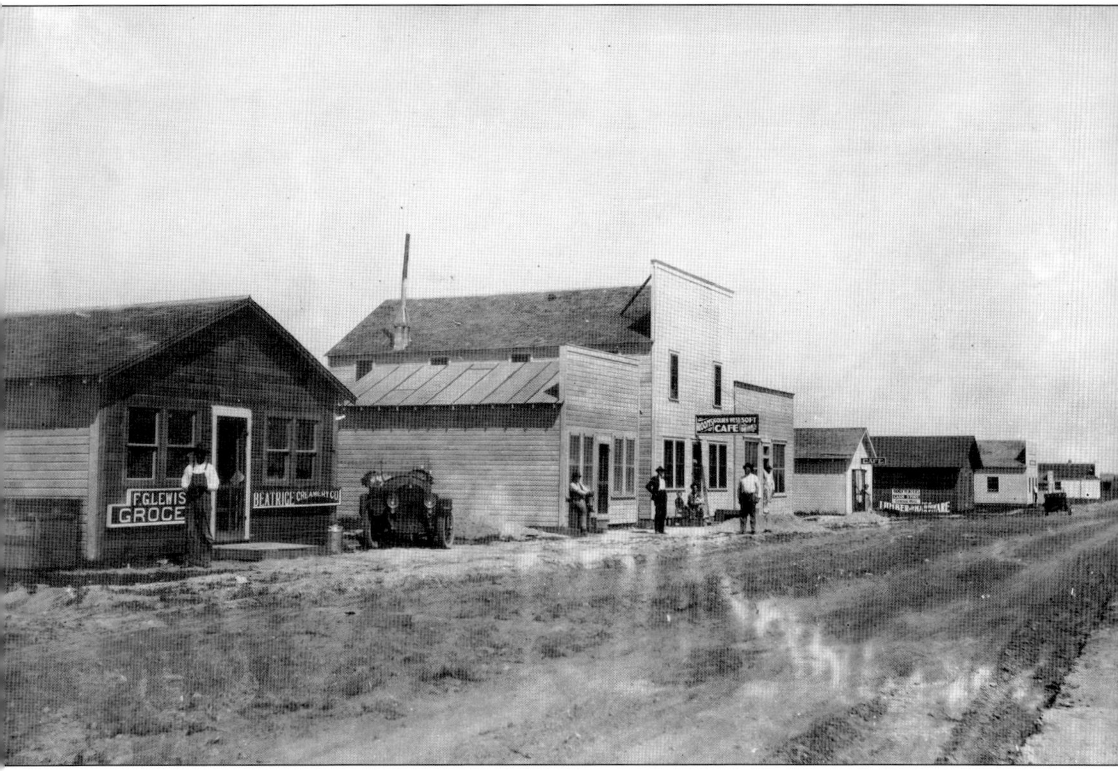

This c. 1920 photograph is looking north on Yoder's Main Street. The buildings from left to right are F.G. Lewis Grocery, Beatrice Creamery, the real estate office, the two-story hotel and café, the blacksmith shop, another café, the Briggs Hardware Store (behind it and across the alley was the lumberyard owned by the same folks), and the Security State Bank. It is not known what was in the final building on that side of the street. (Velma Malone.)

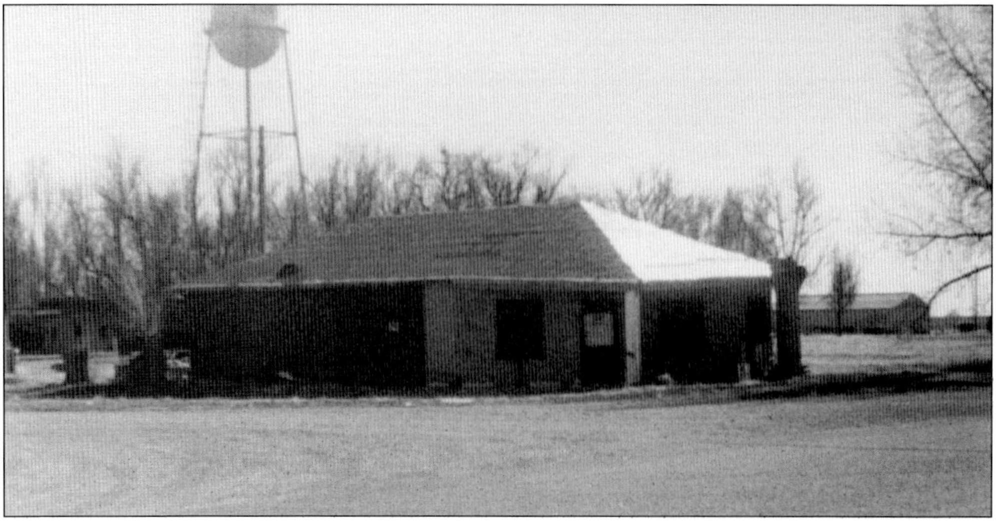

This gas station was built in the 1920s by George Swanson, who sold the service station to W.A. Clemens. His sons Ralph and Vernon helped in the station. It had the only telephone in town, so when someone called, one of the three Clemens men would have to find the person to get them to the phone. The Goshen Hole Grill is now in the station and is run by Tom and Brandy Hiser. (Velma Malone.)

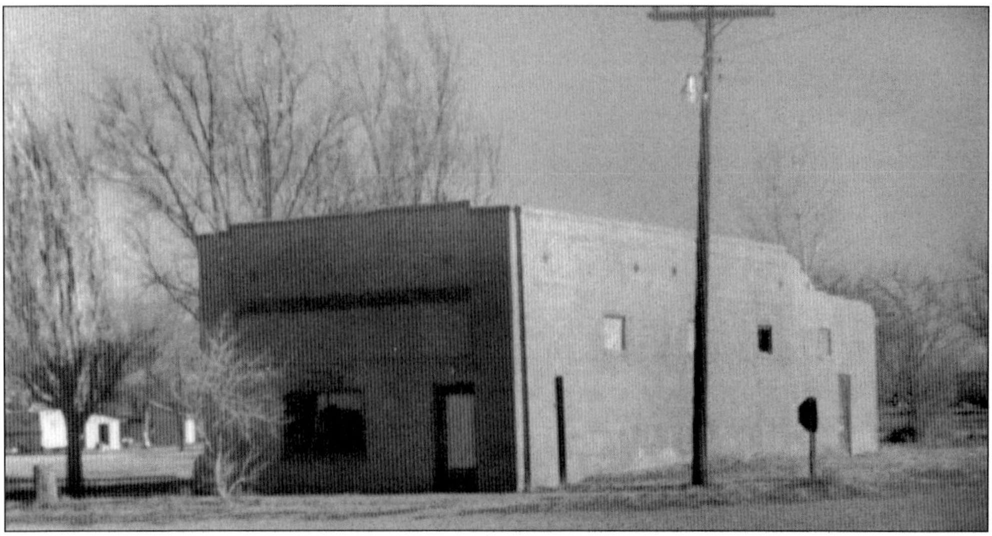

The grocery store was built by George David in the early 1920s. He left town in 1934, and since then, the store has had several owners, including Ted Brown, Violet and Z.O. Yates, and someone named Barnhardt. The building has been torn down. (Velma Malone.)

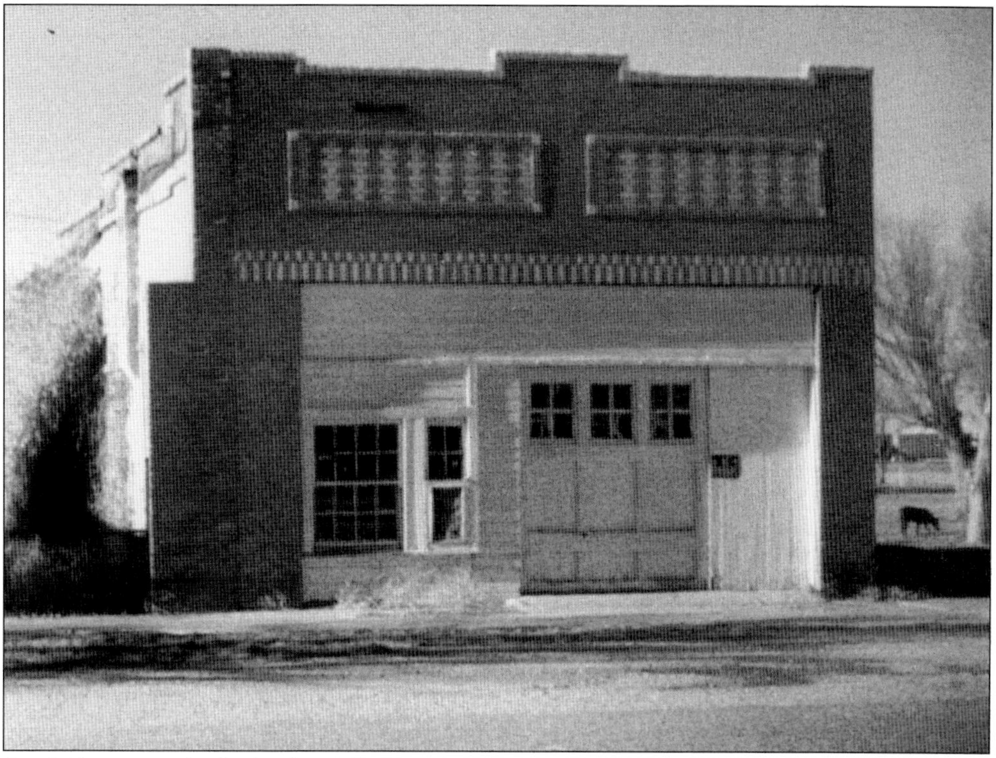

Frank Furney made the bricks and then constructed this building in the early 1920s, and there was an identical one to the left. One of the buildings was a grocery store, and the other was a clothing store. The surround has since been torn off. (Velma Malone.)

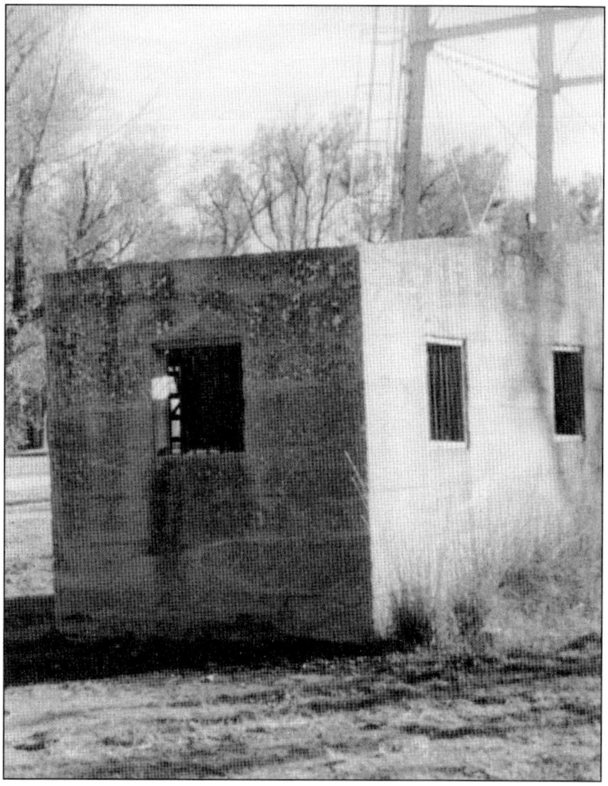

This two-cell jail was built in the 1920s. Oliver Holmes was the first marshal, succeeded by Harve "Red" Holderman. A youngster in town, Jim David, was a constant visitor to the building when it was being constructed. The workers teased him about being the first person to be put in the jail. Many years later, when he was visiting Doug Essert, he asked him to take him by the jail. He proceeded to extract a hacksaw blade that he had placed under the windowsill, which he claimed he would use to escape from jail if he was ever placed there. (Velma Malone.)

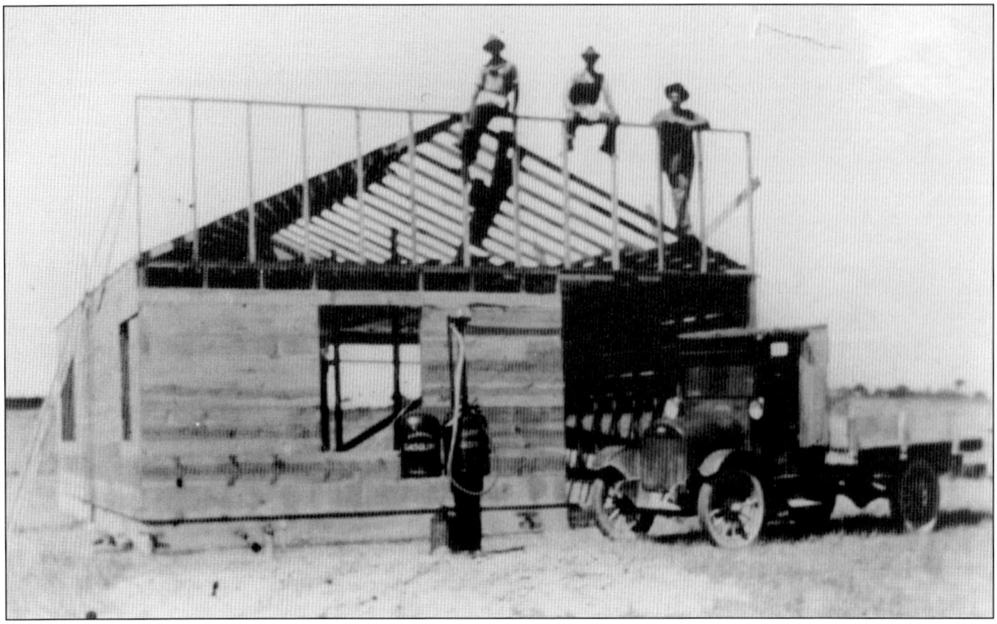

In the summer of 1922, Jay Fowler built his garage. It was one of the first businesses to open, even before Veteran had its name. Hattie May came up with the name and it was approved by the Union Pacific Railroad and the Bureau of Reclamation. (Lucy Purtle Photo Collection, Homesteaders Museum.)

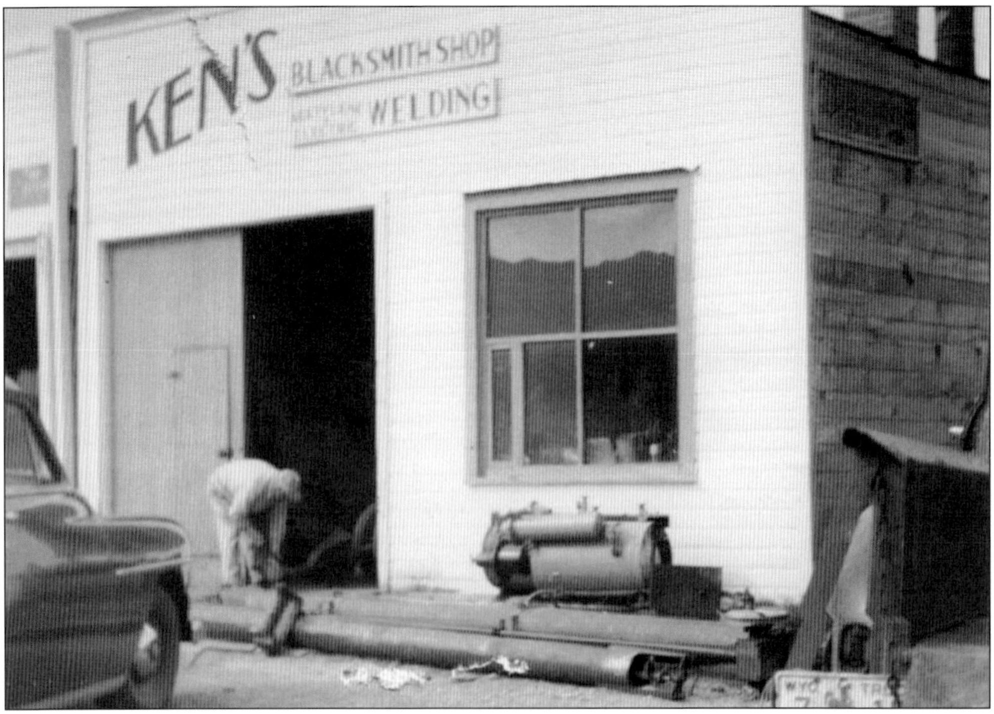

Ken Malone is shown in the doorway of his blacksmith shop. Malone was a 1937 Yoder High School graduate and worked on local farm machinery in this shop. When he went into the military, someone else took over the shop. (Velma Malone.)

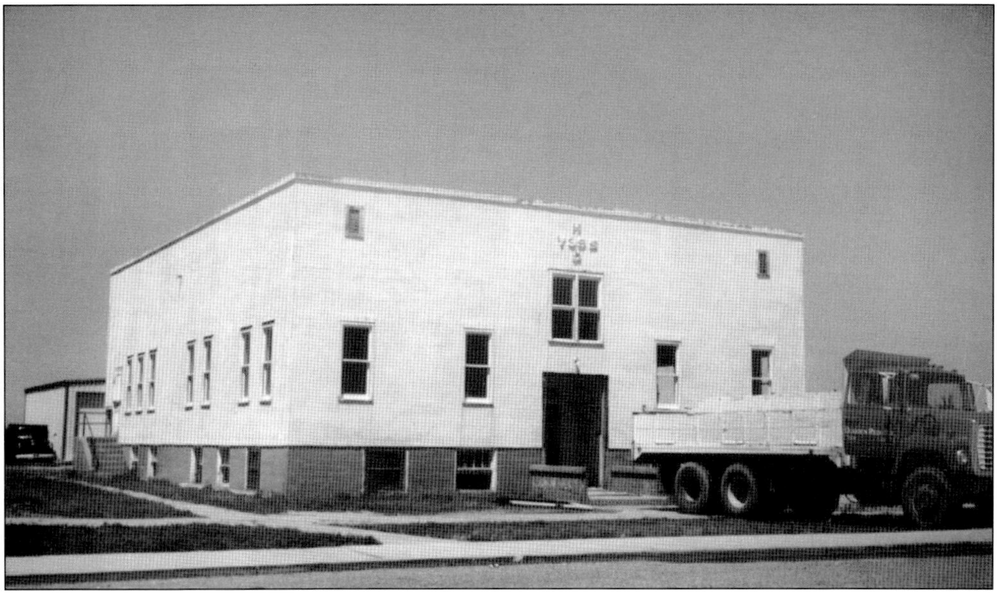

H.L. Malone built Yoder Grade School in 1939. (Velma Malone.)

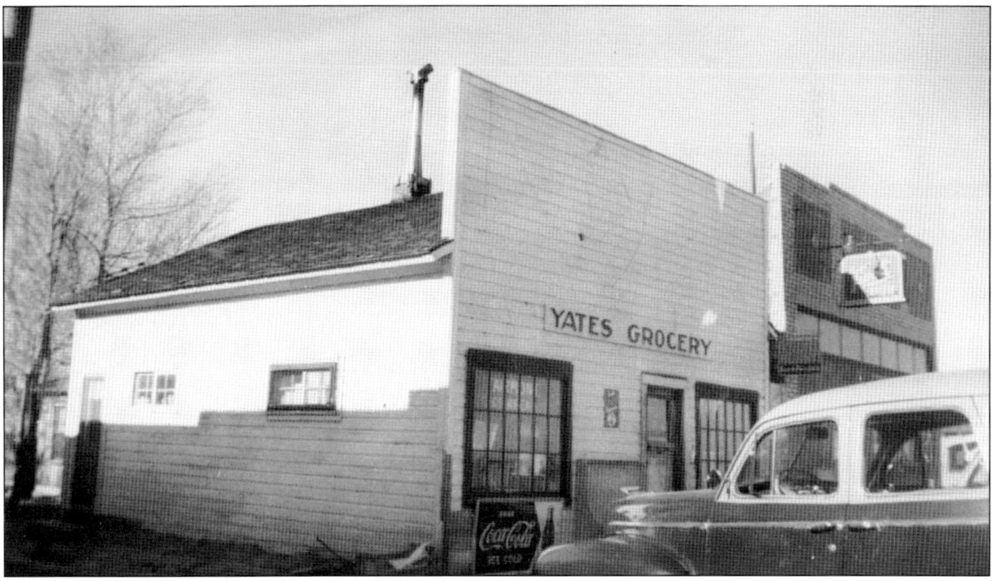

The wooden building on the left was originally the Yoder post office after it was moved from the north side of the building to the right. The building on the right was built by A.F. "Sandy" VerStratten. Dr. Duane NeuShultz, a chiropractor and podiatrist, ran a drugstore in the building and later converted part of it to a six-stool bar. Kate Clemens later operated it as a grocery store. (Velma Malone.)

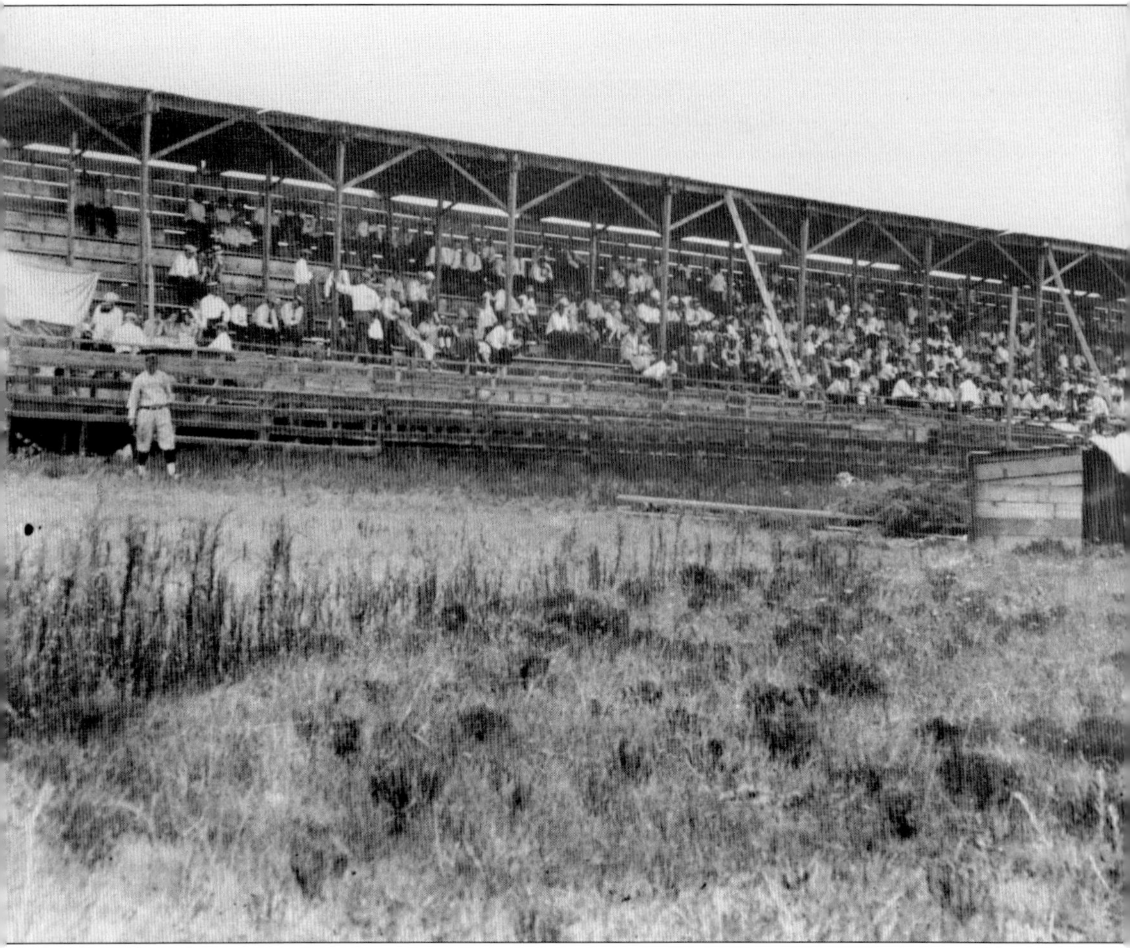

Pictured in 1925 are the Yoder grandstands with a huge crowd. The grandstands had originally been built on the hill south of town for rodeo spectators. The first rodeo was held in 1922. It was estimated that baseball games would draw a crowd of 2,000, with another 1,000 people in cars around the half-mile track. W.J. Essert is walking onto the field on the left. (Homesteaders Museum.)

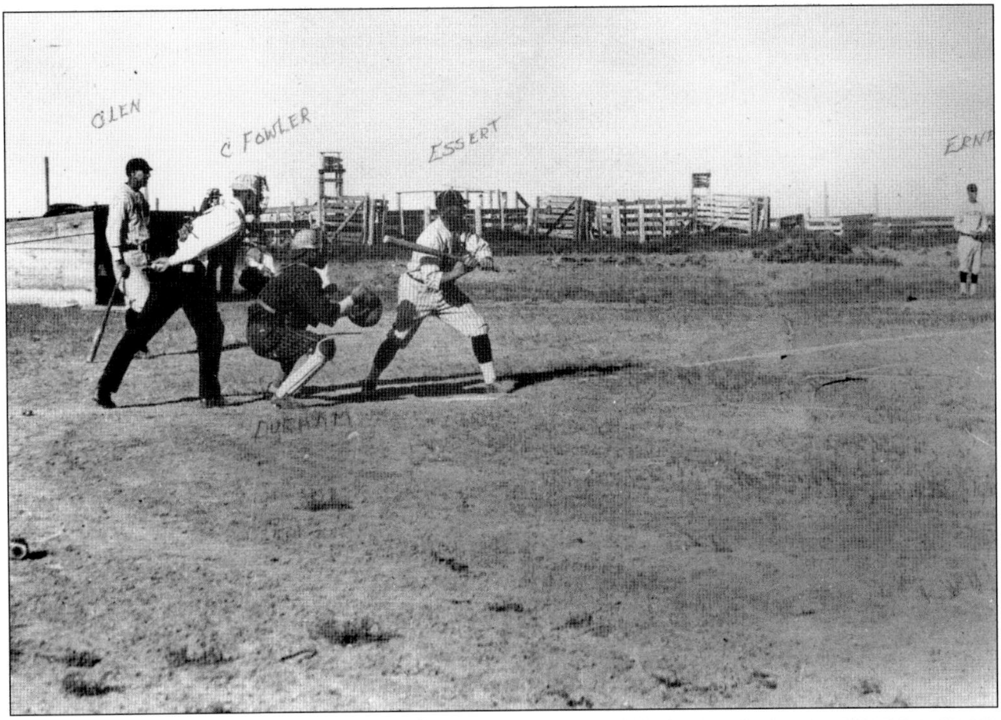

Yoder had a town baseball team in 1925, before the Marlatt Brothers team. Playing ball from left to right are Glen Marlatt, Charley Fowler (umpire), ? Durham, W.J. Essert (batter), and Ernest "Slim" Marlatt in the outfield. This team went to the Denver post-season tournament, which was a semi-world series at that time. (Homesteaders Museum.)

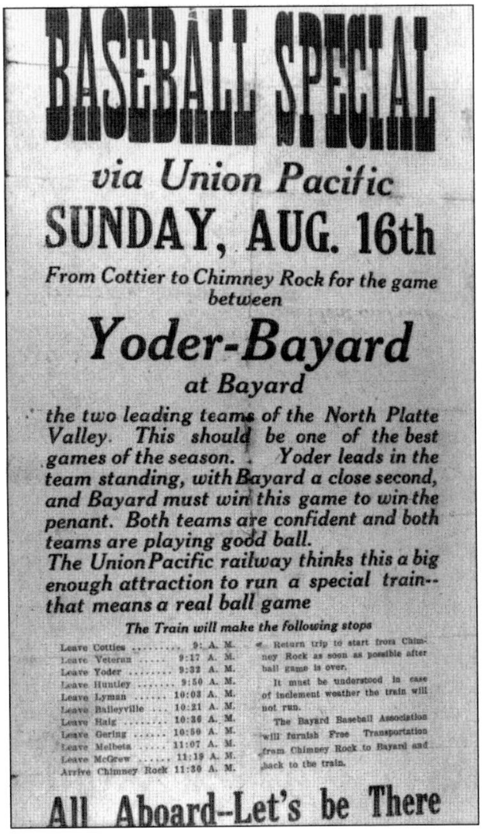

BASEBALL SPECIAL

via Union Pacific

SUNDAY, AUG. 16th

From Cottier to Chimney Rock for the game between

Yoder-Bayard

at Bayard

the two leading teams of the North Platte Valley. This should be one of the best games of the season. Yoder leads in the team standing, with Bayard a close second, and Bayard must win this game to win the penant. Both teams are confident and both teams are playing good ball.

The Union Pacific railway thinks this a big enough attraction to run a special train-- that means a real ball game

The Train will make the following stops

Leave Cotties .... 9: A. M.
Leave Veteran ..... 9:17 A. M.
Leave Yoder .... 9:32 A. M.
Leave Huntley .... 9:50 A. M.
Leave Lyman ...... 10:03 A. M.
Leave Baileyville ... 10:21 A. M.
Leave Haig .... 10:36 A. M.
Leave Gering ...... 10:50 A. M.
Leave Melbeta ..... 11:07 A. M.
Leave McGrew ...... 11:19 A. M.
Arrive Chimney Rock 11:30 A. M.

Return trip to start from Chimney Rock as soon as possible after ball game is over.

It must be understood in case of inclement weather the train will not run.

The Bayard Baseball Association will furnish Free Transportation from Chimney Rock to Bayard and back to the train.

All Aboard--Let's be There

Baseball was the "real deal" in the region during the early days of Goshen County's history. This broadside shows that the game between Yoder and Bayard at Bayard was thought to be so special that the Union Pacific Railroad decided to have a designated train take fans from Cottier to Chimney Rock for the game. Nine other stops would be made for passengers to board. The Bayard Baseball Association was to provide transportation from the last stop to the game. The train would return as quickly as possible to Cottier. (Homesteaders Museum.)

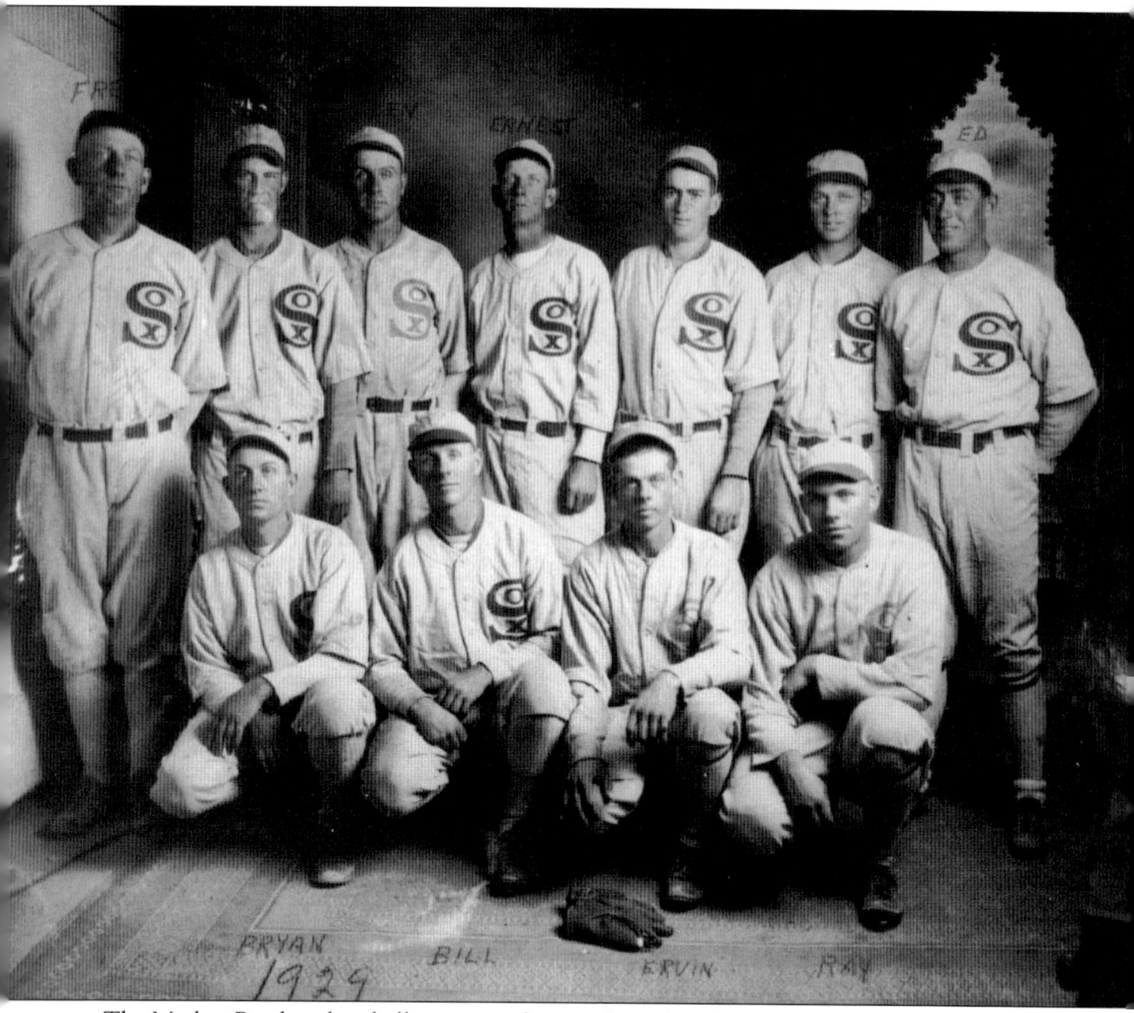

The Marlatt Brothers baseball team was famous throughout the region. In 1929, the family team consisted of, from left to right, (first row) Bryan, Bill, Ervin, and Ray; (second row) Fred, Lloyd, Glen, Ernest, Faye, Jack, and Ed. They were the children of Henry and Arrena Teressa Marlatt. (Homesteaders Museum.)

Seven

LINGLE

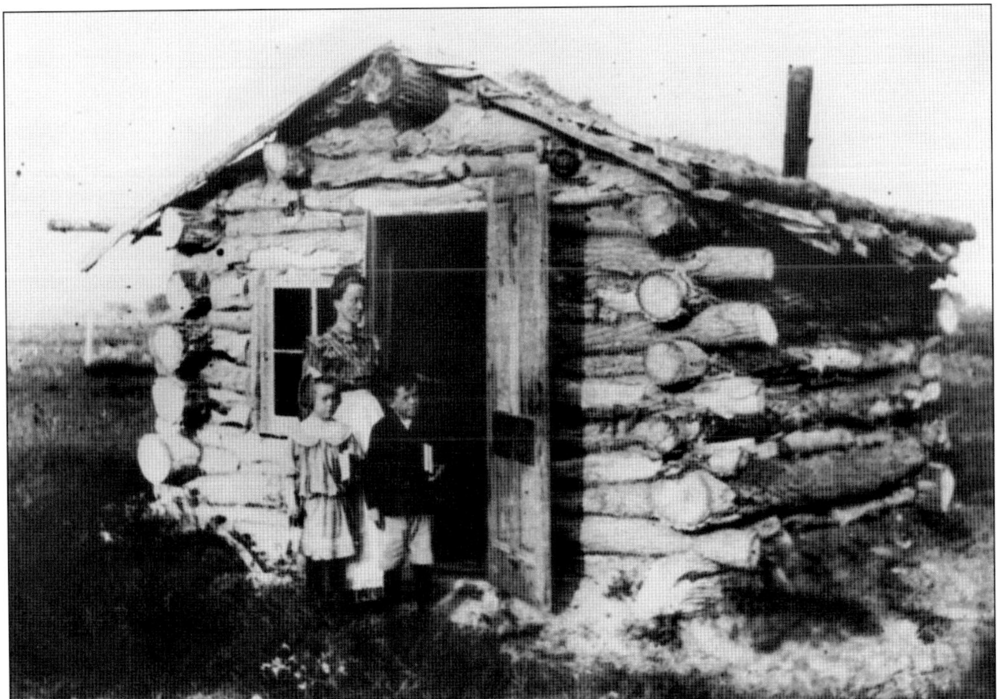

Mrs. Tom Powers (née Abbie E. Chamberlin) and her children John George and Laura M. are standing outside the door of their home. The couple was married in St. Joseph, Missouri, on March 17, 1896. Tom constructed the cottonwood-log building in 1905. It had a sod roof, which needed continual maintenance. It was known as the "Little Log House on the Prairie." Tom had been in the area for some time, freighting and wrangling cattle for the Pratt-Ferris ranch. Abbie served as a postmistress and Tom was the first state senator from Goshen County. (Wyoming State Archives, Department of State Parks and Cultural Resources.)

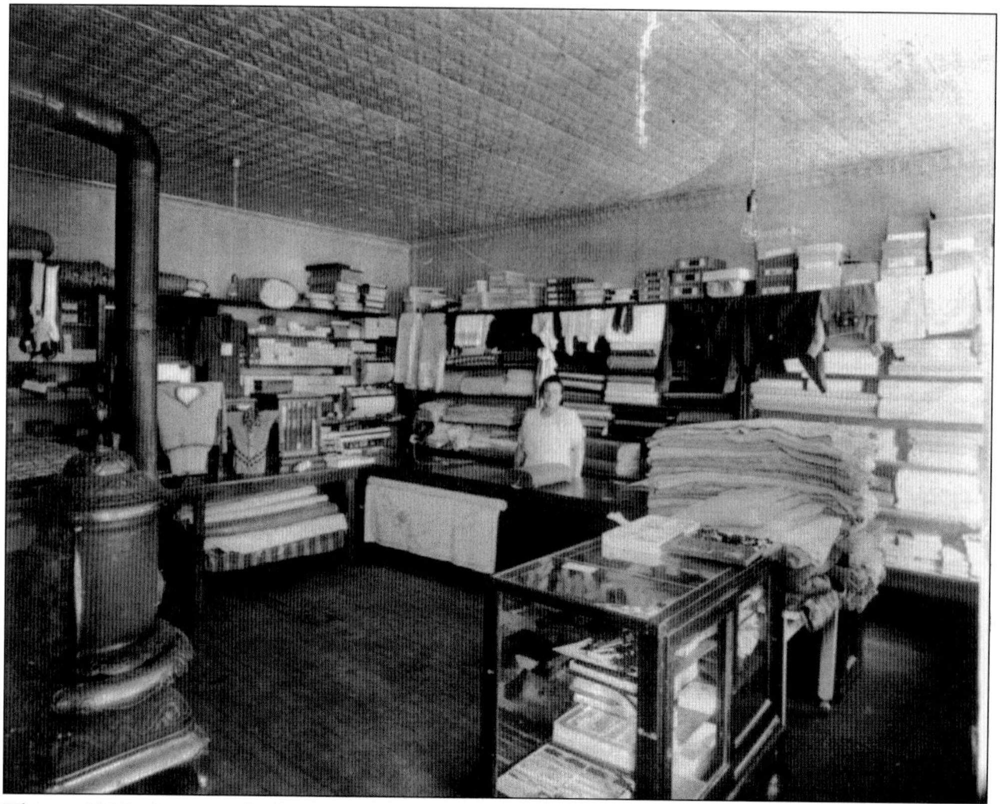

This c. 1926 photograph shows Reitz's General Store. Fred Reitz opened his clothing store in the early 1920s but eventually sold out to Othie Curry. Fred Hinze is pictured as a clerk. He also raised sugar beets and cattle on his farm. (Homesteaders Museum.)

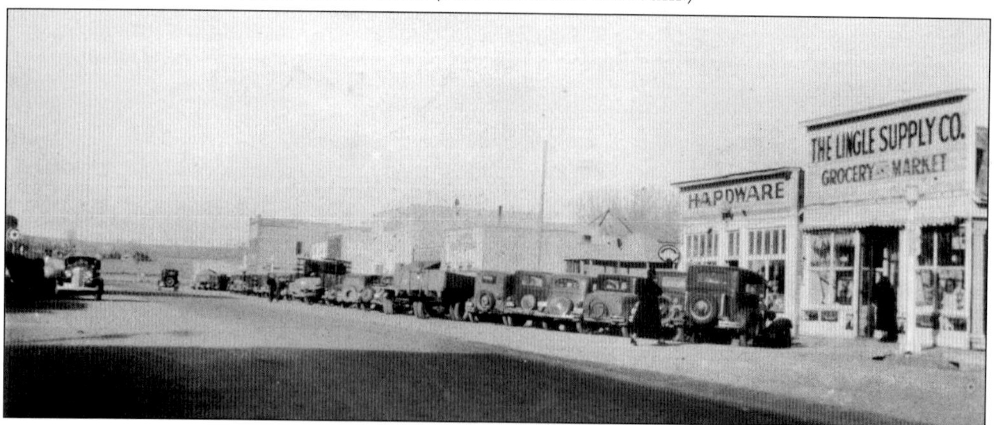

This is an early photograph of Lingle's Main Street. Wyncote was a small town that eventually evolved into Lingle around 1908. The town was named for Hiriam Lingle, who built part of the first irrigation ditch. Some of the buildings were moved from the earlier town of Wyncote. A Mr. Whitehall moved one of these buildings and then sold it to William Connolly, who added another part to the building on the north. The first business in Lingle, called Lingle Supply Company, was established in this building. The business sold groceries, hardware, clothing, fabric, machinery, and Model T cars. Over time, other businesses were established, including a hotel, a post office, a lumberyard, a newspaper, the Lingle State Bank, and a theater. (George Zeimens.)

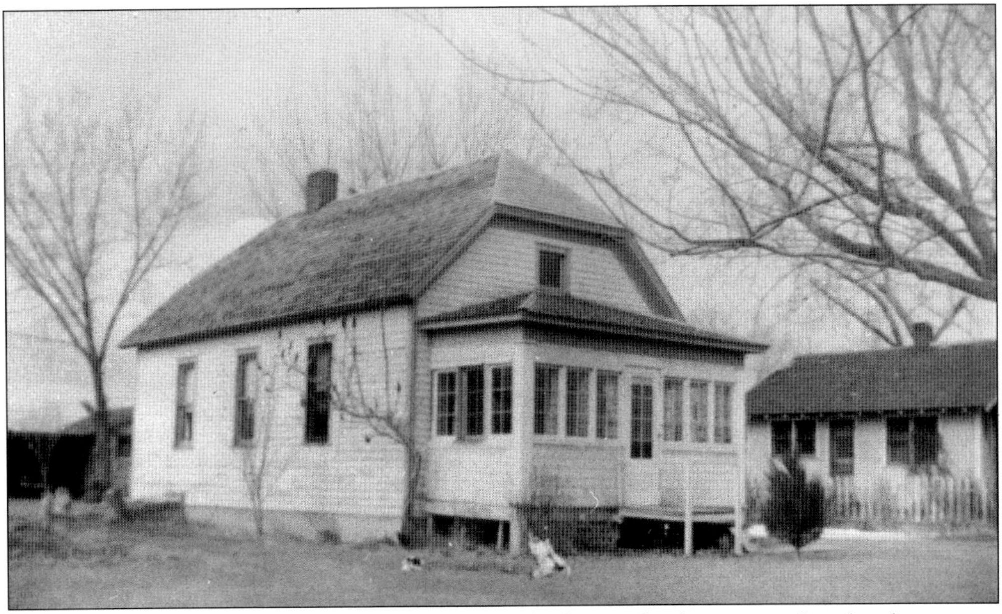

A $10,000 bond financed this school building, which was the first one in Lingle when it was built in the summer of 1915. It was a four-room building constructed by Porter Fowler and Frank Brewer. It housed eight elementary grades and the first two high school grades. Robert Woods was the superintendent. In 1919, because of the consolidation of the Rawhide and Wyncote schools, four more rooms were added on the north side. The first class to graduate was in 1921. The first high school was built in 1923. (Wyoming State Archives, Department of State Parks and Cultural Resources.)

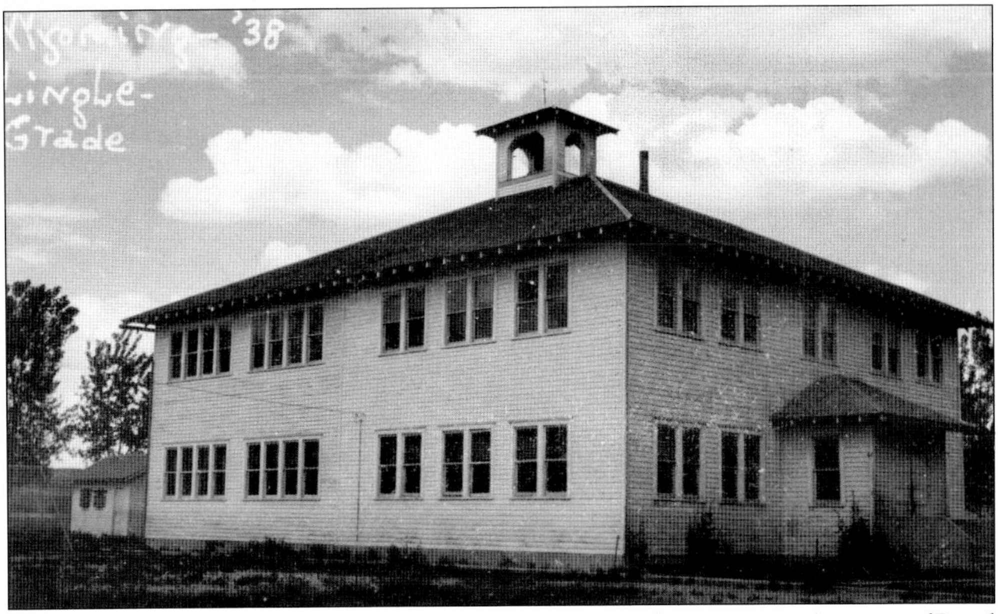

The new grade school was constructed by H.H. Hackett General Construction Company of Rapid City, South Dakota, beginning on November 10, 1938. It was to be finished for school the next fall. The school was financed by a $46,000 bond issue and a federal Public Works Administration loan of $37,000. The school was built west of the high school building. (George Zeimens.)

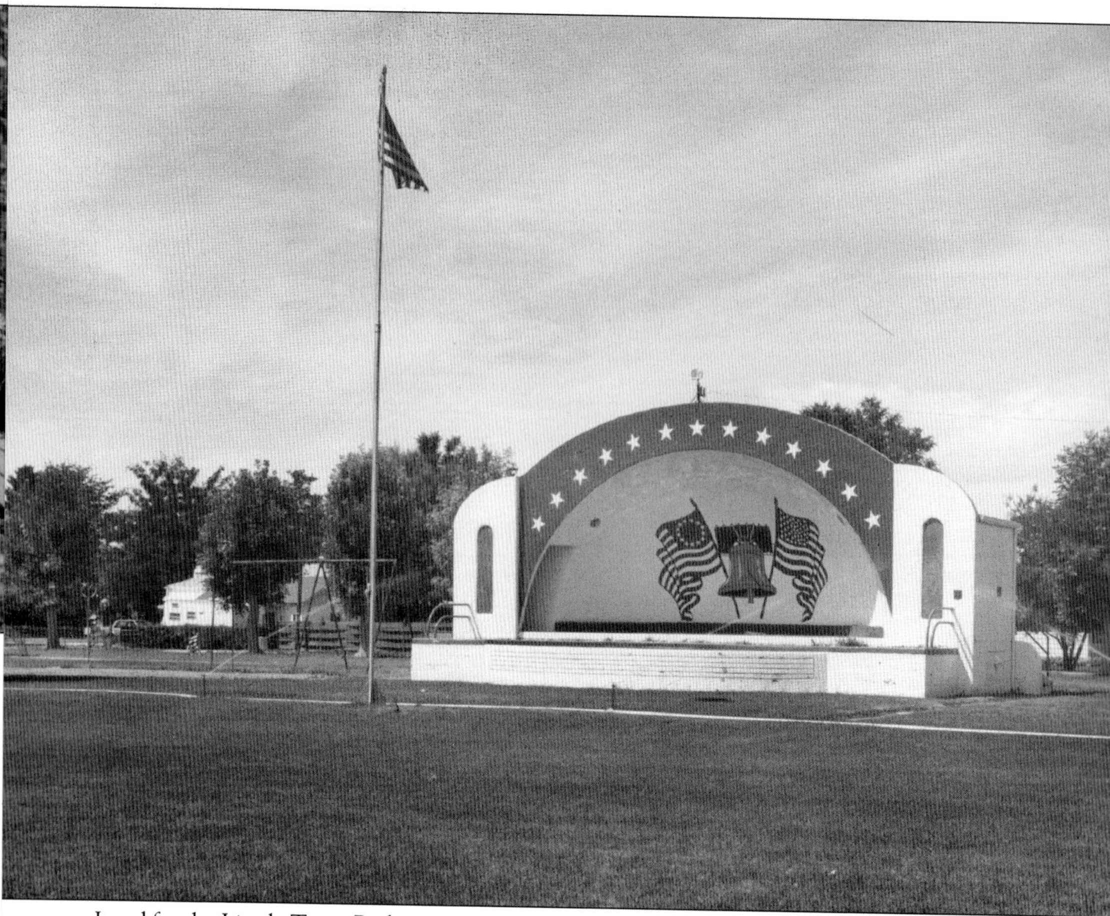

Land for the Lingle Town Park was given to the city in the last will and testament of Levi Z. Leiter. In ordinance No. 49, the Lingle City Council, having all three readings in one meeting, accepted the donation on January 30, 1936. On December 7, 1994, the name of the park was changed to Whipple Park. Ivan Whipple was a lineman employed by Wyrulec Company, a distributor of electricity. The band shell was built as a WPA project in 1941 and 1942. William Carr designed and painted the patriotic bell and flags in July 1987. On March 30, 1993, the design logo was registered with Wyoming's secretary of state as a trademark as part of the celebration for Lingle's 75th anniversary. The design has been faithfully repainted about every four to five years by city staff. (Homesteader Museum.)

Eight

Jay Em

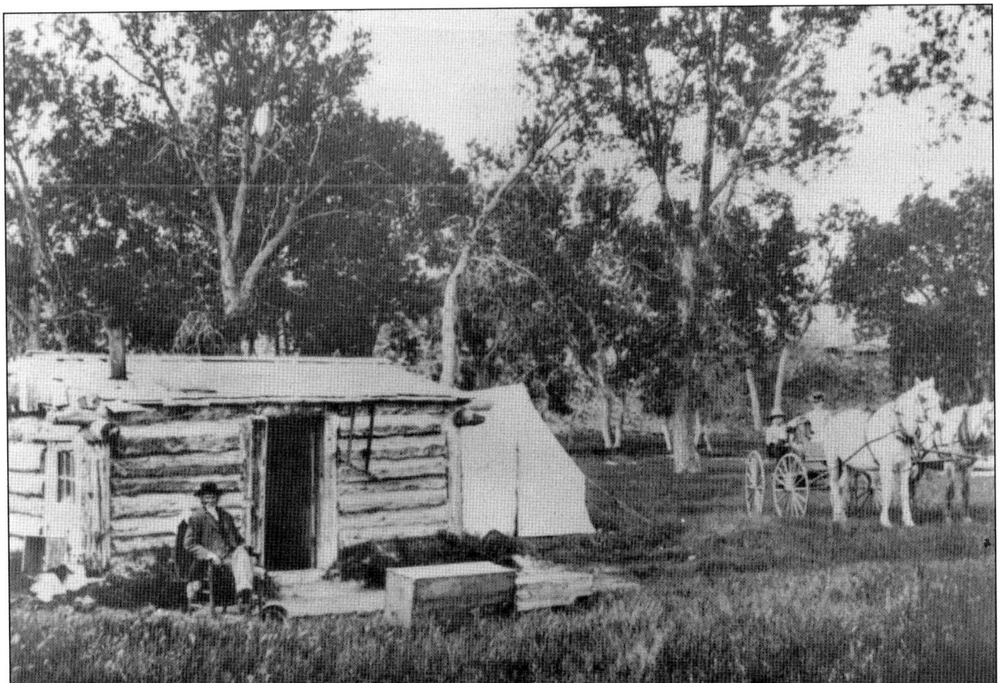

Jack Hargraves sits in front of the post office in 1908, just around the time it closed. The post office was located one mile south of Jay Em and had officially opened in 1899. Silas Harris reopened the post office, but for three months, he had to ride 11 miles to the Rawhide Buttes station three days a week to get the mail before he was named postmaster. Silas's son Lake took over in 1910 and served in the position for nearly 50 years. (Homesteaders Museum.)

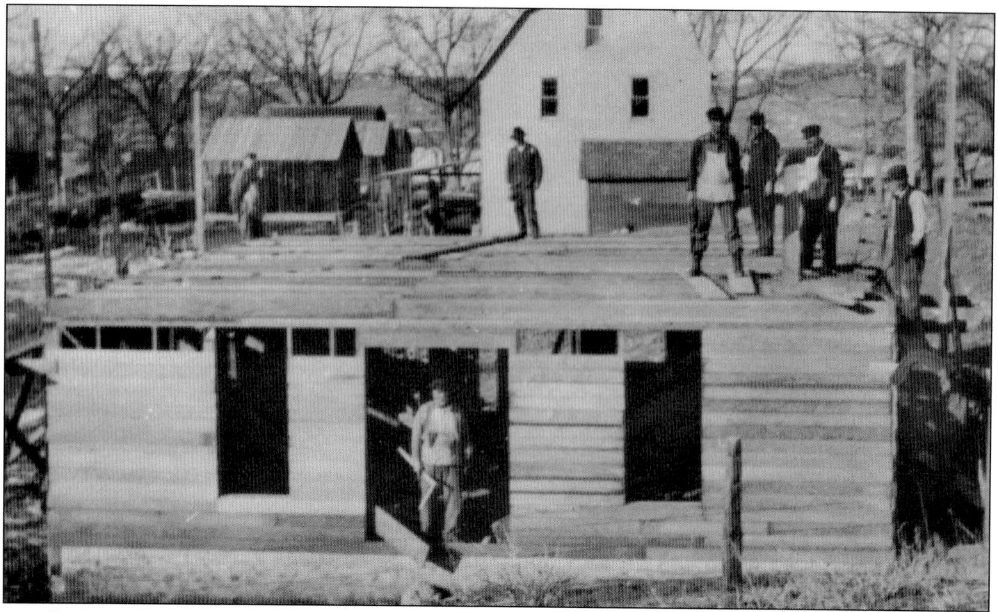

J Rolling M was the brand of James Moore, a Texas trail driver, cattleman, and freighter who was associated with the naming of the town of Jay Em. He homesteaded a large ranch in 1850 in the area of Rawhide Creek. Moore was killed when his horse spooked while he was feeding cattle and he fell into the hay wagon. His widow remarried, and her husband sold the ranch to a Dr. Johnston and his brother Will from Wapaun, Wisconsin. Will was the ranch manager. Dr. Johnston met Silas Harris, a Wisconsin cattle buyer who was interested in land in the West. Harris moved his wife, Annie, and their three sons, Art, Lake, and Frank, to the ranch in 1905. In 1909, Silas bought the ranch from the Johnstons. This photograph shows the beginnings of the lumberyard. The large building in the background to the right was the hardware store and gas station, and later, the upstairs was where movies were shown. (Homesteaders Museum.)

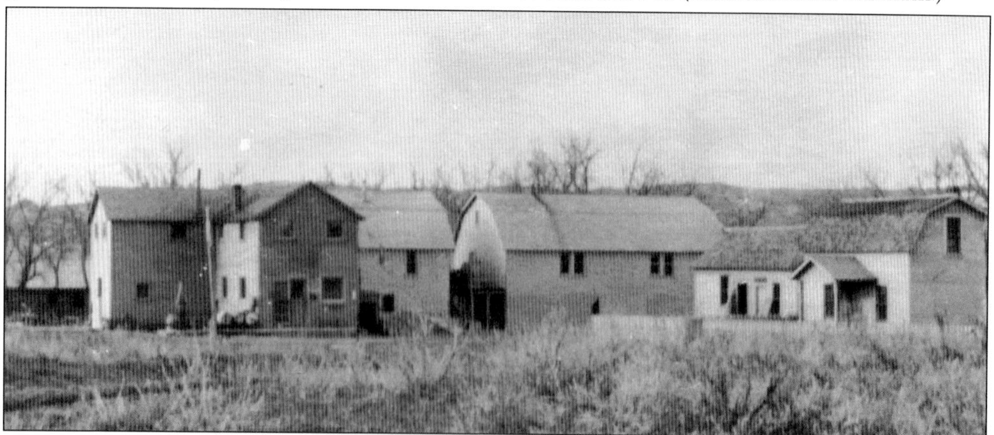

Lake founded the small settlement of Jay Em in 1912 by starting a grocery store in his homestead house. He saw the need for such a place for the neighboring homesteaders instead of having to travel to Lusk or Torrington for their necessities. One of the other services the store provided was buying local dairy cream. This part of the business was the largest of its kind at that time in Wyoming. From 1912 to 1917, other businesses sprang up. A large mill produced and sold cattle feed, cereals, and flour from the corn, wheat, and barley grown in the area. There was a potato cellar for storage and a place to get certified-seed potatoes. (Homesteaders Museum.)

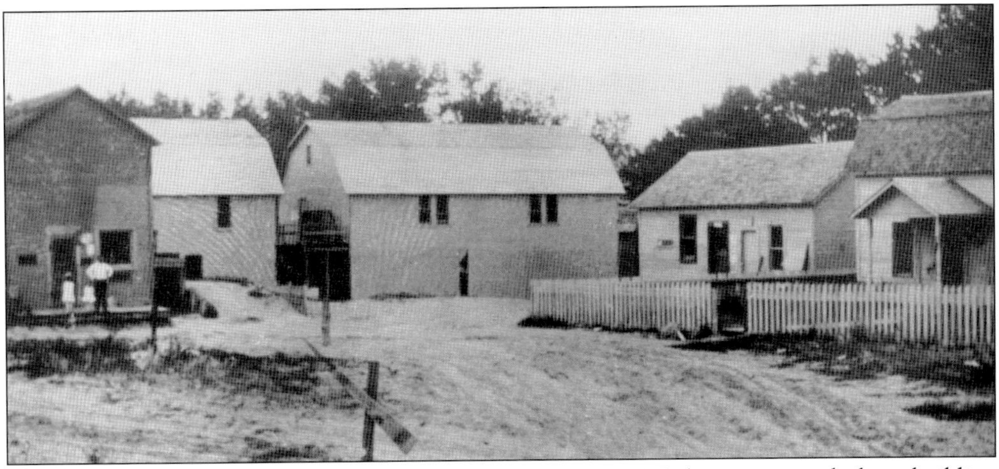

There was also a combination ice house and restaurant. In 1917, Lake constructed a large building to house the grocery store, drugstore, and hardware business. The hardware store had a soda fountain and handled appliances, veterinary and ranch supplies, stock tanks, and windmills. Lake and his wife, Autumn, started publishing the *Fort Laramie Signal* and *Jay Em News*. There was also a millinery shop, a shoe and harness shop, a cream station, and a blacksmith shop. In the 1920s, a barbershop, gas station, and garage were also available. It never had a saloon. Many area youngsters remember attending summer 4-H, Boy Scouts, and football camps in its park. (Homesteaders Museum.)

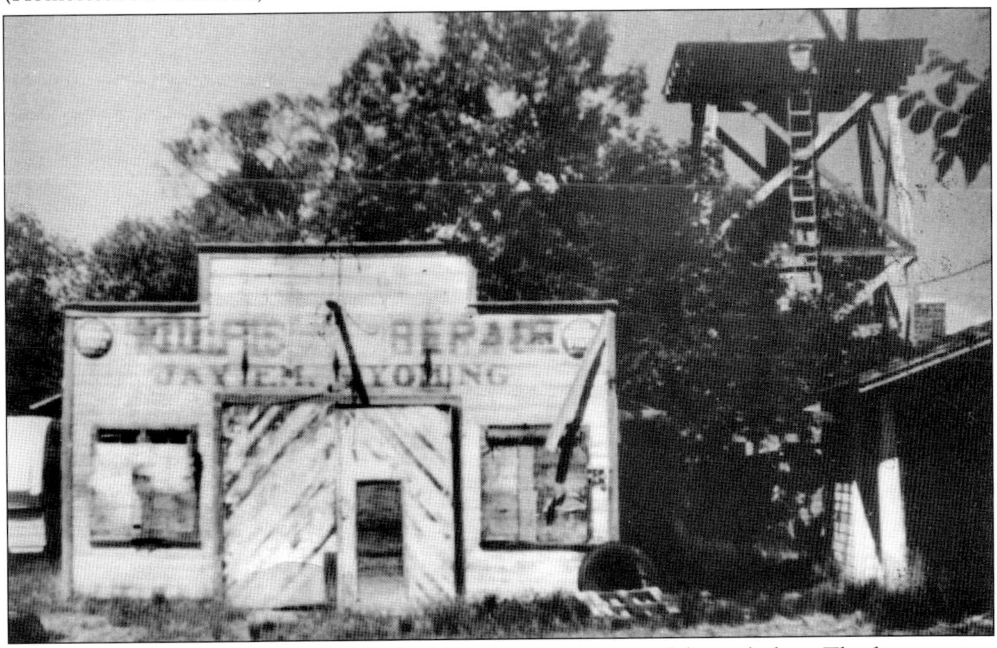

Jay Em Repair Shop was located in the building that is now part of the rock shop. The first meeting for the election of a board of directors was held to start a bank, which received its charter on October 18, 1919. The Farmers State Bank of J.M. opened for business in 1920. The first president was J.W. Newell. On April 5, 1945, the bank was granted a national charter and became the Farmers National Bank of Jay Em. The board of directors received permission to move the charter to Torrington, and the name was changed to Farmers National Bank of Torrington. Thirteen years later, the bank changed its name to First National Bank. (Homesteaders Museum.)

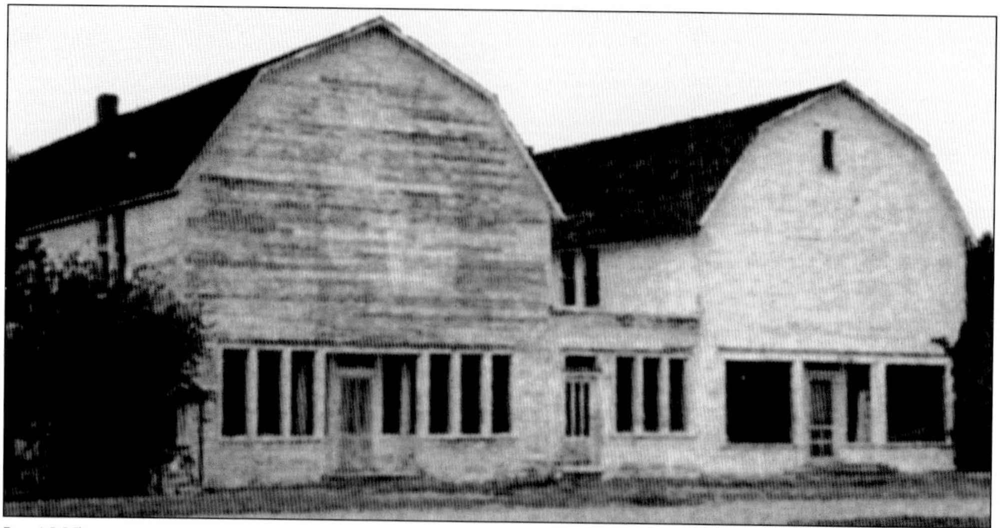

In 1935, a grocery store was built close to the hardware store. This photograph shows these two almost identical buildings. About this same time, a rock shop opened for business and sold fireplaces, mantels, headstones, salt and pepper shakers, bookends, tabletops, lamps, and jewelry. The stones came from Hartville, Wheatland, and Muskrat Canyon, as well as from South Dakota, Minnesota, and Virginia. (Hazel Mudgett.)

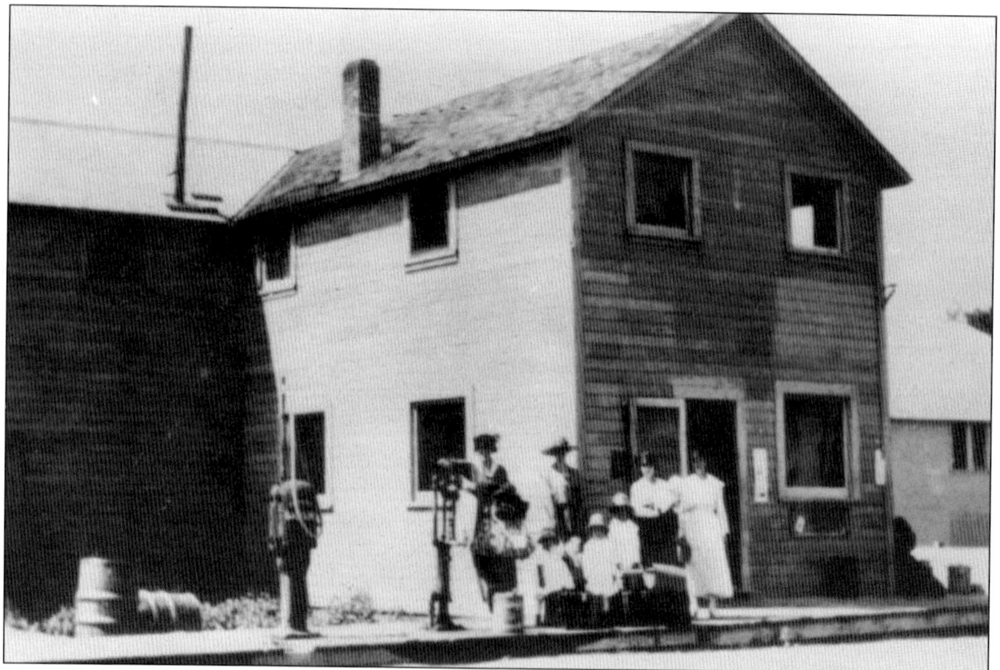

Most of the buildings in the town of Jay Em are closed now, though they are being kept intact as though the business is just closed for the day. In 1984, the town was designated as a historic district and placed in the National Historic Register. Family members continue to clean and maintain the existing buildings. There are few people who live in the town now, and they must go to Lusk or Torrington for services, doctors, and groceries. Tours by appointment are given through all of the buildings from May through September each year by two of Lake Harris's granddaughters, with some help from a few other family members. (Homesteaders Museum.)

Nine

Torrington

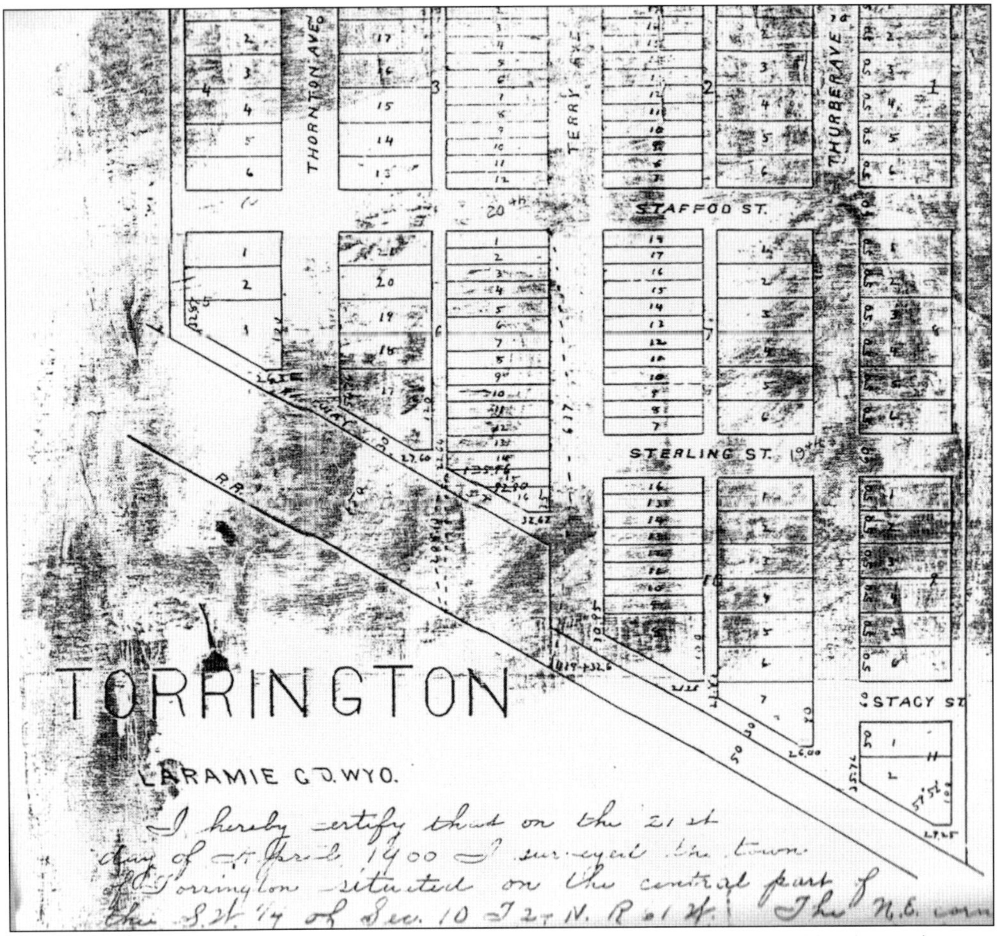

This is a copy of the 1900 original Torrington plat. The land had been deeded by the Burlington Railroad and was owned by the Lincoln Land Company of Nebraska. (Homesteaders Museum.)

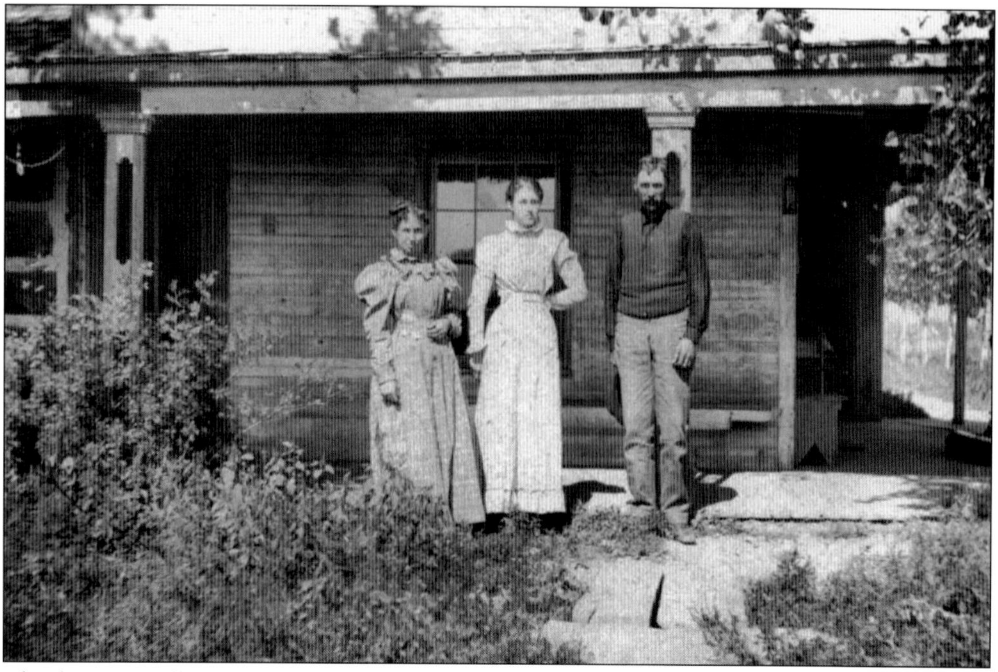

The first post office in Torrington was in a building that had been moved from Fort Laramie to a location just west of town, opening on July 20, 1889. Standing in front of the home/post office are Delia E. (also known as Dehlia Curtis), Matlee L. Curtis, and William G. Curtis, first postmaster. (Homesteaders Museum.)

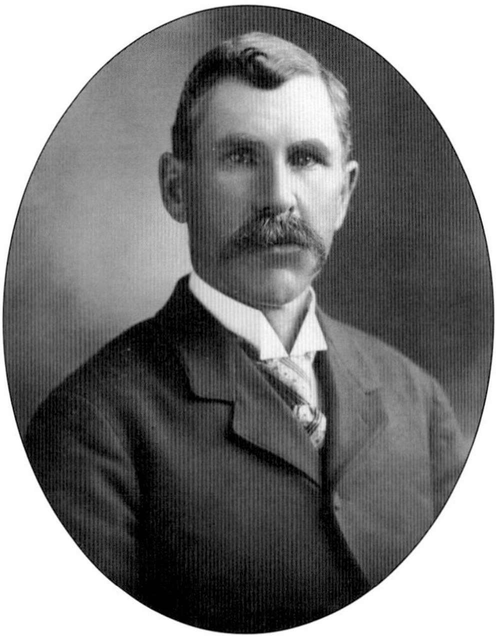

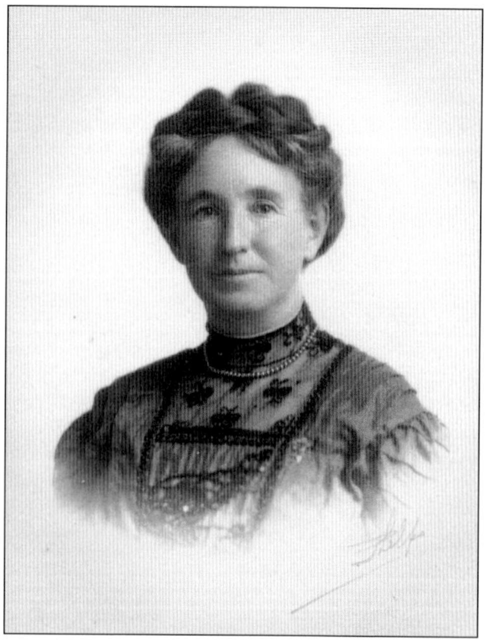

William G. Curtis was the founder of Torrington in 1889. He was the first postmaster and maintained it in his home. The mail went from Cheyenne to Fort Laramie and then to Torrington twice a week. After the town was incorporated in 1907, Curtis served two terms as mayor. The portrait of his wife, Dehlia, was taken around 1910 or 1912. (Homesteaders Museum.)

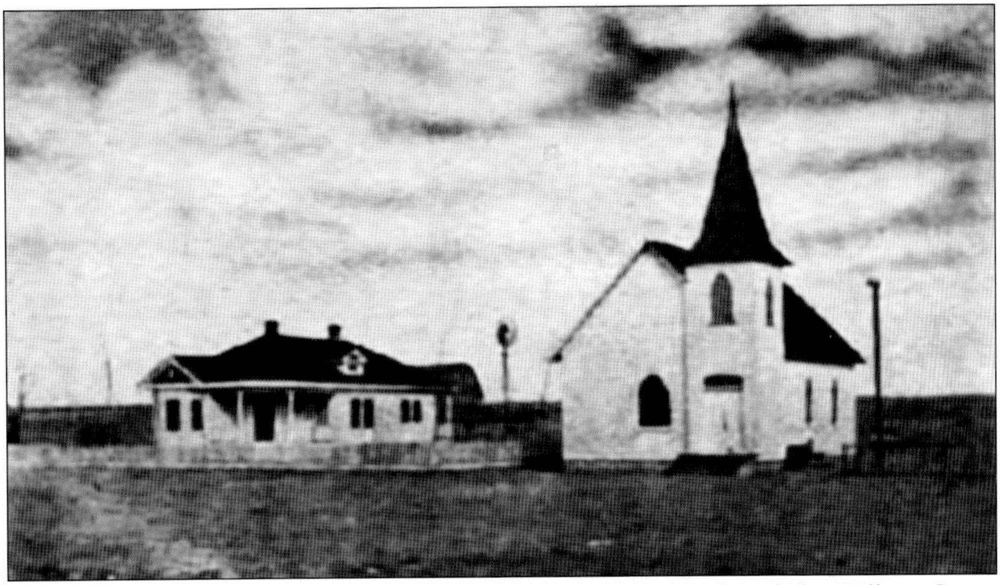

This photograph is of the 1908 Congregational Episcopal Church and the William Curtis residence to the left. The church was where the Goshen County Library is now at 2001 East A Street. The Congregational Church was the state church in Connecticut, so Curtis thought it would be proper to have one here. The church building was later sold to the Episcopalians in Torrington. (H.W. Yoder.)

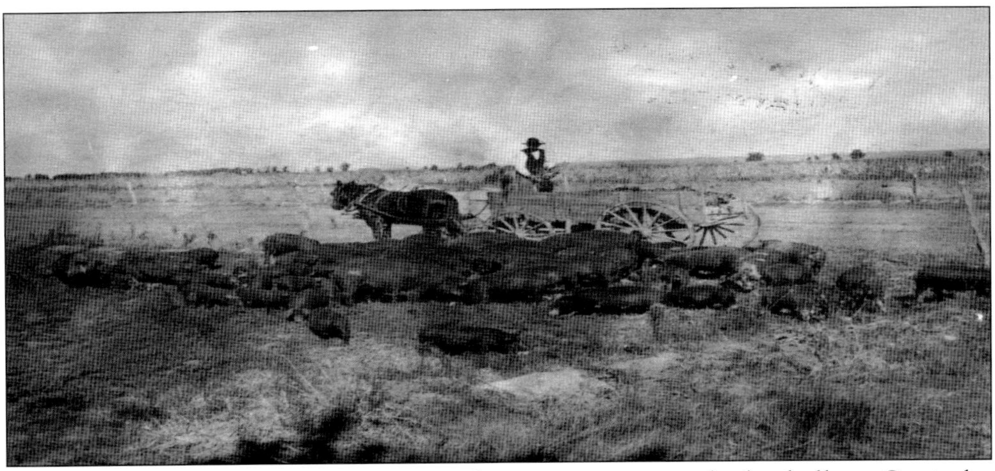

Torrington founder William Curtis is pictured in a wagon surveying his herd of hogs. Curtis also raised and grazed cattle at his truck farm, where the Goshen County Cooperative Extension Service is now located on West Highway 26. (Homesteaders Museum.)

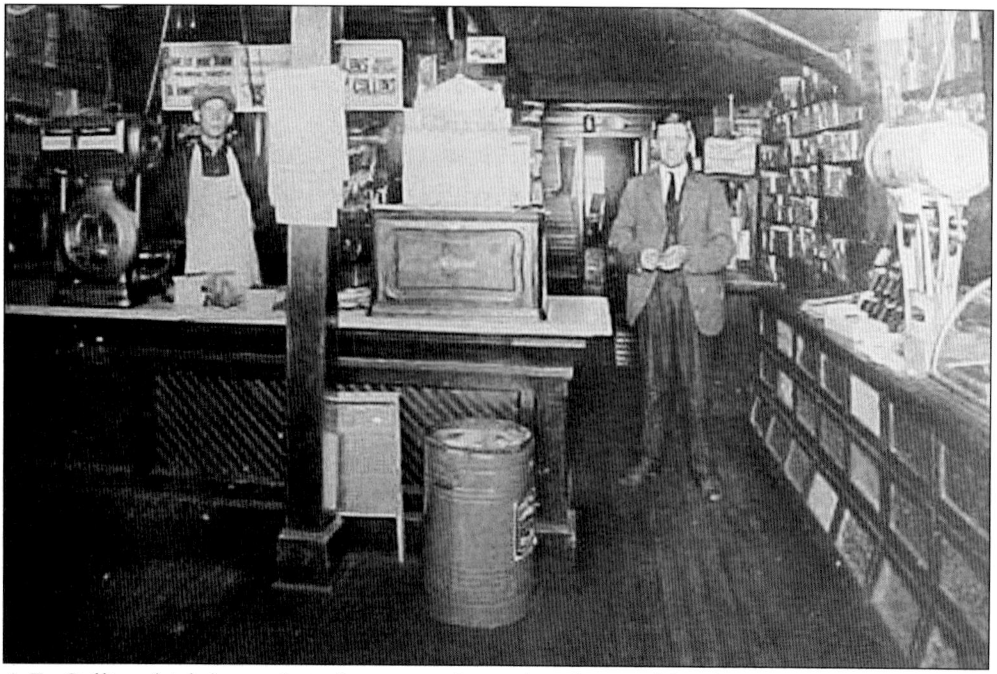

A.E. Collins (right) stands in his general merchandise and hardware store around 1905. (Homesteaders Museum.)

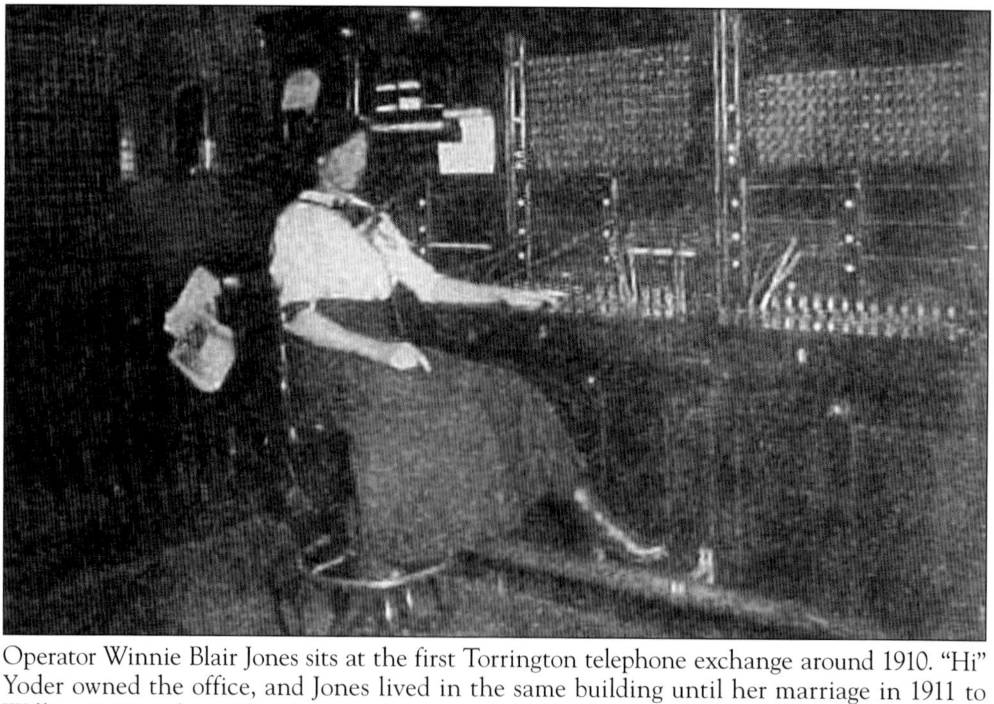

Operator Winnie Blair Jones sits at the first Torrington telephone exchange around 1910. "Hi" Yoder owned the office, and Jones lived in the same building until her marriage in 1911 to William J. Knowlton. Winnie was sometimes visited by her sister Eula Blair and Winnie's son Vernon. Knowlton and Winnie met while attending the Presbyterian church in Torrington. They had five children: Lois (Stephens), Eula (Martinez), Jay, Betty Lou (Bayless), and Richard. (Homesteaders Museum.)

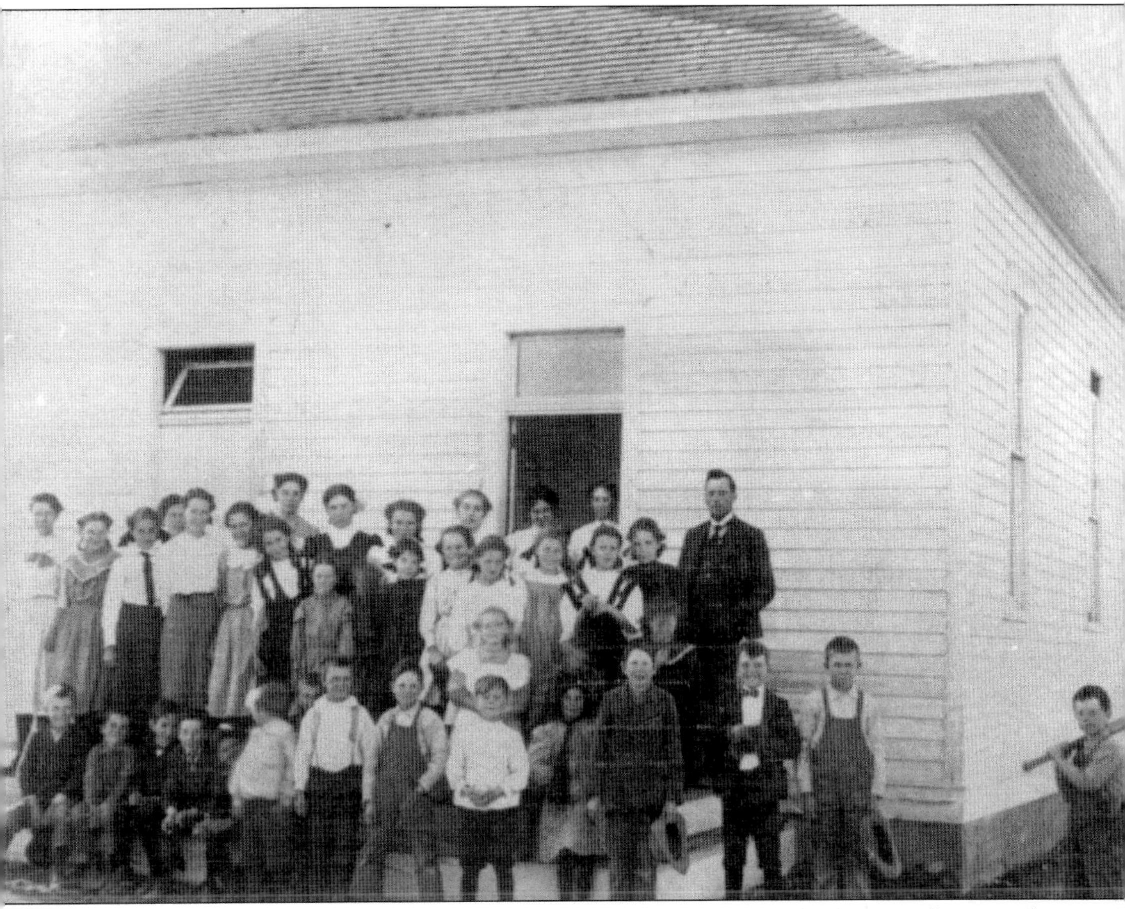

The first school was built in 1905 by M.L. Snyder, Byron Vining, and Charles S. Hollingsworth at the present-day West A Street between Twentieth and Twenty-first Avenues. It was used until 1908. Teachers standing in the open doorway are Miss Eaton and Miss Wasson. Superintendent L.L. Cassell is the man in the suit to the right. This photograph is of the first class of students. (Homesteader Museum.)

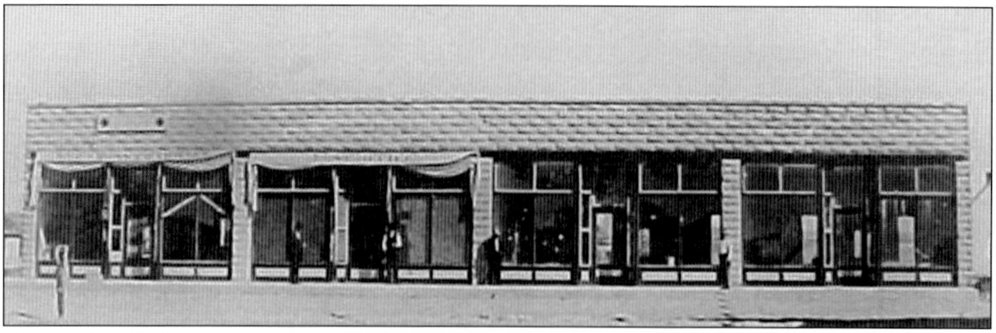

Originally called Terry Avenue, this photograph of Torrington's Main Street dates to 1906. On the left is the Red Cross Pharmacy, established in 1906 by W.S. Miller and E.S. Empey. The business was sold to H.W. "Hi" Yoder, who renamed it the Palace Pharmacy. It had a full soda fountain. Next to it was the post office and land office operated by W.G. Curtis. (Homesteaders Museum.)

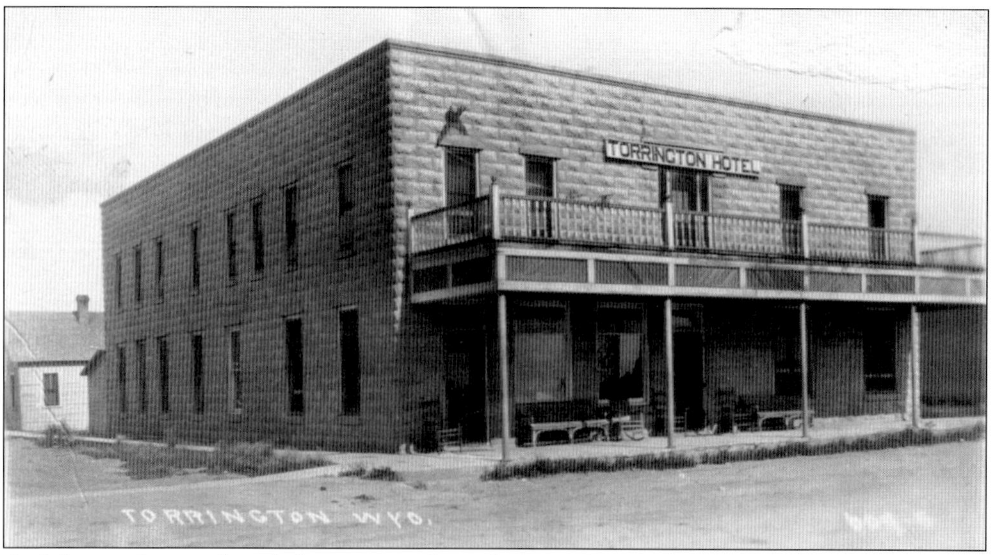

Carl Stein, who purchased the property from the Lincoln Land Company, built the two-story Torrington Hotel in 1906. He emigrated from Germany in 1890 and lived in Lingle. E.A. Bolinger was the first manager, and the hotel was located at the current address of 1841 Main Street. The building has been modified and remodeled over the years, and Gary's Gun Shop and Reed Insurance are located in it now. Hiram W. "Hi" Yoder took this 1919 photograph. (Homesteaders Museum.)

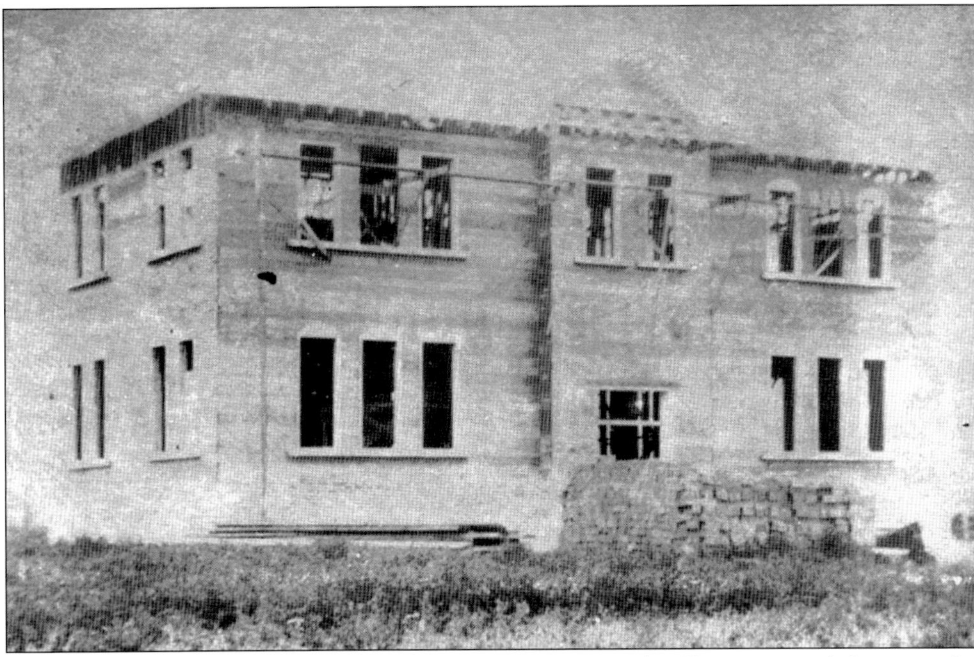

The redbrick school is pictured in 1907 under construction. Walter Kimzey, an early homesteader, was one of the workmen on the school building. The bricks were possibly made in Scottsbluff. It later served as the home of Goshen County Community College before being turned into Cottier Apartments at the corner of Twenty-third Avenue and East A Street. (Homesteaders Museum.)

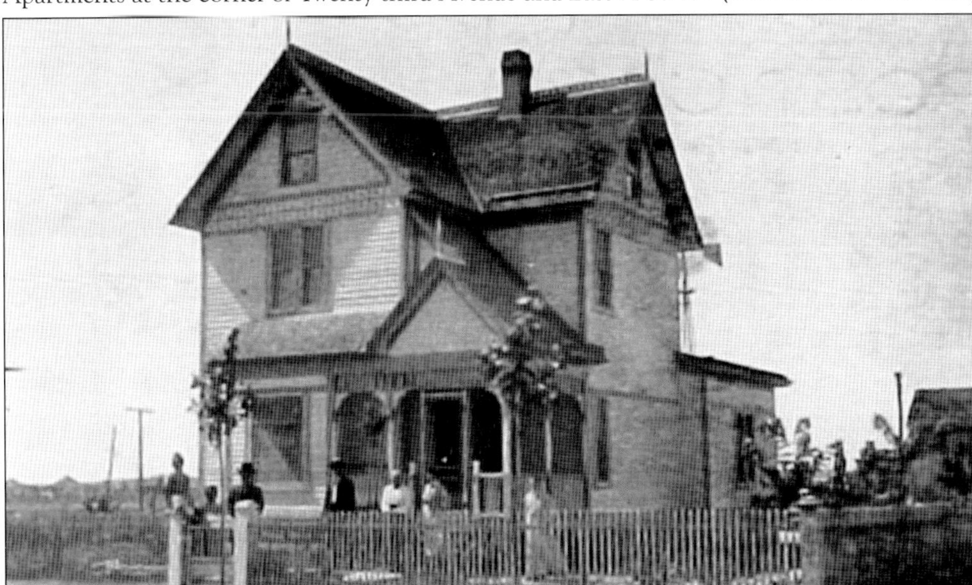

This 1908 photograph shows the Victorian-style John Travis Snow home. The house is located at 2142 West A Street. Snow established the Snow and Clarke Bank in December 1904 with a capital of $25,000. H.S. Clarke Jr. was the president. The following year, it was renamed the Torrington State Bank. Still privately owned in 1908, it became the First National Bank of Torrington. John's nephew Travis Snow was the first World War I casualty from Torrington, so the local group named the American Legion Travis Snow Post No. 5 after him. (Homesteaders Museum.)

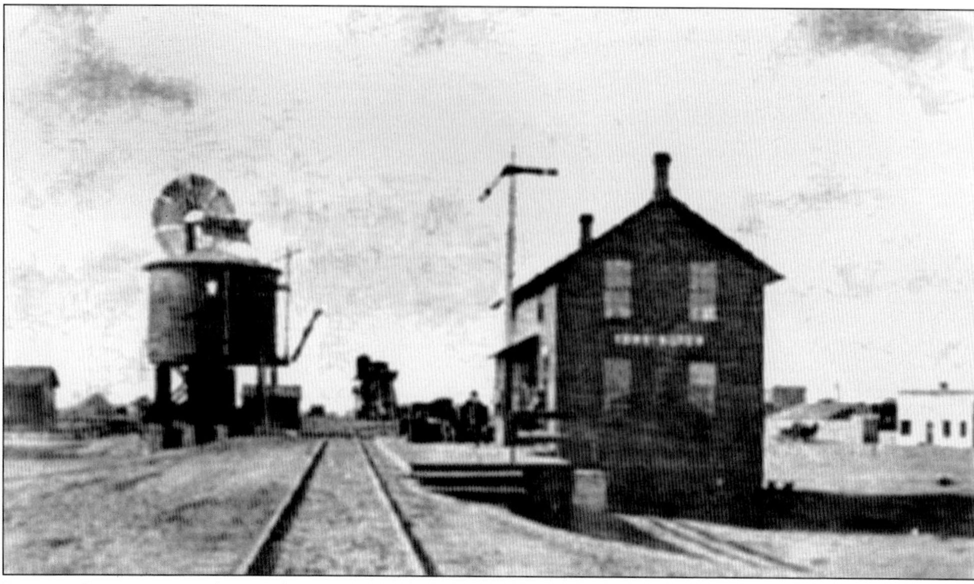

Pictured in 1908 is the Burlington Northern Railroad depot. The building was wooden, and to the left are the water tank and coal chutes. (Hiram W. "Hi" Yoder.)

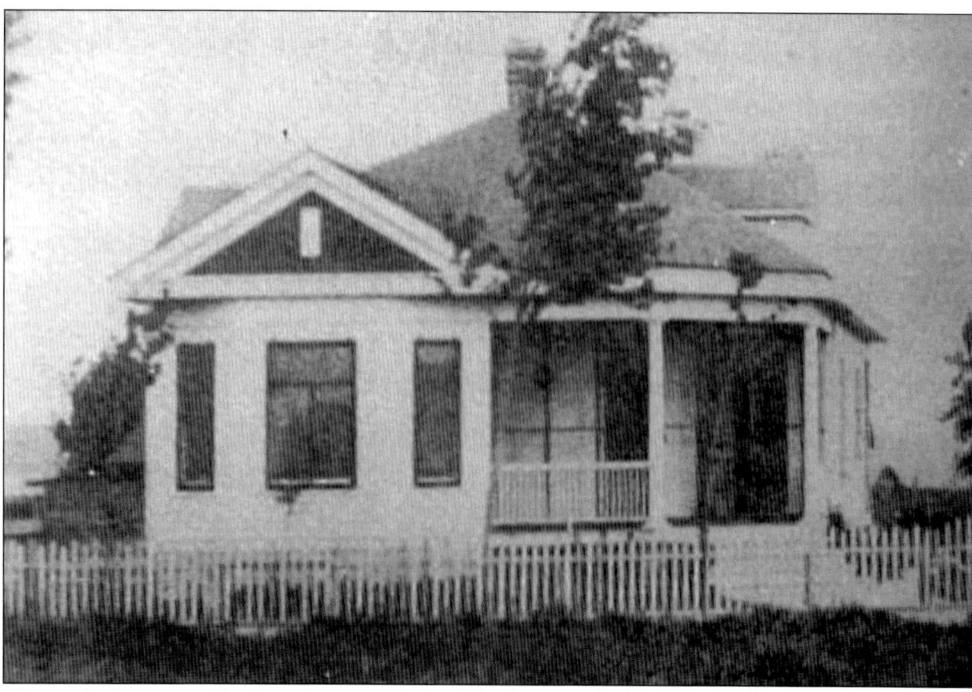

This is the William G. Curtis home in 1908. The house, which was moved into Torrington from his farm south of town, was later razed. (Homesteaders Museum.)

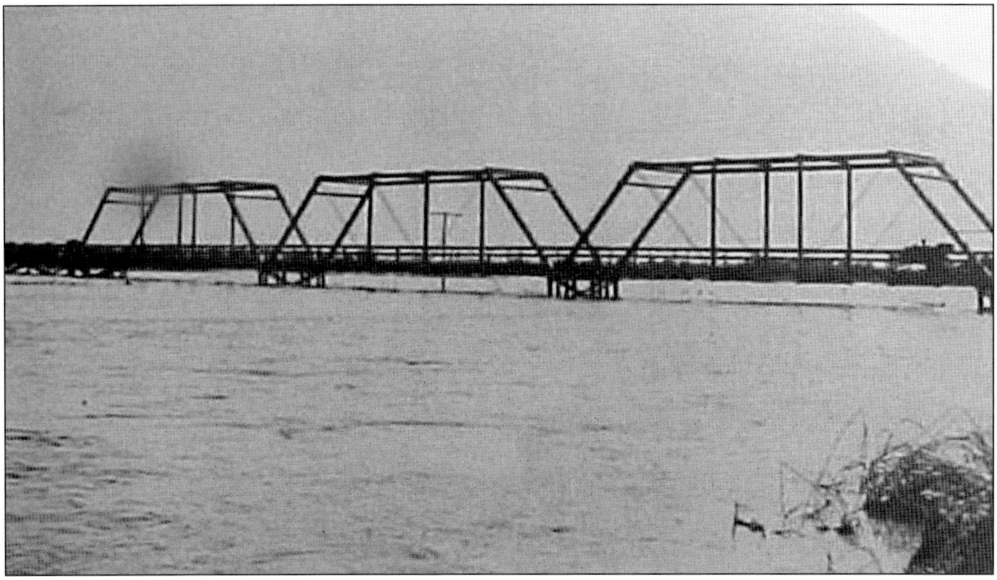

Just east of today's Torrington golf course was the location of the original Platte River Bridge. *Platte* is a French word for "flat," and the river was described as one mile wide and one inch deep. West C Street was the highway to West Fifteenth Avenue. This photograph was taken in 1911. (Homesteaders Museum.)

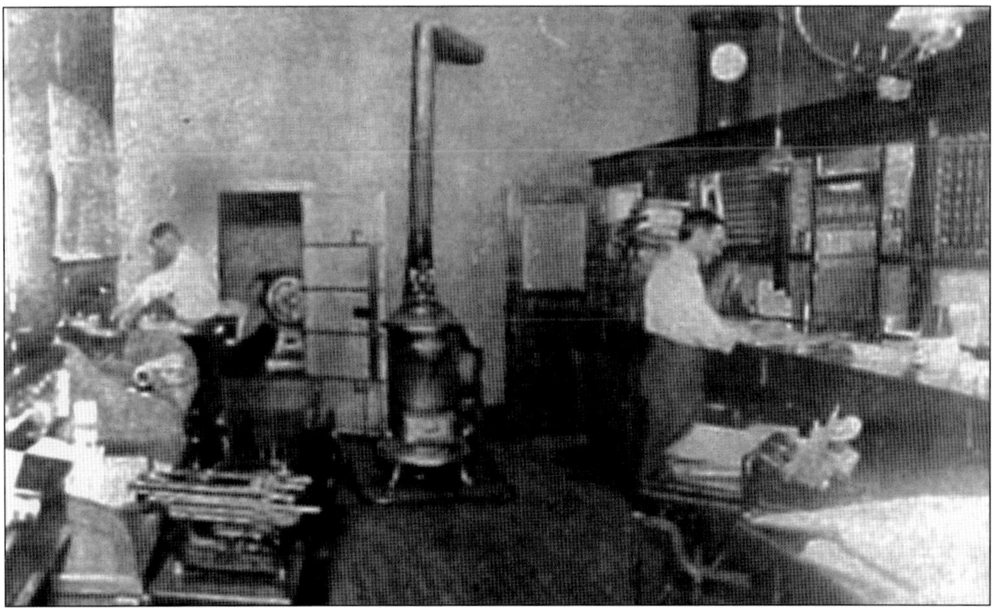

This 1911 photograph shows Royce Tebbet (left), who was an assistant cashier at the First National Bank for 11 years. In January 1918, he moved to the Citizen's National Bank, which had just received its national charter. The organizers for this new bank were W.O. Eaton, president; E.B. Dearing, vice president; and Tebbet as cashier. Tebbet eventually became the chief executive officer of the bank and held that position for over 50 years. Joe McDonald (right) became the vice president of the First National Bank at the same time that Tebbet moved to Citizen's National Bank. (Homesteaders Museum.)

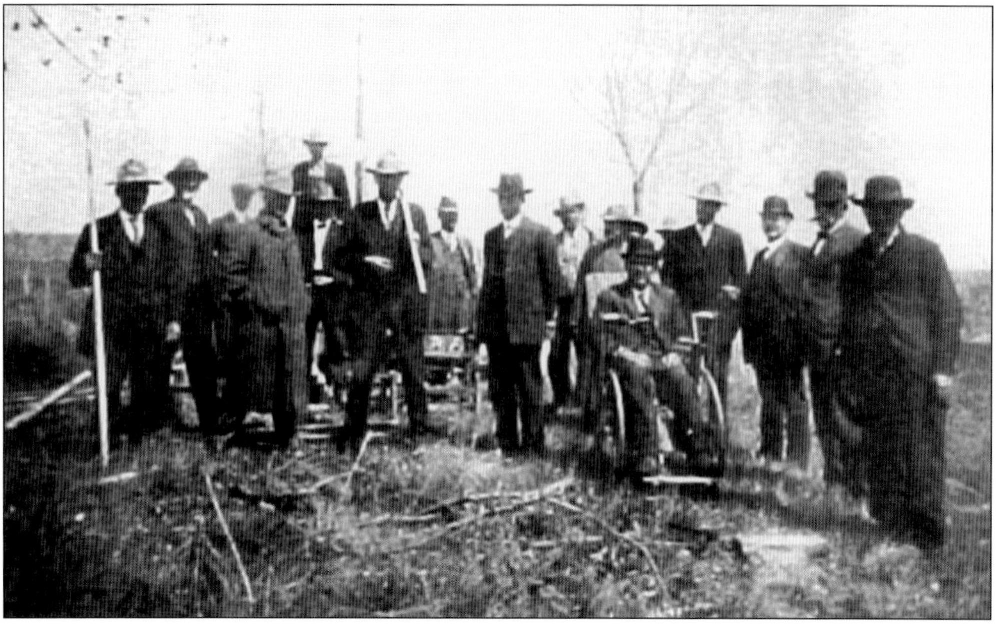

Ground-breaking for the Goshen County Courthouse occurred in the spring of 1912. Lingle and Torrington had been in contention for the county seat. Citizens of Torrington pledged $20,000 for the building, and the Lincoln Land Company donated a site. In an election of the people, Torrington won by 299 votes. Harry Little, in the wheelchair, was the county clerk and clerk of court. (Homesteaders Museum.)

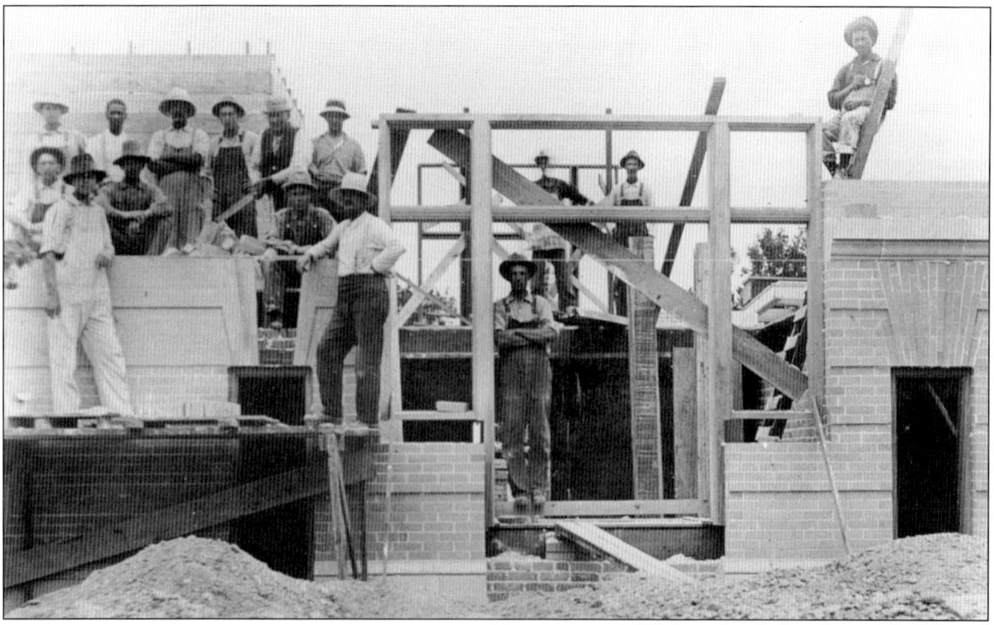

The construction crew for the new courthouse is pictured in 1912 with William Knowlton in the doorway. Knowlton, the county surveyor, worked on several buildings in the area, such as the first high school, the lumberyard in Lingle, and some of the buildings at F.E. Warren Air Force Base in Cheyenne, Wyoming. On January 6, 1913, the first elected board was Jess Yoder, E.B. Hudson, and W.C. Vance. (Homesteaders Museum.)

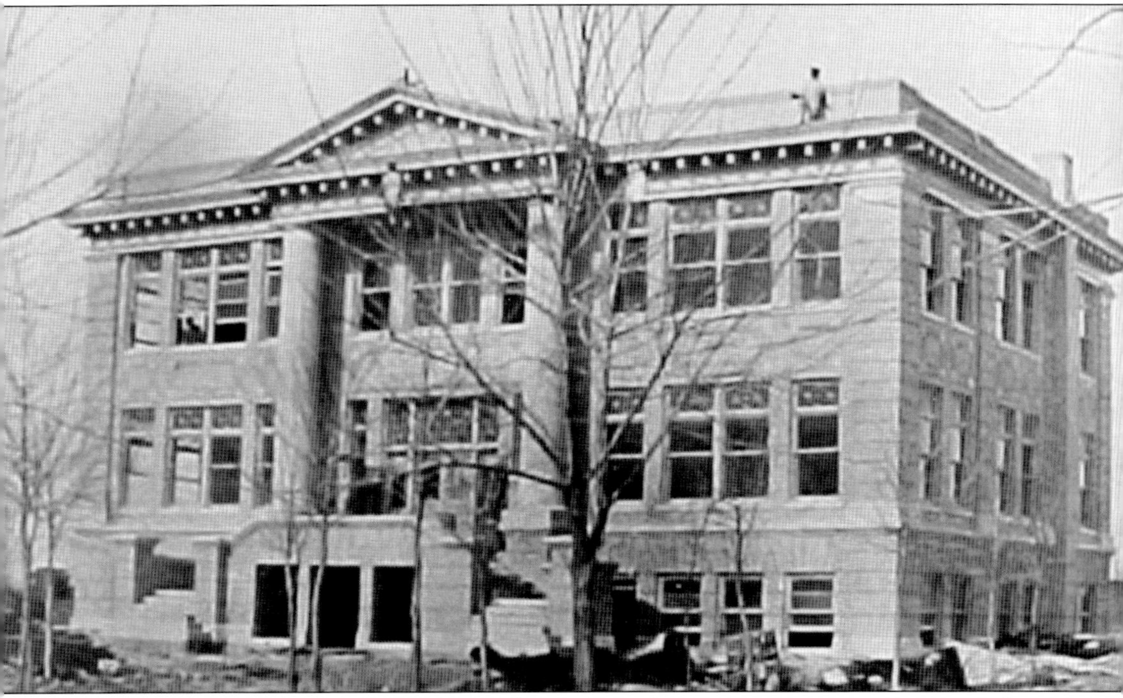

The finishing touches were applied to the Goshen County Courthouse in 1913 in preparation for the next round of land drawings. The cost of the courthouse was $25,177.14, and the cornerstone was laid on July 4, 1913. Even though the trees were planted, notice all the construction materials around the base of the building that were still waiting to be cleaned up. The county officials included Mike Hayes, sheriff; I.E. "Ike" Yoder, assessor; C.A. Elquest, coroner; C.P. Johnson, justice of the peace; C.O. Downing, superintendent of schools; J.L. Sawyer, attorney; Marlin Snyder, treasurer; and Harry Little, county clerk and clerk of court. (Homesteaders Museum.)

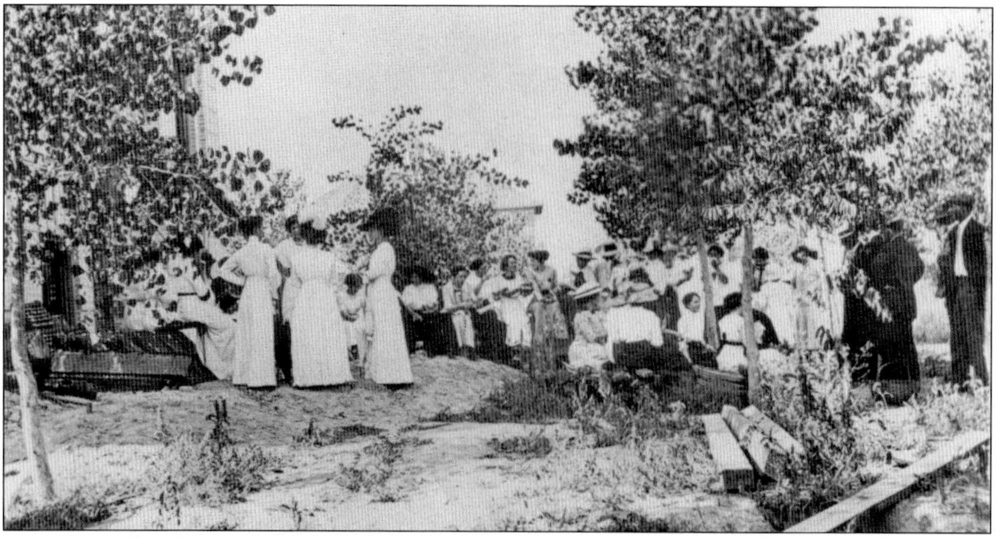

A Wyoming legislative act was approved for state teachers institutes. These were to be maintained in part by nominal fees required of all teachers in the state. At these meetings, the specific needs and problems of the teachers and schools were discussed, generally in connection with a series of lectures. Two counties could meet together, and the first meetings dealt with textbooks. This group, at the first of these meetings in Goshen County, gathered on the grounds of the new courthouse. Behind the trees, the redbrick schoolhouse is visible. At this time, there were 1,127 children enrolled in 55 county schools with 89 teachers. They received $11,209.81 as the apportionment to run the schools. (Homesteaders Museum.)

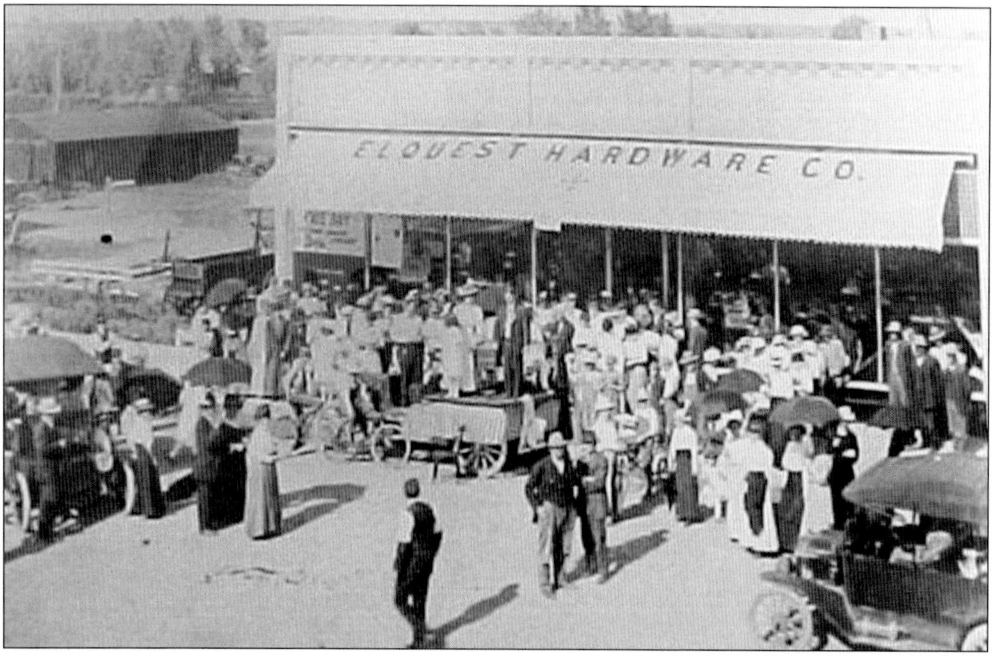

In 1912, the Elquest Hardware Store opened on Terry Avenue. The owner, Charles A. Elquest, had come to Torrington from Scottsbluff, Nebraska, in 1910, where he had also been engaged in the hardware business. He was elected the first coroner in Goshen County in 1912 and served in that position until 1917. (Homesteaders Museum.)

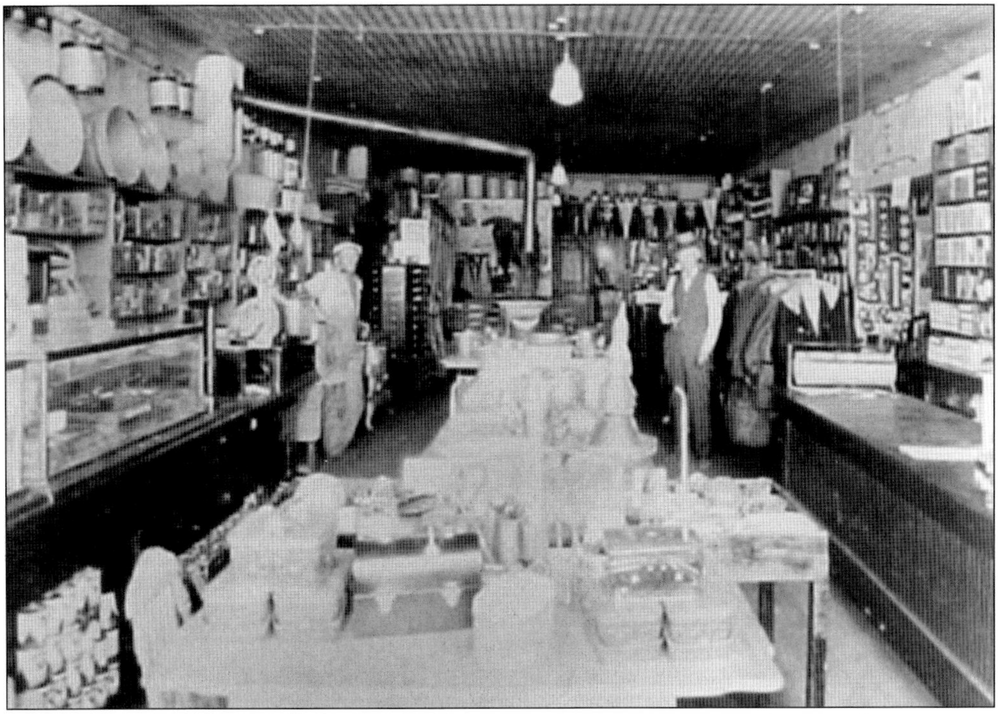

This 1918 photograph shows the inside of the Elquest Hardware Store. Farm implements were becoming sought-after commodities, and the store had them available. At that time, Charles Elquest and William W. Austin were advertising as licensed embalmers and funeral directors. (Homesteaders Museum.)

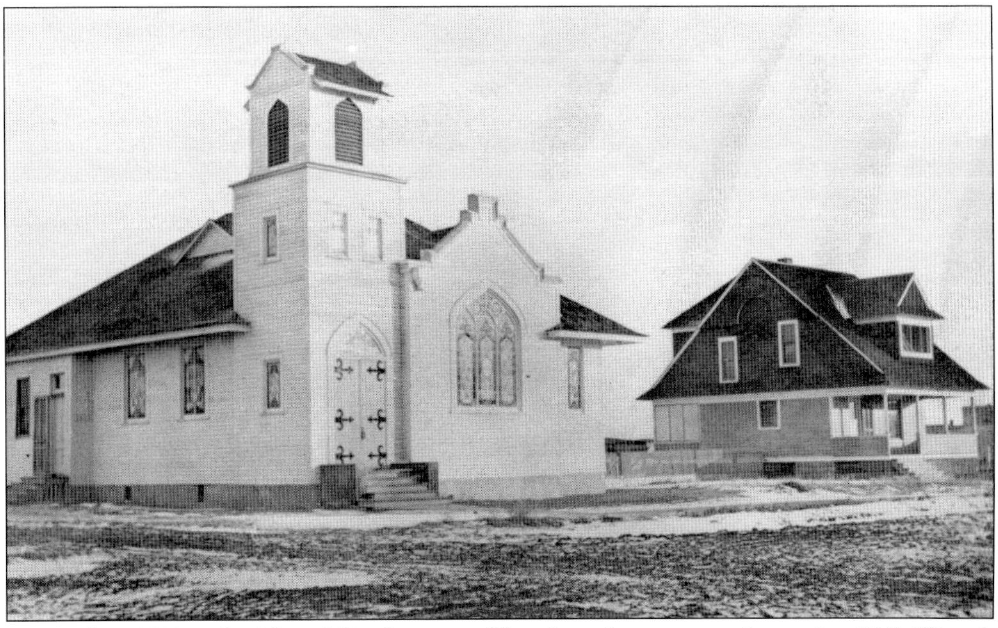

Pictured in 1914 is the United Presbyterian Church and parsonage, located at 2141 West A Street. The first church was built in 1906 but burned down one year later. It was replaced with this building in 1909. (Homesteaders Museum.)

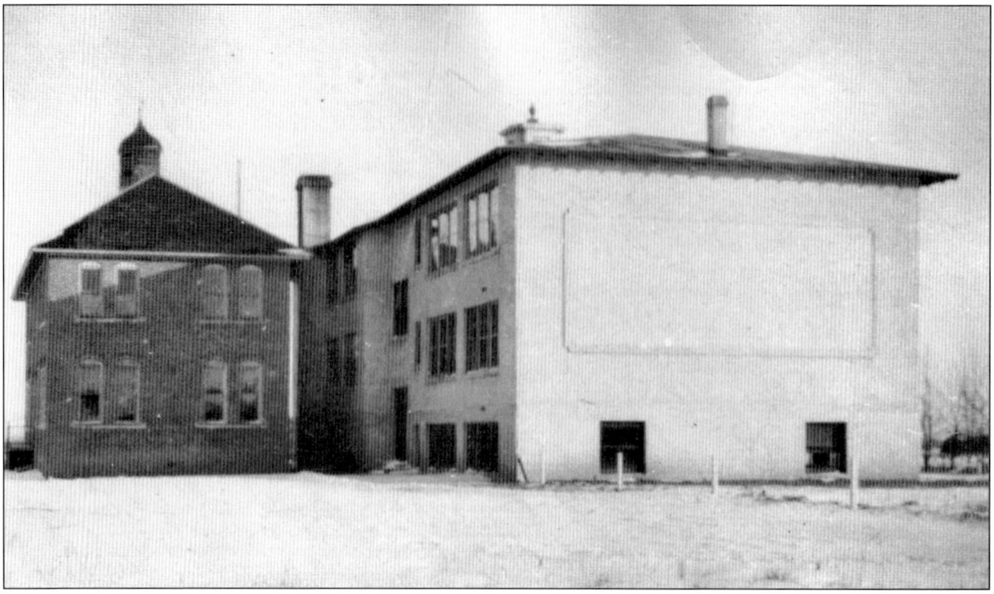

The new Torrington High School was built in 1915 just 20 feet south of the redbrick schoolhouse that had educated students from grades one through six. The brick building was later used as a rooming house for 10 to 12 years and was torn down in 1926. (Homesteaders Museum.)

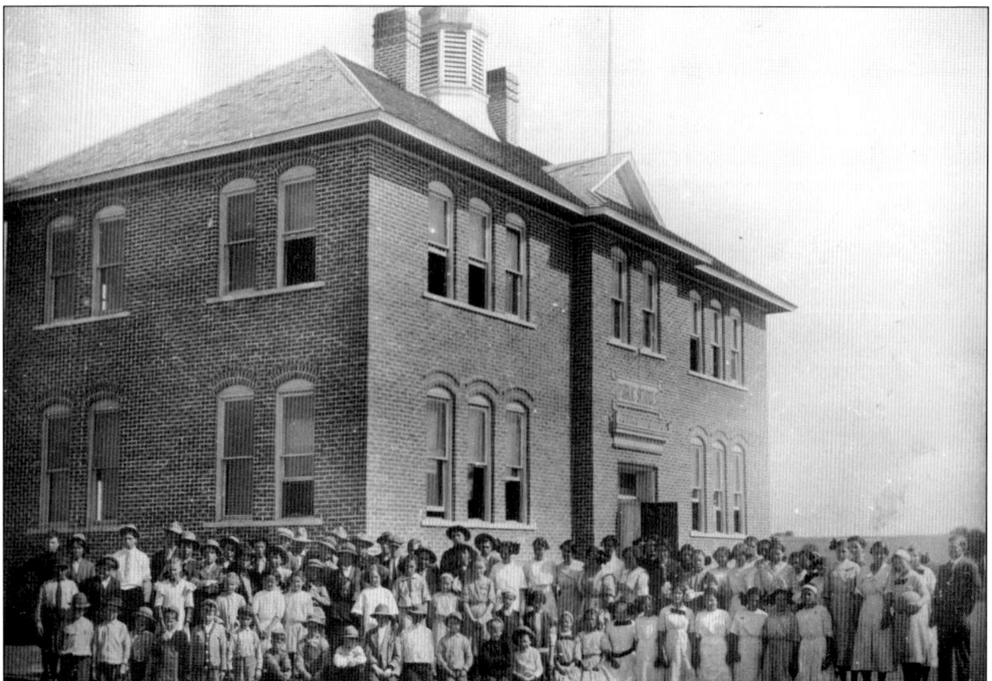

The redbrick schoolhouse is pictured in 1916. All the grades came out on the lawn to have their photograph taken. Notice that the windows are open; the school did not have air conditioning. (Homesteaders Museum.)

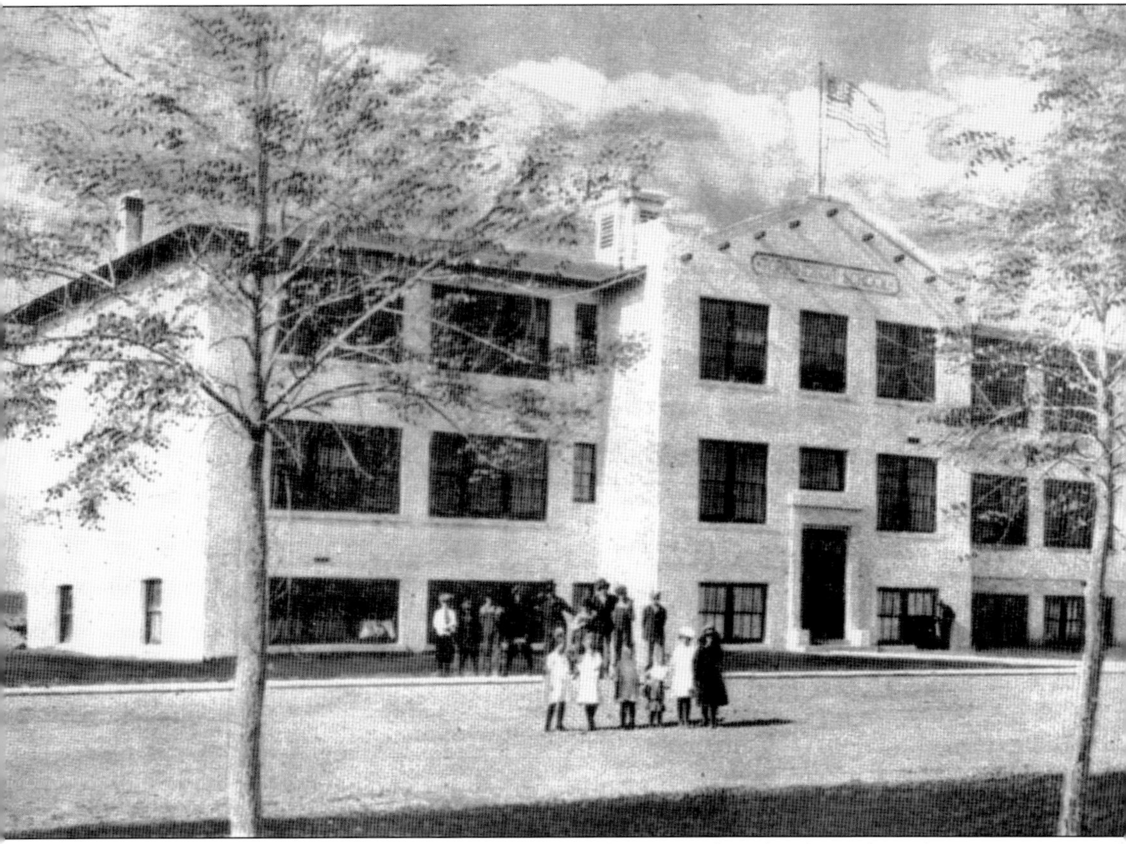

The front of the first Torrington High School is pictured in 1916. The school was the only Mission-style school built in Wyoming at that time. This school later became the facility for the fifth and sixth grades and was called the Pioneer School. It is located at 202 East Twenty-second Avenue and now sits empty. Larry Cottier purchased the building in 1981 from the City of Torrington, which had been given the building by the local school district. Cottier planned to remodel it into condo apartments but found the project too costly. (Homesteaders Museum.)

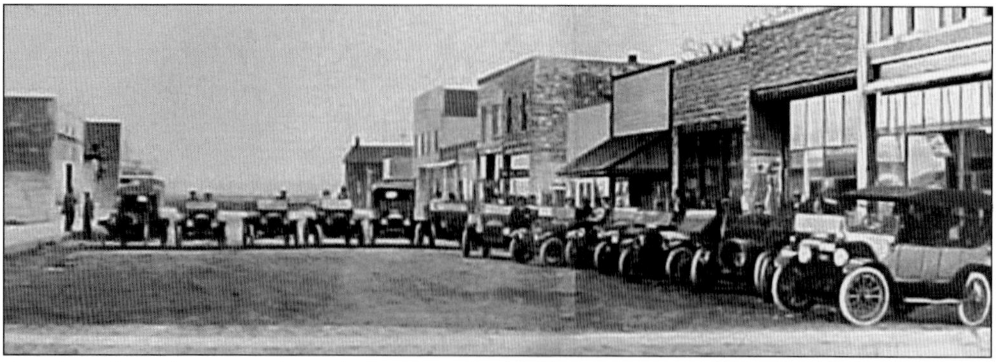

Car shows have been popular in Torrington for decades. A number of cars are displayed in this 1919 picture. There was a car race as part of this show as well. The first car in Torrington arrived in 1908 and belonged to William Copeland. It was an International high-wheel, solid-rubber-tire, two-seated buggy with a horizontal engine under the seat. It was used to carry mail to the sand hills, since wagons had a hard time making the trips. (Homesteaders Museum.)

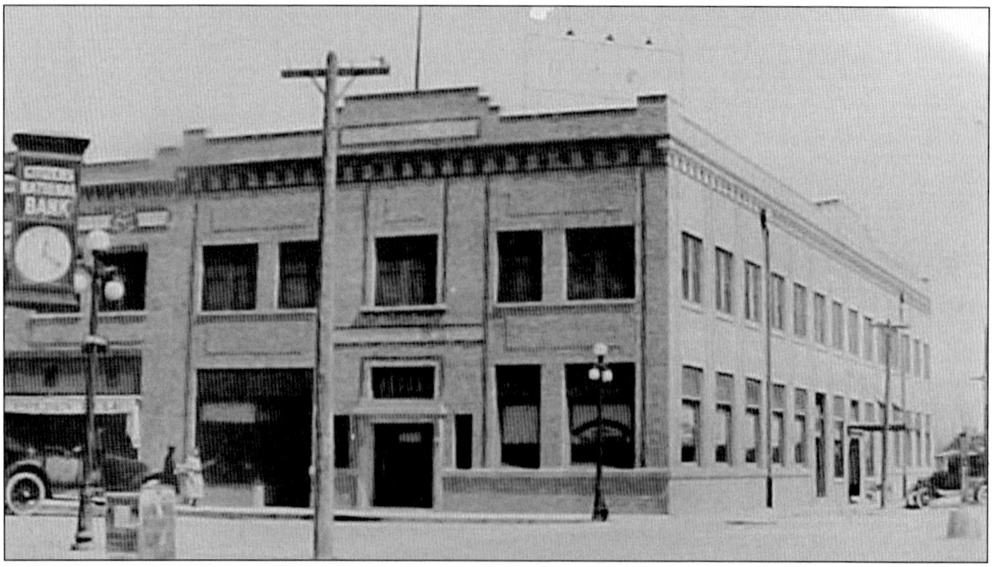

The Trail Hotel, located at 2001 Main Street, is pictured in 1918. At a cost of $50,000 to $60,000, B.F. Yoder began construction on this Torrington hotel on April 10, 1918. On the ground floor was to be a drugstore and the Torrington State Bank. In the middle of the building on the south side was the entrance to the hotel lobby and restaurant. Upstairs, there were accommodations in 35 sleeping rooms. The building was to have vapor-steam heating. Officers in the bank were B.F. Yoder, president; J.T. Snow, vice president; and A.H. Woolever, cashier. Currently, Greg Knudsen's Law Offices and Kendra Knudsen's CPA offices use only the lower level. (Homesteaders Museum.)

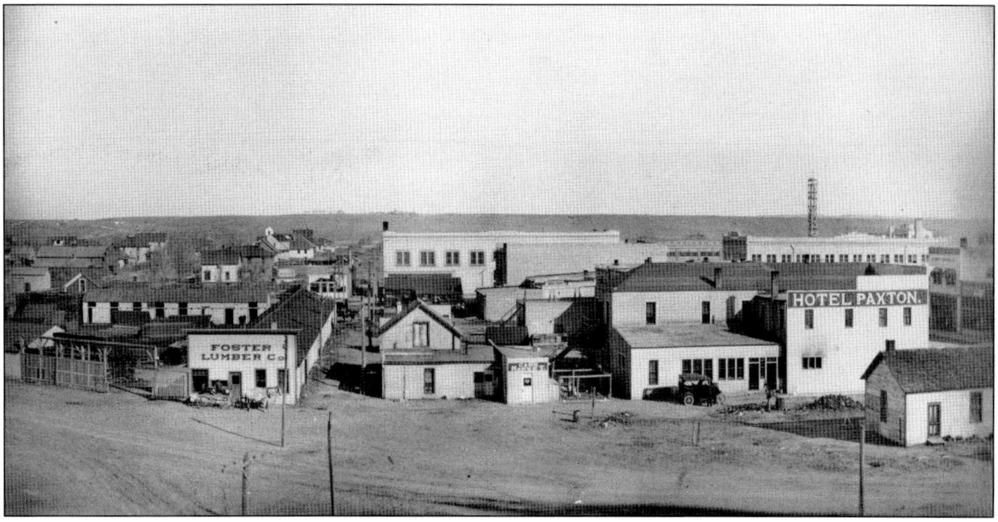

This 1919 photograph shows Torrington looking west from Railroad Avenue. The Foster Lumber Company was at 119 West Twentieth Avenue. To the right of it was Cash Grocery, and facing Main Street was the Hotel Paxton. (Homesteaders Museum.)

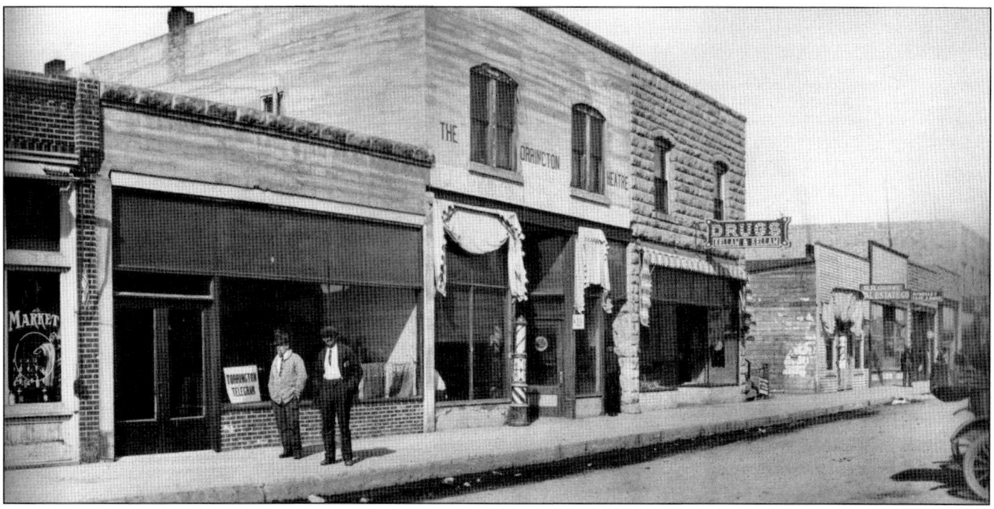

This c. 1919 photograph shows the west side of Terry Avenue. From left to right are the Jack Beatty Meat Market, the *Torrington Telegram*, the Torrington Theatre, Kellam and Kellam drugstore, the R.R. Grouse Real Estate Office, and the Torrington State Bank. (Homesteaders Museum.)

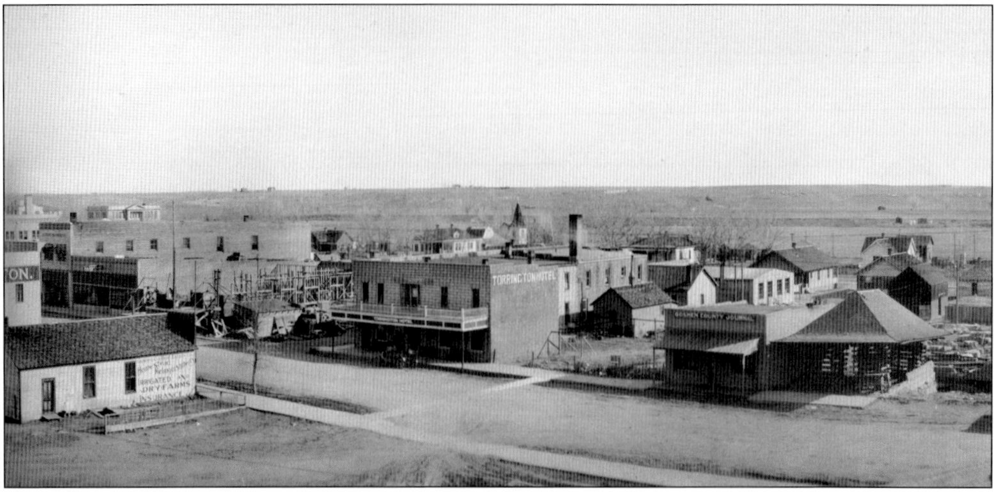

Another c. 1919 photograph looks northeast from Terry Avenue, showing the Goshen County Real Estate Company on the left. Across the street is the Torrington Hotel, and to the right of it is the *Goshen County Journal*, a local newspaper. (Homesteaders Museum.)

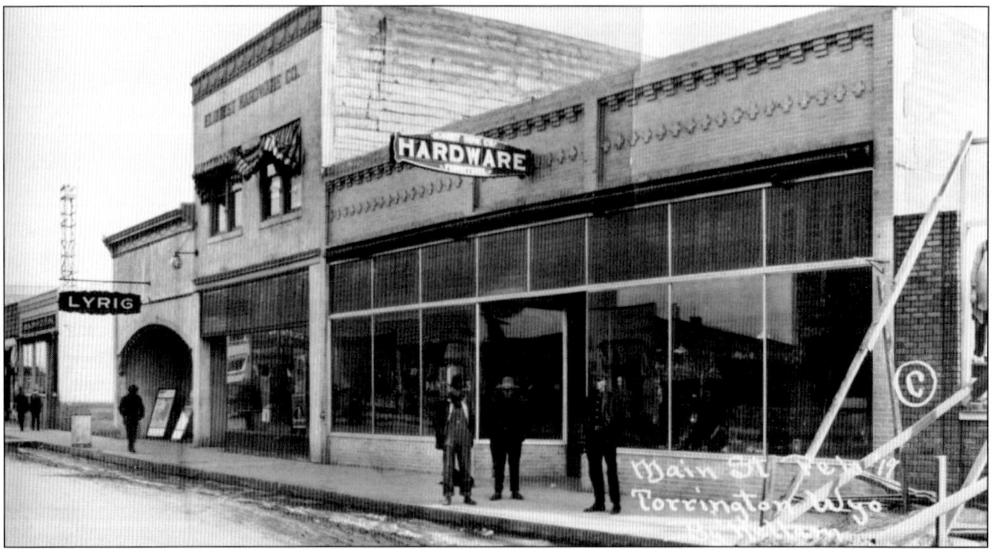

This 1919 photograph of the east side of Terry Avenue shows the Lyrig Theater, Elquest Hardware Company, and the Elquest Hardware Furniture Store. (Homesteaders Museum.)

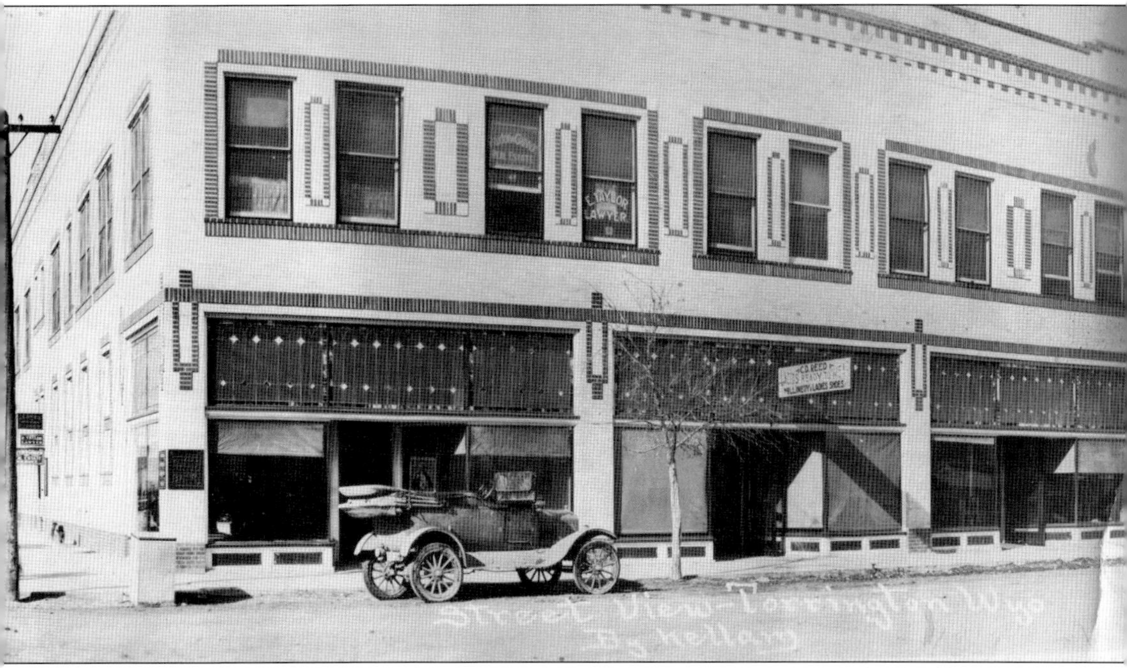

Large multistory buildings were coming to Torrington's Main Street in 1919. This building was constructed that year and was known as the W.O. Eaton building. It was the first one on the north section of Main Street, located at the corner of Terry Avenue and Stafford Street. There was an elm tree planted in front of the building that remained until the street was paved. The building housed the Citizen's National Bank and the Valley Mercantile Furniture Store. Eaton was founder and president of the bank, which opened the first week of April. E.B. Dearing was vice president, and Royce Tebbet was cashier of the bank. The upper floor housed the Paxton and Gamon Real Estate and Insurance Offices and Everett Taylor, lawyer. To the right is C.D. Reed Ladies Ready-to-Wear, Millinery, and Ladies Shoes. (Homesteaders Museum.)

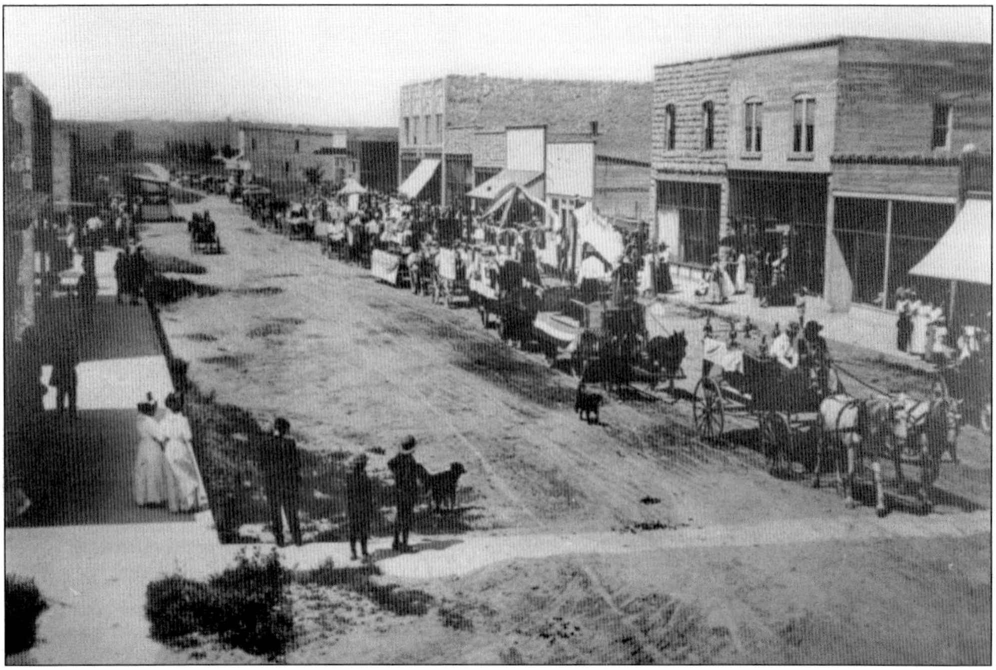

Pictured in 1919 is the Goshen County Fair Parade on the unpaved Terry Avenue. Tom G. Powers, H.W. Yoder, Boyd M. Reid, Lee A. Root, H.M. Porter, Charles A. Elquest, George Power, Charley Willand, and a few others organized the first Goshen County Fair and Rodeo in 1915. This group purchased the land for the original grandstand and a few other buildings. In 1925, county commissioners William W. Austin, W.A. Nelson, and Frank Davis purchased the property and took over the fairgrounds. (Homesteaders Museum.)

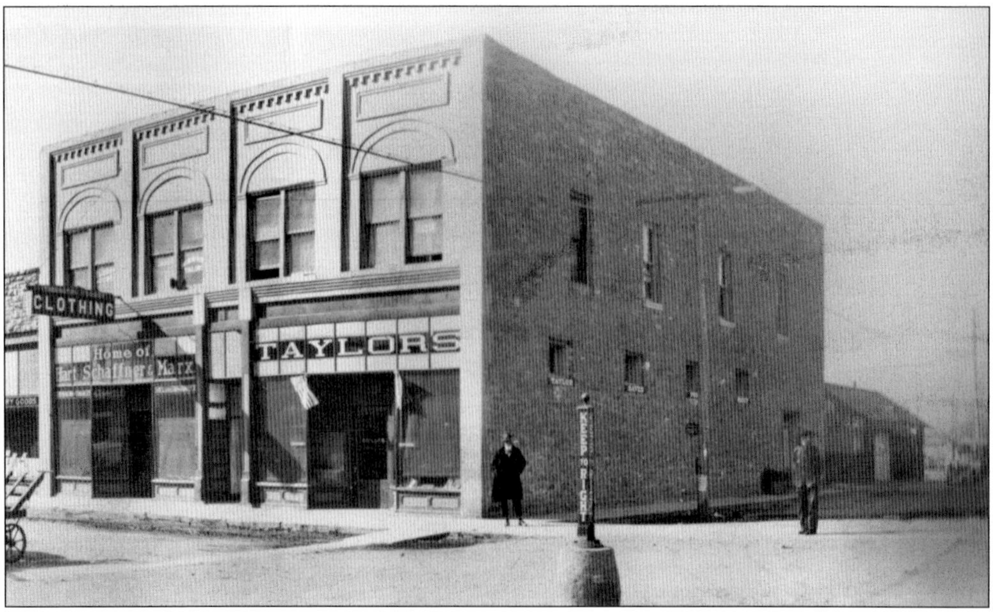

This photograph shows the 1940 Main building as it appeared in 1917; it was owned by Clyde Smith. On the right is Taylor's Grocery, and on the left is the home of Hart, Schaffner & Marx. The sign says Torrington Toggery Clothing. (Homesteaders Museum.)

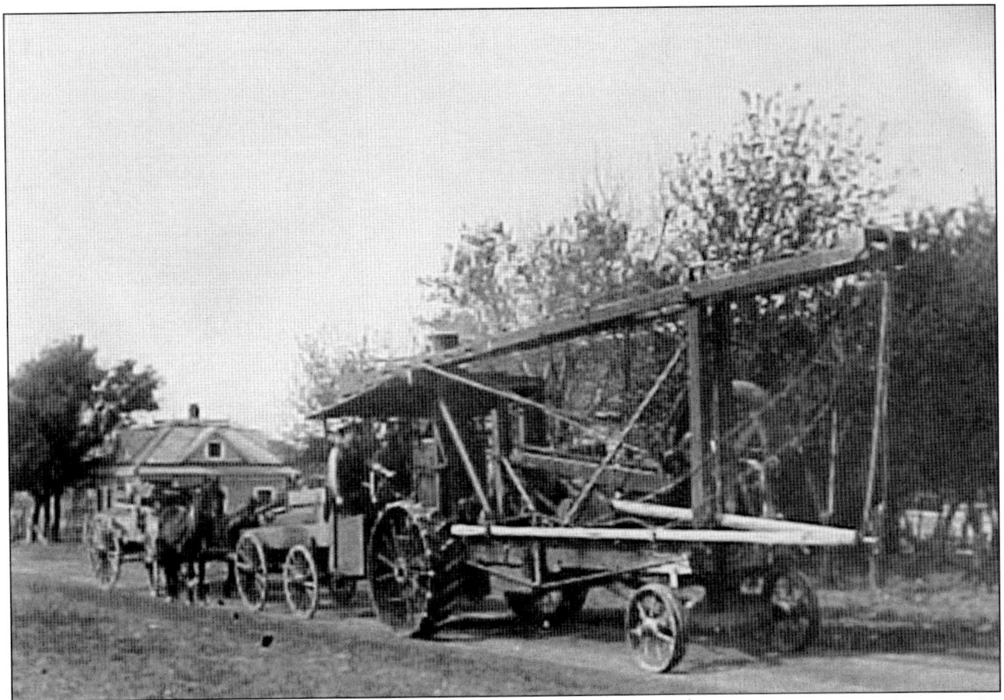

This 1890s well-drilling rig was still being used in the 1920s to drill water wells in the area for homesteaders. The rig came from Nebraska. (Homesteaders Museum.)

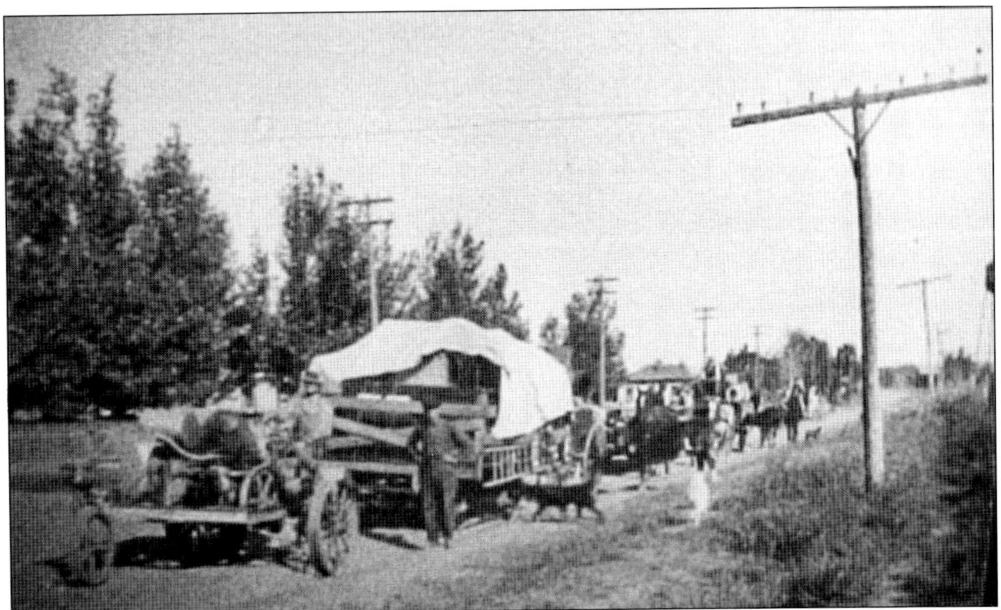

Even though Goshen County was first populated by ranchers and then by persons who had applied for and received 160 acres as part of the federal land law since the 1860s, there were still homesteaders heading out of Torrington in the 1920s. This group was traveling out of town with supplies on the old highway, now West C Street, possibly on its way to the Veteran/Yoder area. Notice the water tower on the right edge of the photograph. (Homesteaders Museum.)

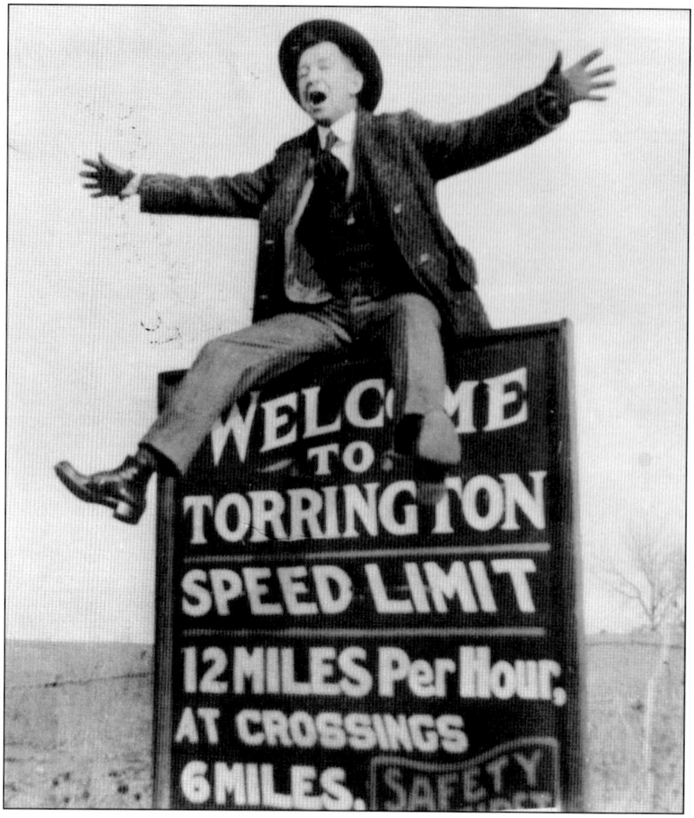

This 1920 welcome sign to Torrington was placed before the crossing of the old bridge out by the current golf course. It is not known why this man was sitting on the sign or who he was. (Homesteaders Museum.)

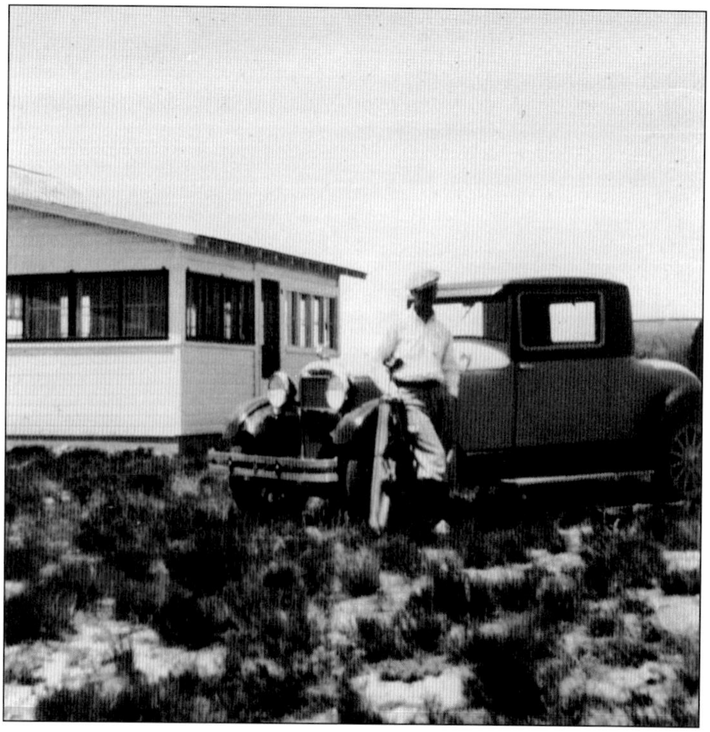

Russ Cloos is pictured some time in the 1920s wearing golfing clothes of the day—a newsboy hat and striped short pants called knickers. His Essex-model car was parked outside the Torrington Municipal Golf Course Clubhouse. The club at that time was south of town near the old airport. (Homesteaders Museum.)

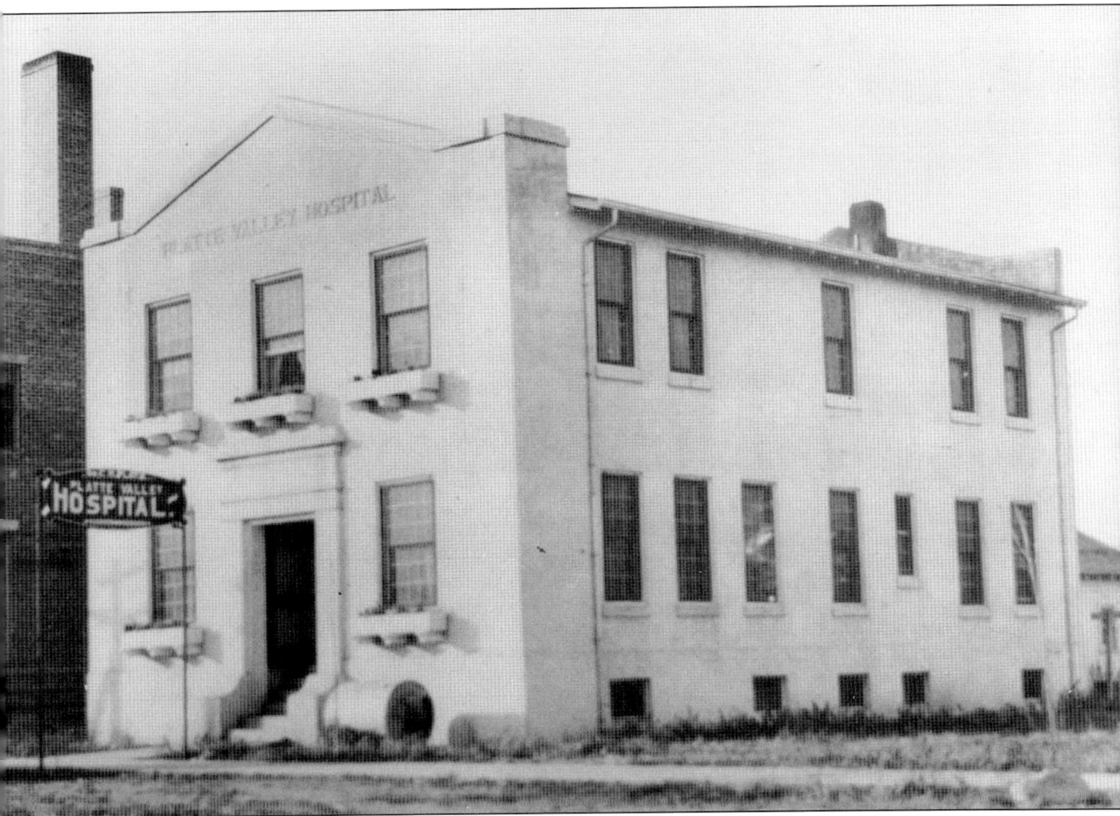

Dr. Charles H. Platz built Platte Valley Hospital, the area's first hospital, on East Twentieth Avenue in Torrington in 1916. He had come here in 1906 at the request of Dr. Elizabeth Sawyer's father. Practicing medicine in Goshen County at that time were Dr. E.S. Empey, Dr. C.B. Conoway, Dr. George O. Dunseth, and Dr. William J. Brownrigg. Dr. Platz moved to Casper in 1927, and the building became an annex for the Trail Hotel. It now houses the Elks Lodge and Clubroom. (Homesteaders Museum.)

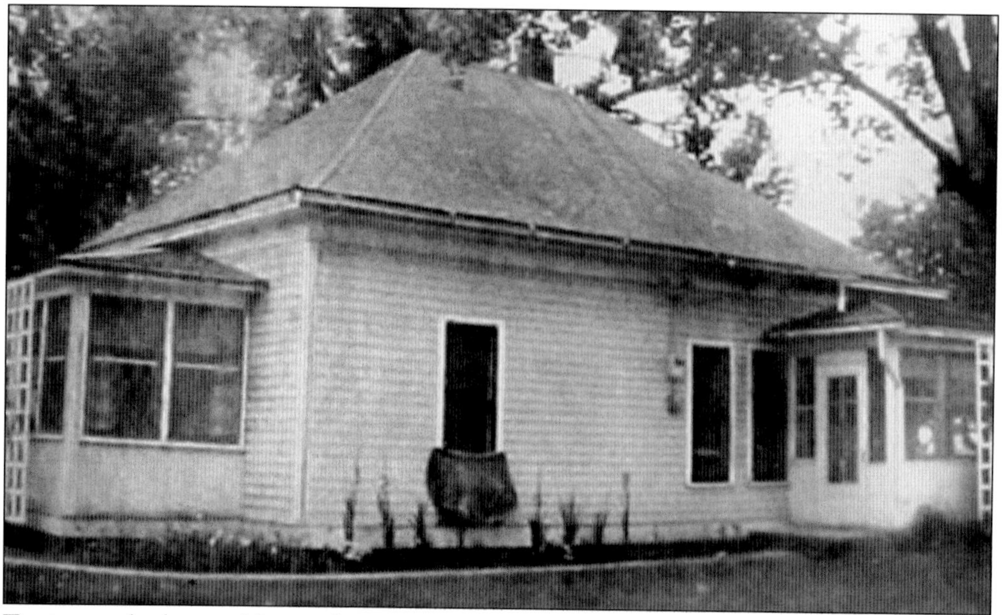

Torrington had several hospitals running at the same time, including this one at 426 West Nineteenth Street. It was under the control of Mrs. J.A. Hays (Hattie Mae) from 1923 until 1933. (Homesteaders Museum.)

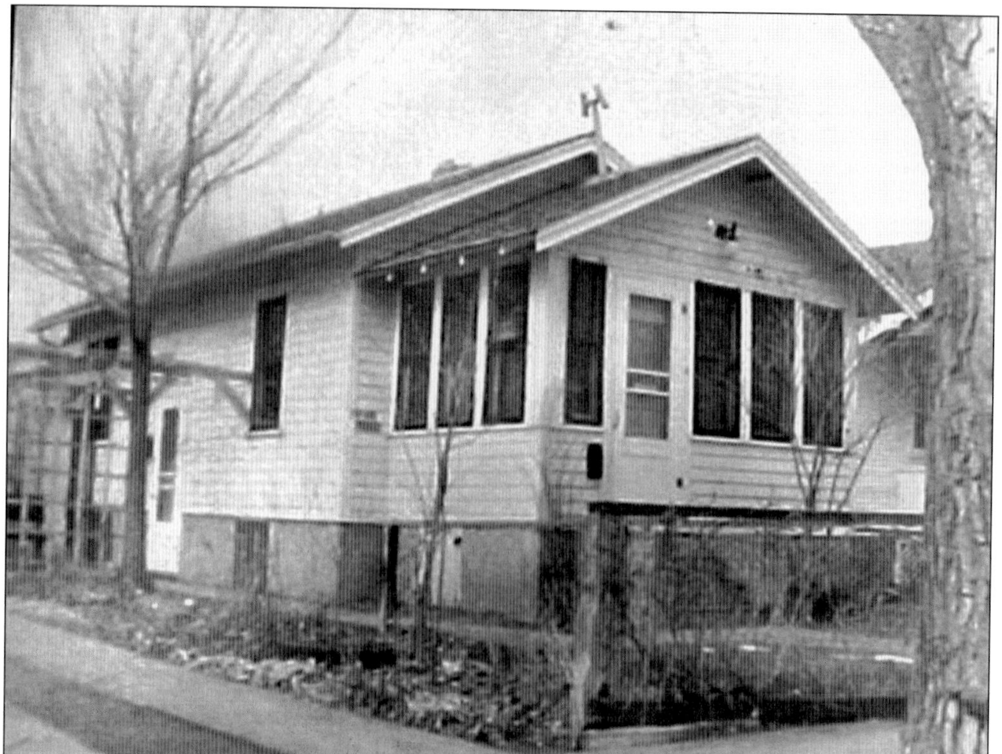

Essie Hisey operated a hospital in her home at 2220 East A Street from 1923 until 1928. The charge for a mother and her baby was $2 per day. (Homesteaders Museum.)

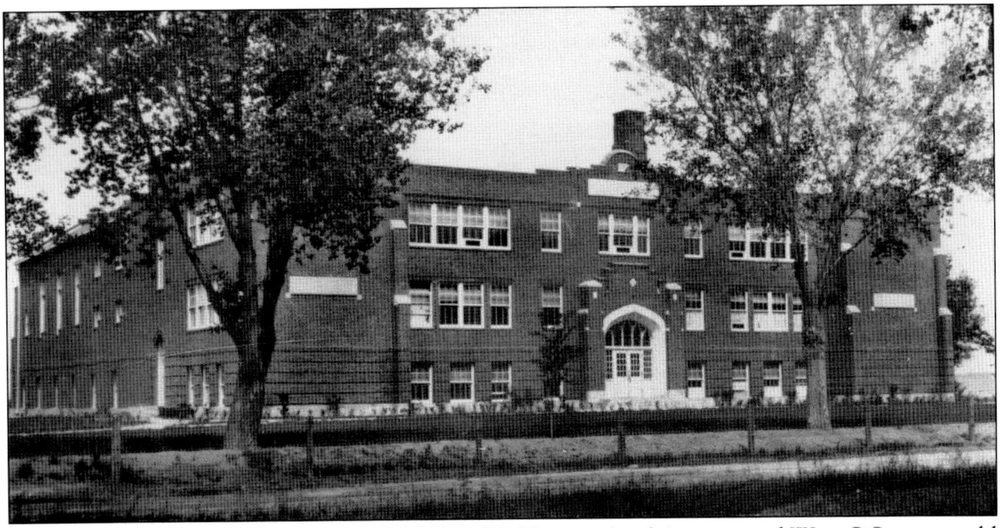

Built in 1923, the new Torrington High School at Twenty-third Avenue and West C Street would replace the one on East A Street. An addition was completed in 1937. To the north of the school is Willi Gymnasium, built in 1954 at a cost of $300,000. This second high school building was torn down, and a new school was built in the same location in 1981. (Homesteaders Museum.)

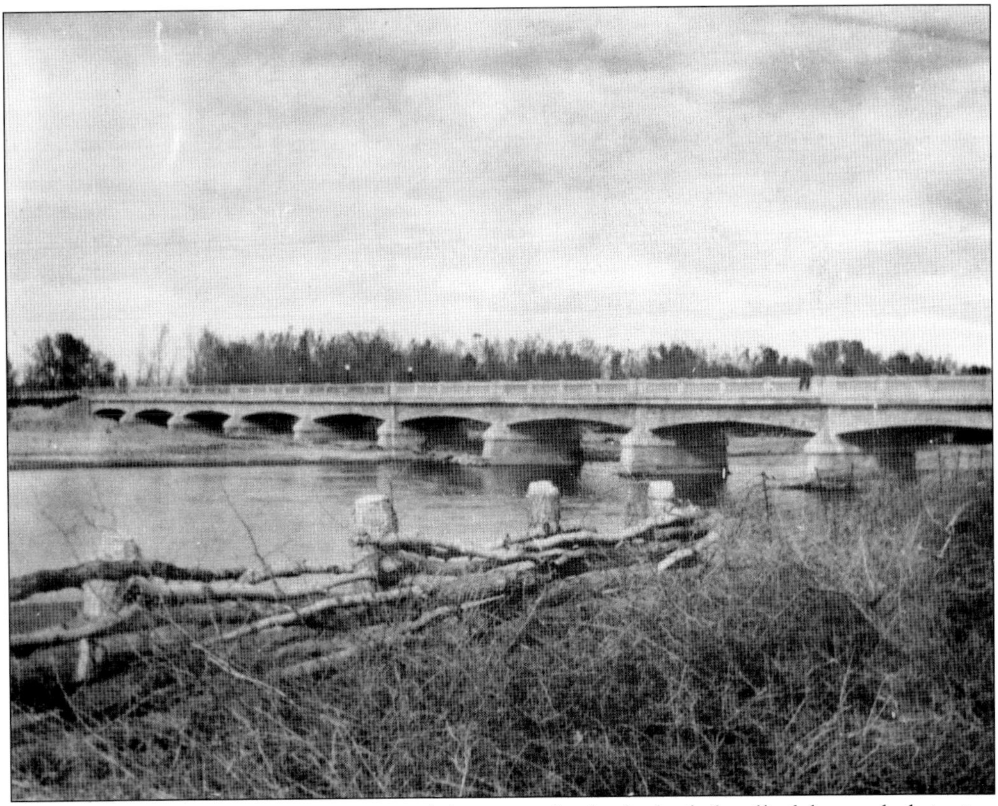

In 1924, the Holly Sugar Factory required that a new bridge be built for all of the trucks bringing in beets. This photograph shows the new Platte River Bridge on Highway 85 that would replace the previous bridge, which was built in 1905. (Homesteaders Museum.)

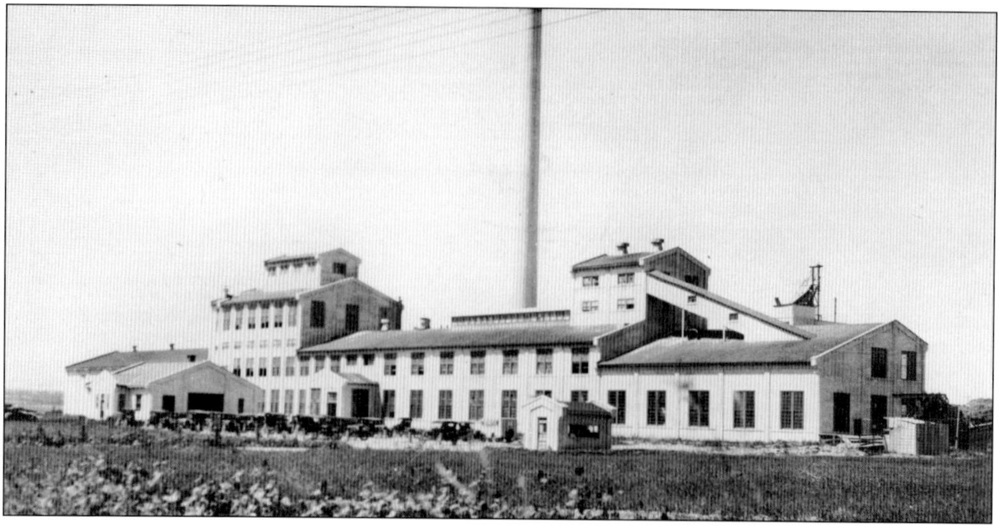

Farming commodities were expanded in 1926, when the Holly Sugar Factory was built. This photograph was taken in 1928. Holly Sugar's parent company was established in 1905. The factory had a Union Pacific Railroad spur that served as a stage for shipping sugar products. Many other tanks and buildings have been added to the factory over the years, and it is currently being operated by Western Sugar Cooperative. (Both, Homesteaders Museum.)

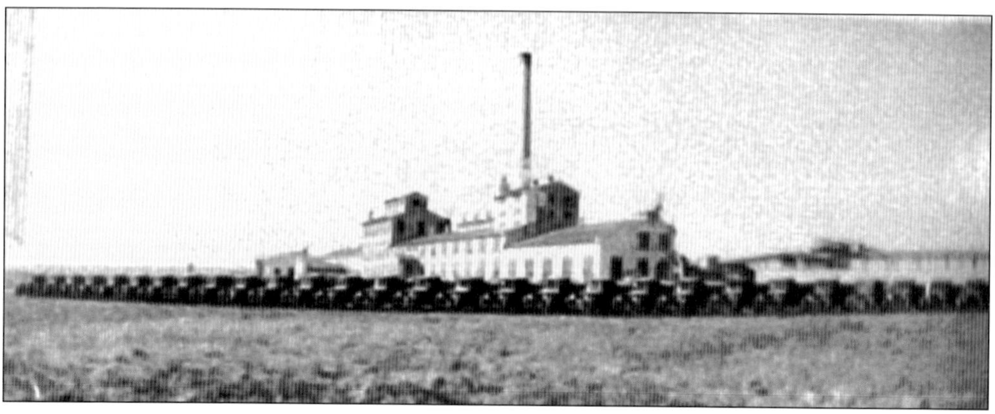

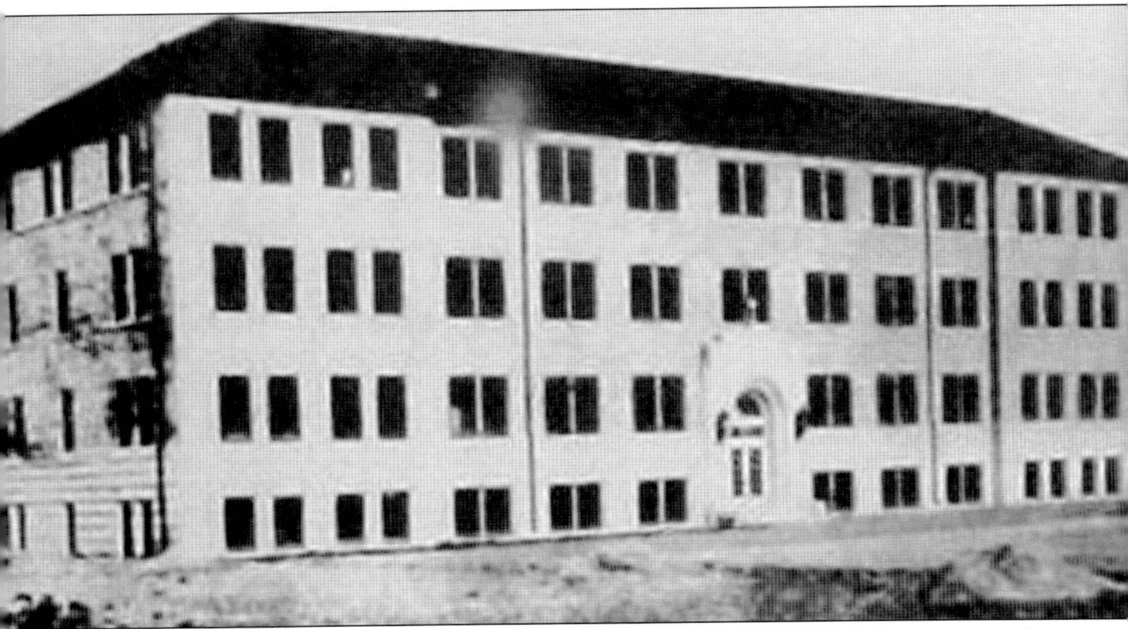

St. Joseph's Children's Orphanage opened on September 1, 1930. Bishop Patrick A. McGovern and John T. McDonald were instrumental in getting the permission of the Catholic diocese to build the facility. Architect William Dubois designed the fireproof building to house 80 children, and it was built at a cost of $175,000. Later, another building was constructed behind it for the laundry area and a place for the hired man, who did the farming, to live. (Homesteaders Museum.)

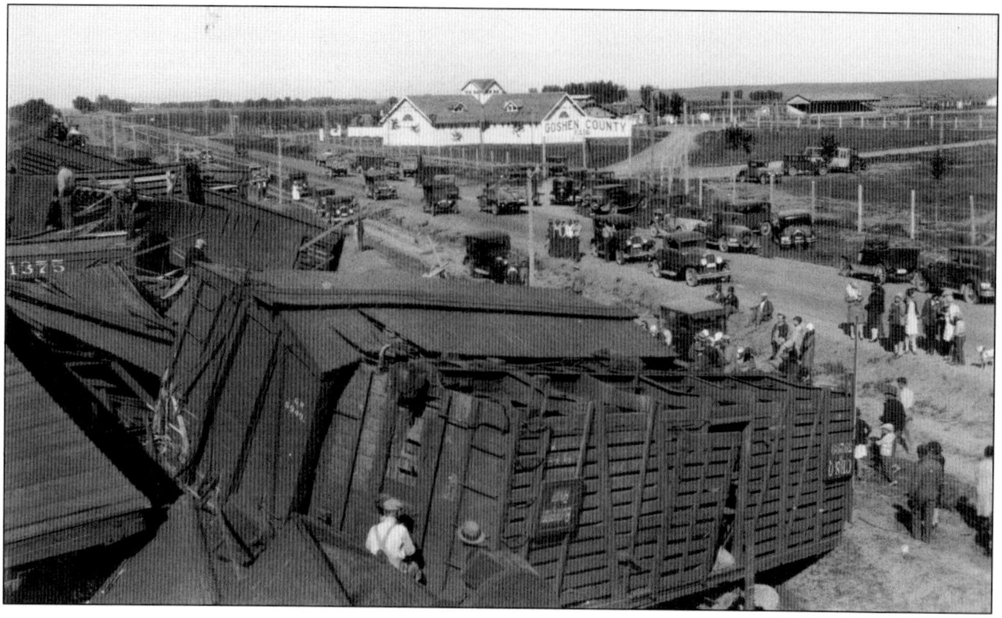

On October 14, 1929, a train carrying freight cars wrecked near the present-day fair grounds. The Burlington freight was heading east about 5:05 a.m. when the engine hit a brake shoe wedged between the rails, which was thought to have been lost from the previous train. There were 13 cars of sheep on the train when the wreck occurred, and about 1,000 of the 3,500 sheep were killed. The National Guard was called out to help with traffic control as hundreds of cars and thousands of people came to look at the wreck. Astonishingly, the engine remained on the track. By about 7:15 p.m., the wreck was cleared so that other trains could proceed. None of the freight crew was injured. Wood from the wrecked cars was sold for $1 per load. (Both, Homesteaders Museum.)

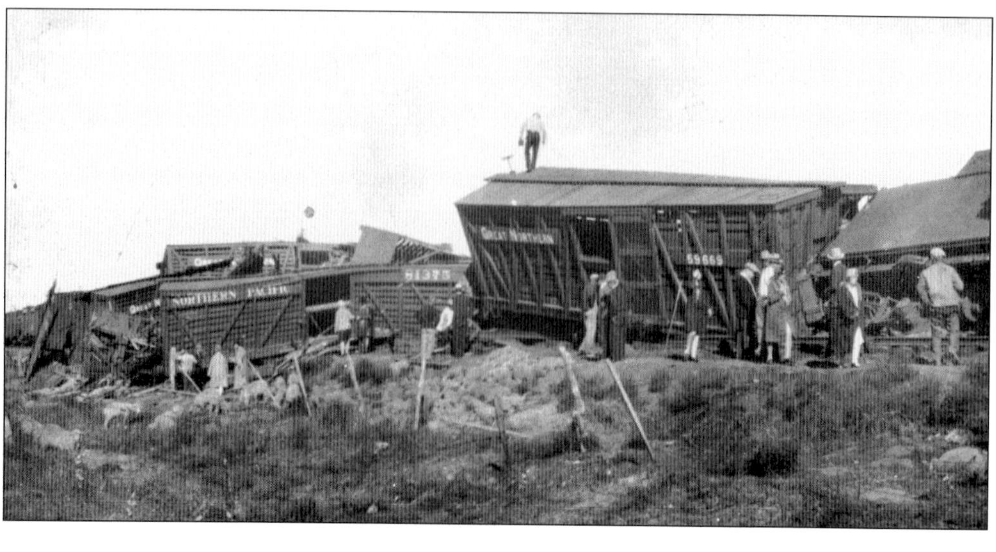

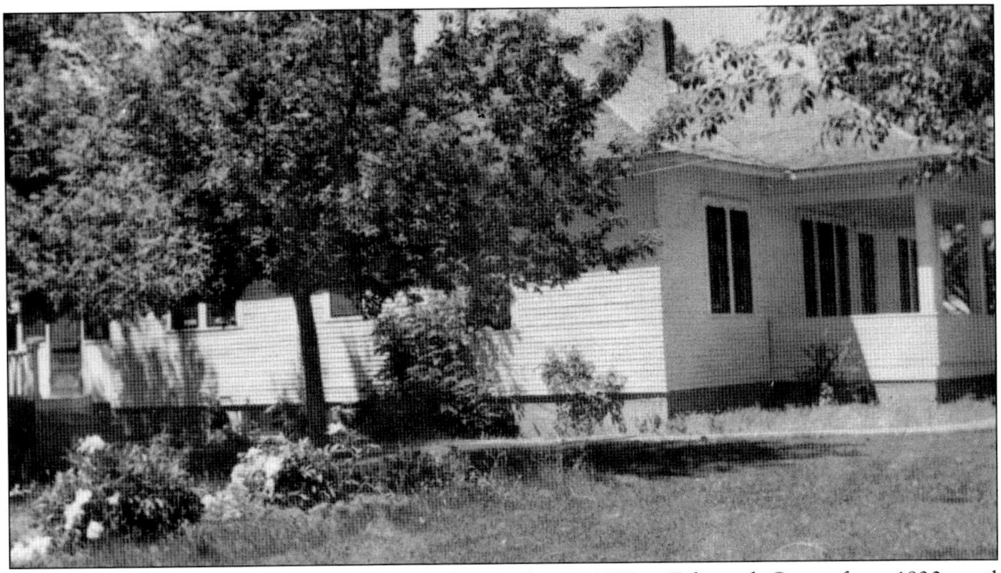

Mrs. John "Brownie" Scott (Muriel) had a hospital at 620 West Fifteenth Street from 1930 until 1933. The house was built in 1917. (Homesteaders Museum.)

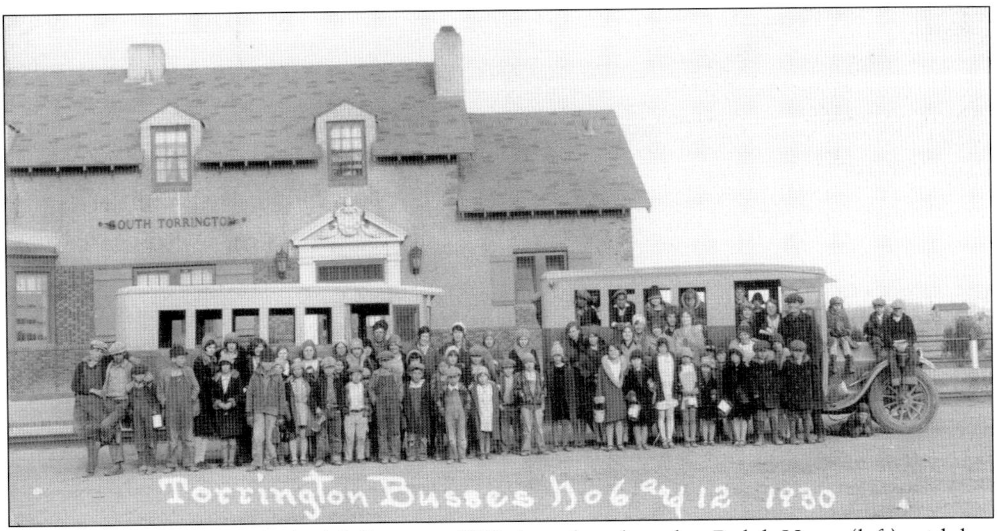

Torrington school buses looked different in 1930 than they do today. Ralph Hayes (left), with bus 6, and Judge James Johnston (right), with bus 12, are pictured in front of the South Torrington depot before they begin the Cottier Circle run. (Homesteaders Museum.)

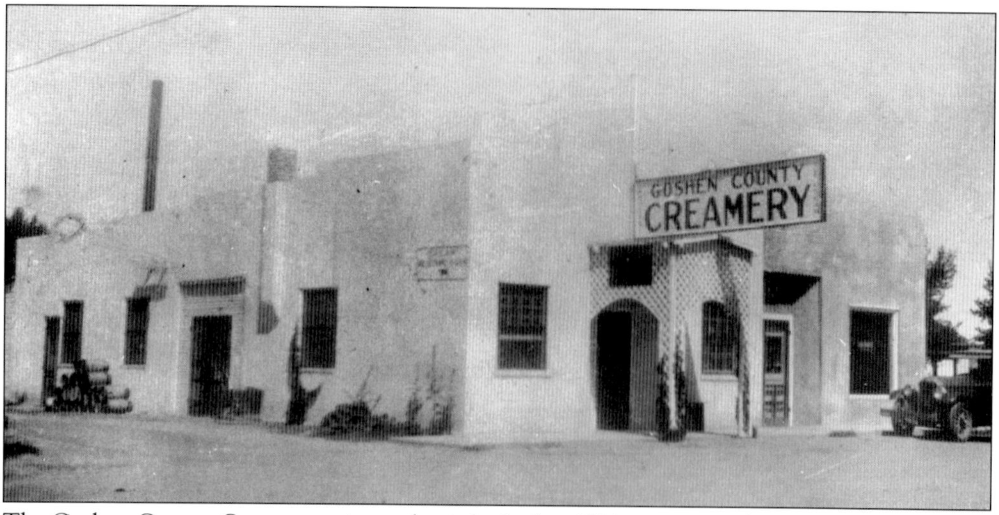

The Goshen County Creamery, pictured as it looked in 1934, was opened in 1926 at 220-222 East Twentieth Avenue. The owners were Ralph Woodruff and Fred Woodruff. They purchased milk and cream from local farmers and sold the milk in returnable glass containers. They also sold cream and butter, and almost everyone in the area remembers the delicious ice cream. In 1949, the building was purchased by Bernie M. Woodruff. Bernie and spouse Elda moved from Laramie to Torrington and began operating the creamery. In 1950, two apartments above the business were constructed. Son Bernie J. Woodruff became owner of the property when his father passed away in 1964. Ray Harris managed the creamery until his retirement in 1973. Bernie and spouse Sandi then took over. In the mid-1970s, creameries began closing nationwide. The Goshen County Creamery closed in 1976. Since then, the property has included various businesses, including the Harry (Leithead) Appliance Repair Store and, later, the Goshen County Ministries, operated by Lester and Florence Snow. In 2010, this property was purchased by Jerry and Ann White. Shown working in the creamery below are Ralph Woodruff (left), his sister, Alice, and Willard Ainsworth. (Both, Homesteaders Museum.)

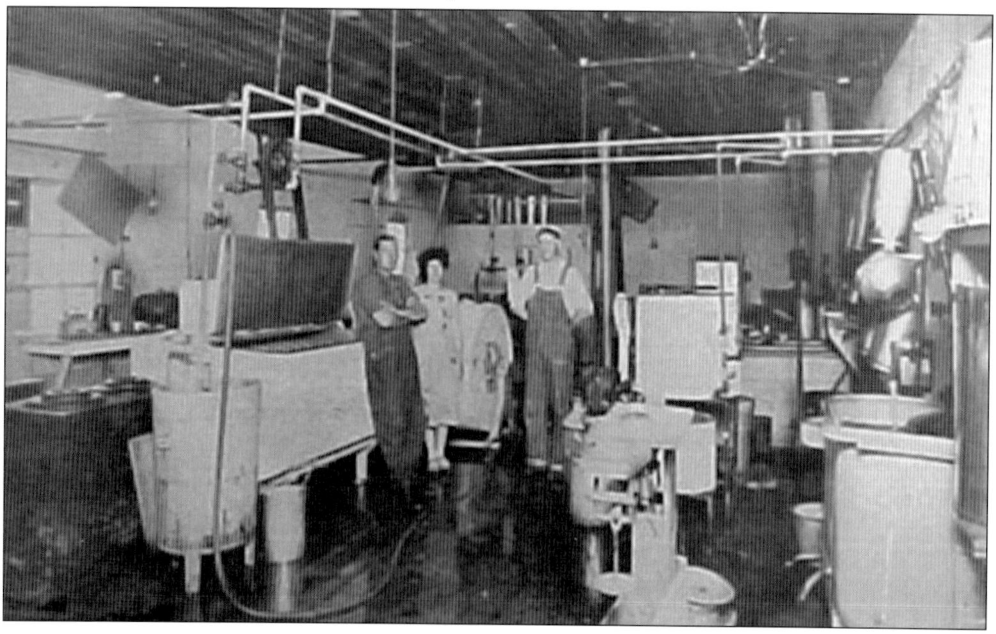

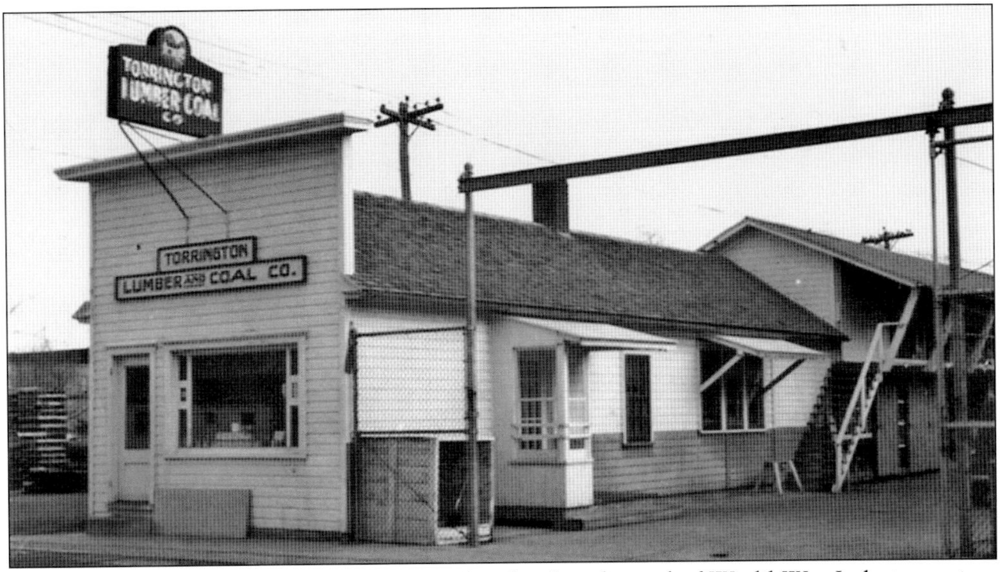

The Bloedorn family arrived in Wyoming shortly after the end of World War I, during a time of westward expansion. The town of Torrington, Wyoming, was beginning to flourish. Due to this development, founders C.F.W. Bloedorn and A.O. Bloedorn purchased lumberyard sites in Torrington and the nearby town of Lingle. In April 1919, original stockholders C.F.W. Bloedorn, A.O. Bloedorn, B.J. Hilsabeck, and H.B. Bloedorn incorporated the Torrington Lumber & Coal Company. The lumberyard purchased in bulk and supplied other lumberyards in Wyoming as well as in Nebraska. As time passed, the lumber company grew, and eventually A.O. Bloedorn began focusing his attention on the development of Bloedorn Lumber Company while business associate Charlie D. Cook managed the Torrington lumberyard. (Homesteaders Museum.)

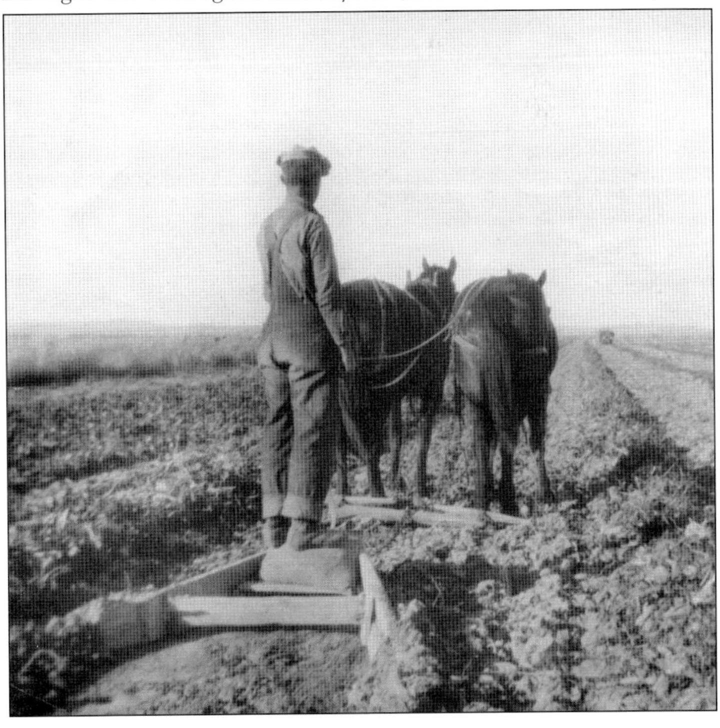

This c. 1930 photograph shows Alley Clowe on the "A" being pulled to smooth the row for topped beets. (Homesteaders Museum.)

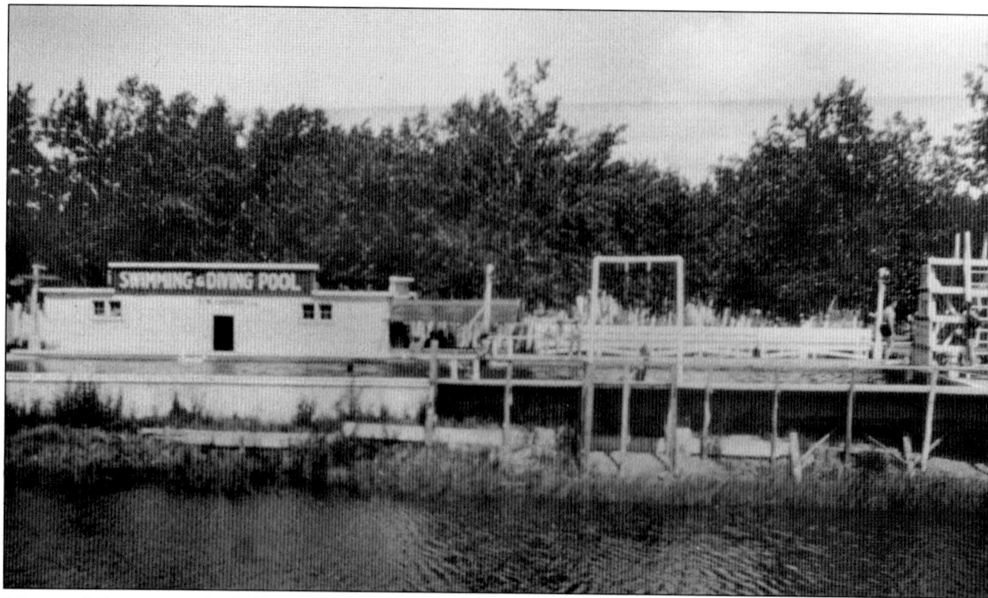

Many of Torrington's children swam in Frank Cannon's Pool and Bathhouse, shown here in 1930. Part of the facility included a traveler's court, where there were cabins for rent. In June 1949, owner E.L. Richardson installed a regulation diving board. In the 1960s, many people remember Dale Jones as a fixture there, since he was a swimming teacher and threw pennies in the water for children to dive after. He always wore a white rubber swimming cap and was extremely tanned in the summer. (Homesteaders Museum.)

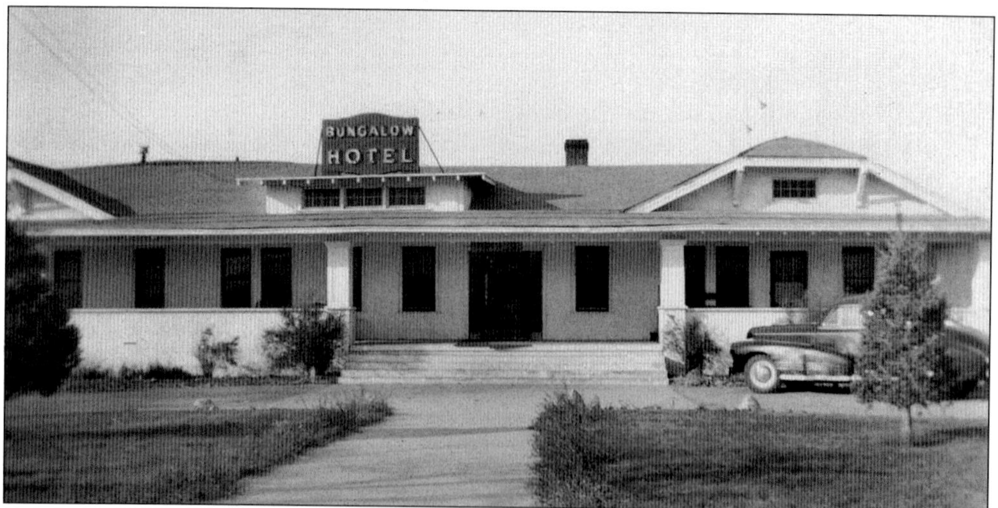

Owned and operated by Clyde Smith in 1932, the nine sections that comprised the Bungalow Hotel were moved to Torrington from Lusk and located on South Main Street. Clyde Smith, John Agnew (a rancher), John McDonald, and Victor Ellis (both bankers) purchased the building. Smith and Ellis went to Chicago, where they purchased new furnishings for the hotel. The hotel contained 60 rooms as well as a coffee shop, a dining room, a kitchen, and a parlor–writing room, where dancing classes were held with Smith's daughter Ruth as the teacher. The hotel closed in the fall of 1969. Razing of the building began on March 5, 1973, and it was replaced by a new A&W restaurant, which replaced the one being operated by Gene and Verna Matthews on the west highway. (Bill Law.)

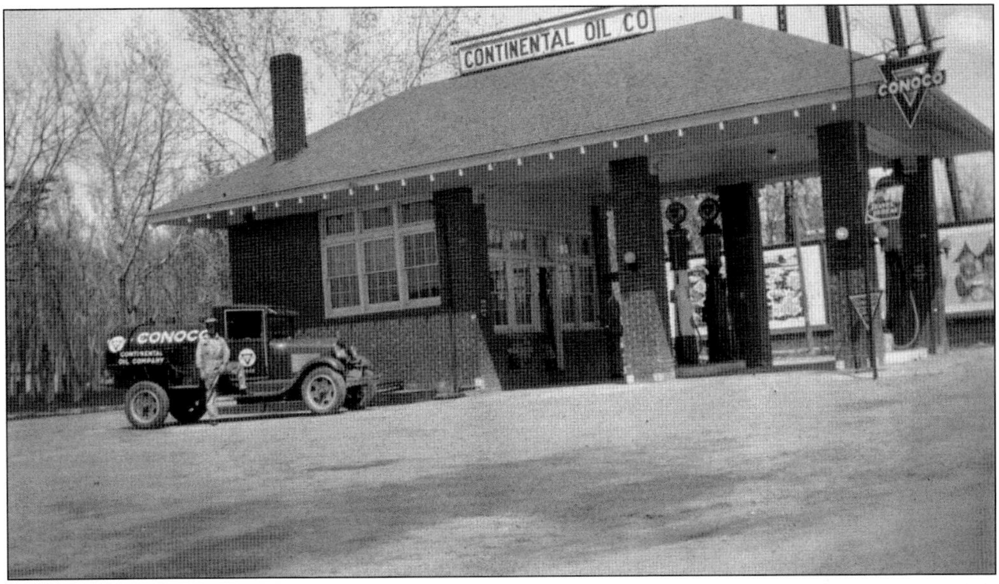

This Conoco filling station was located on West C Street and Highway 26 and 85 in 1932. Ralph Hayes is shown here as the driver of the delivery truck. L.J. McManaman leased the business and operated it. Behind the truck to the left was the bulk plant owned by Henry Zilk, who purchased the fuel from Continental Oil Company. George Ochsner, who wanted to use the materials on another building, tore down the structure in the early 1960s. (Homesteaders Museum.)

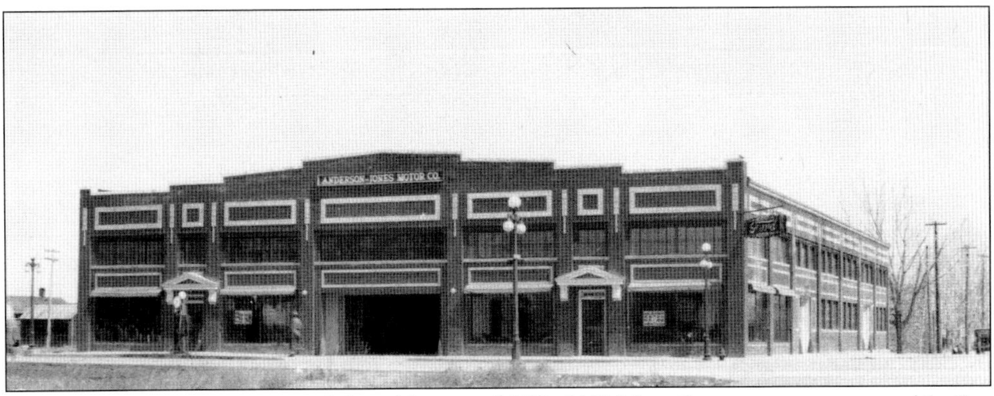

This building, which comprised the addresses of 2113–2101 Main Street, was constructed for Jim Nolan to be used as a car dealership. Albert Eaton Motor Company operated it next, and then it became the Neal Willhite Motor Company, which sold Chrysler and Plymouth cars for a short time. The Wyoming Grill was operated out of the north end of the building by the Matthews brothers. It now houses the Pineapple Grill. (Homesteaders Museum.)

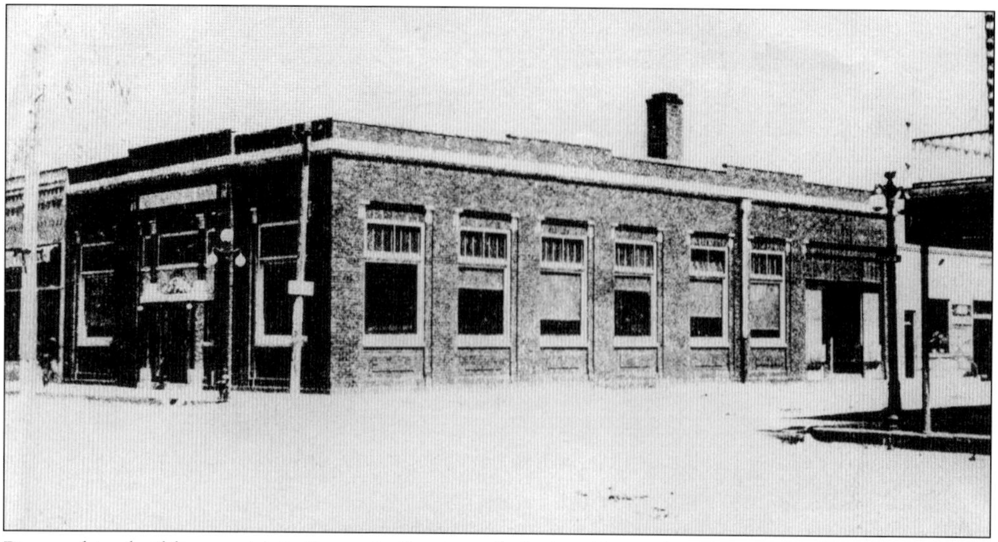

Pictured is a building on Main Street before it exploded on December 7, 1933. (Deloris Q. Kaufman Collection, Homesteaders Museum.)

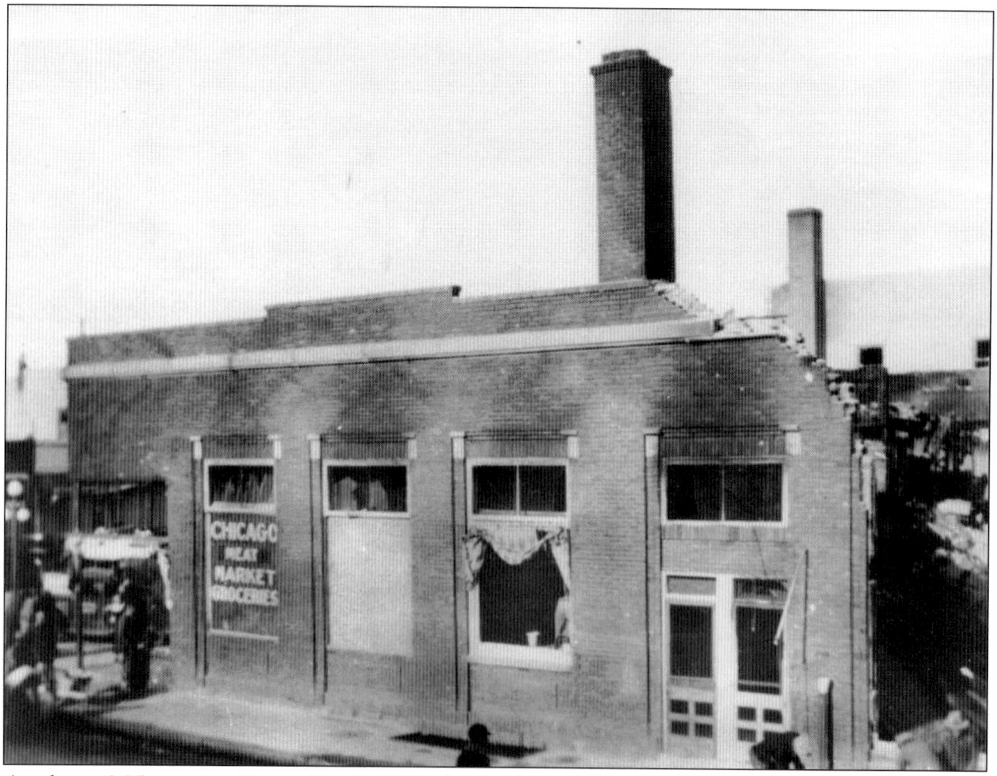

At about 6:05 p.m. on December 7, 1933, this building, along with several other buildings and residences, were destroyed or damaged by a minor—and then major—explosion. This building, constructed in 1919, was the old First National Bank, and next to it was the old post office. A falling wall crushed Virgil Duckwork, and H.C. Stovall and Mr. and Mrs. Elmer Goltry, operators of a secondhand business, were injured. Goltry's store had only been open a few days. (Homesteaders Museum.)

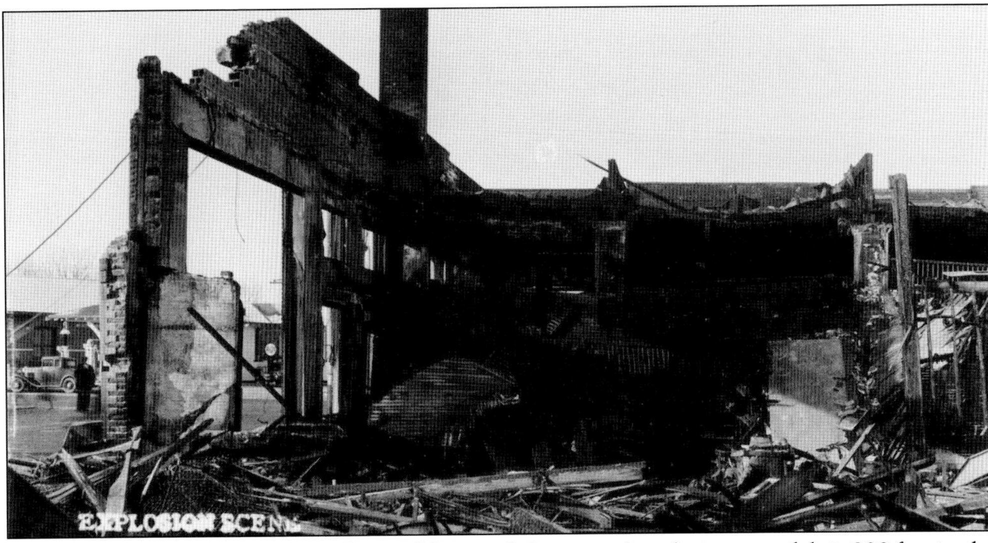

The first explosion raised the roof several feet, and the second explosion sent debris 300 feet in the air. All four walls of the post office blasted outward. A gas line in the basement of the Bloomer Variety Store had let out a stream of gas that ignited, sending flames 10 feet or more up the front of the store. Fire fighters sprayed water so that the Standard Hardware Store on the north and the Torrington Hotel on the south weren't destroyed. Plumbers worked to turn off the gas valve until 8:30 p.m. Electricity was also shut off so that loose wires could be disconnected. City crews hauled away broken glass that had littered the street. Carpenters boarded up the store fronts to eliminate any chance of further vandalism. (Homesteaders Museum.)

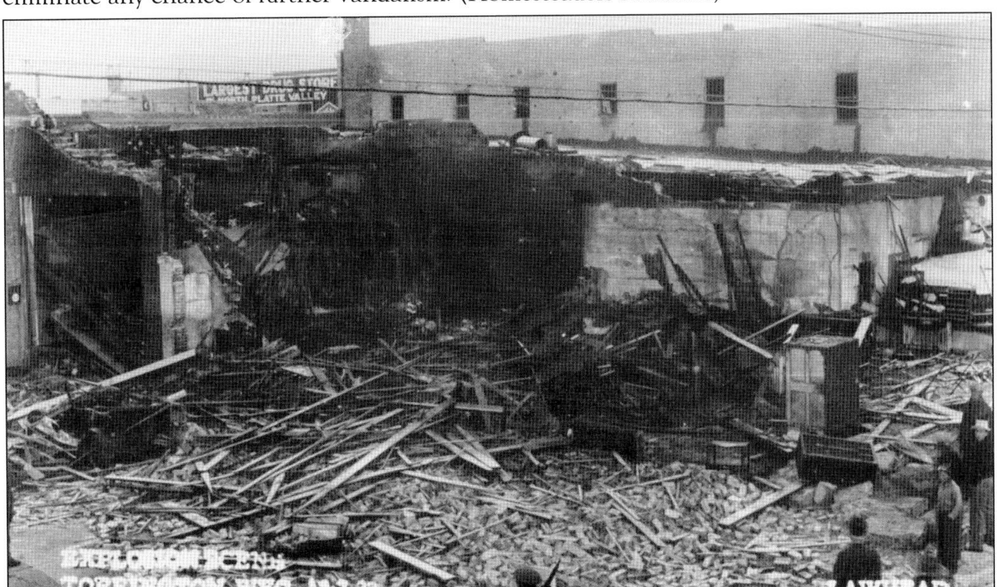

Other businesses that were damaged included E.A. Collins's Chicago Market, which lost grocery and clothing items and several tons of beans, Cruse Hat Shop, Bloomer Variety, and other nearby residences. Damage was estimated at more than $100,000. The Scottsbluff radio station broadcasted news of the blast, and the Associated Press had reporters here in two hours. Thousands of cars with plates from most of the western states came to see the damage. The local telephone office was swamped with inquiries following noise of the explosion. (Homesteaders Museum.)

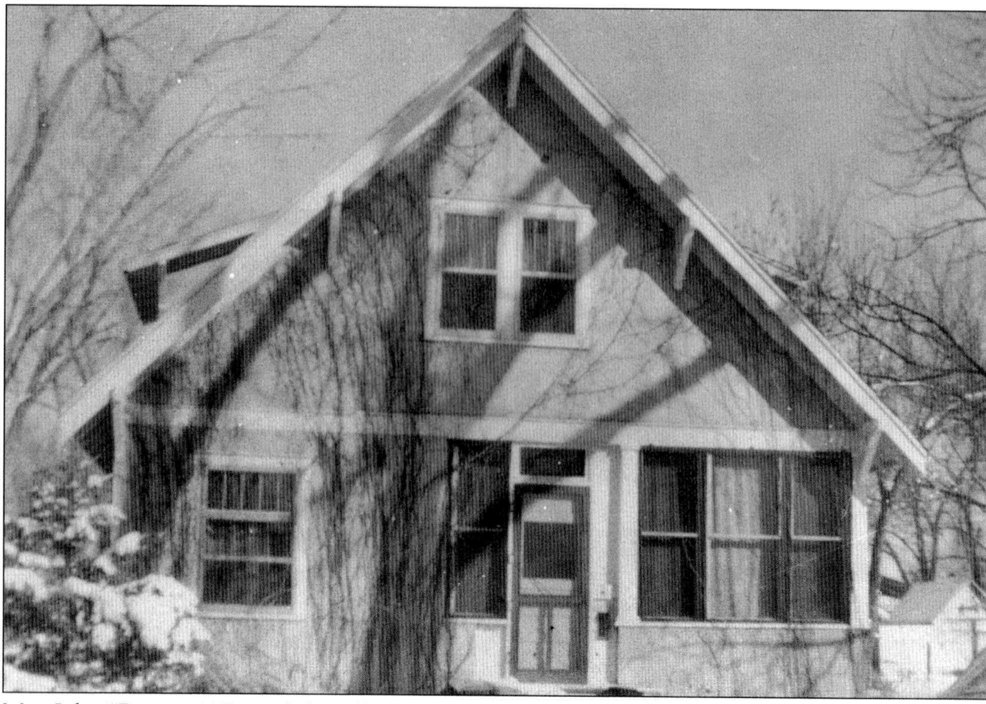

Mrs. John "Brownie" Scott (Muriel) operated a hospital first at 620 West Fifteenth Avenue from 1930 to 1933 and then at 2241 West B Street from 1933 until 1942. She had 10 beds and six baby baskets. Surgery was done on the kitchen table. Doctors Keenan, Downing, and Barbee reopened the Platte Valley Hospital in 1933 and ran it until 1942, when they left for the service. Brownie, along with Doctor Sell and Doctor Reid, operated the hospital until 1946, when it was perceived that there was a need for a larger hospital than the 14 rooms currently available. (Homesteaders Museum.)

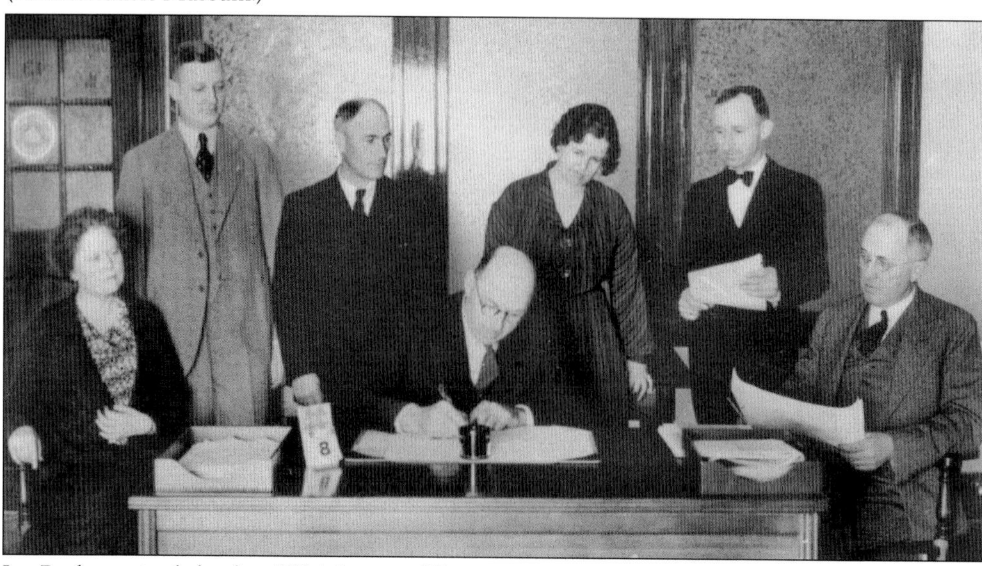

Jay Burk received the first FHA loan in Wyoming in 1935. Helping with the signing are, from left to right, Mrs. Warren Russell (Berea), two unidentified, A.O. Bloedorn (seated), Asa Rooth, Jay Burk, and unidentified. (Dorothy Rooth Collection, Homesteaders Museum.)

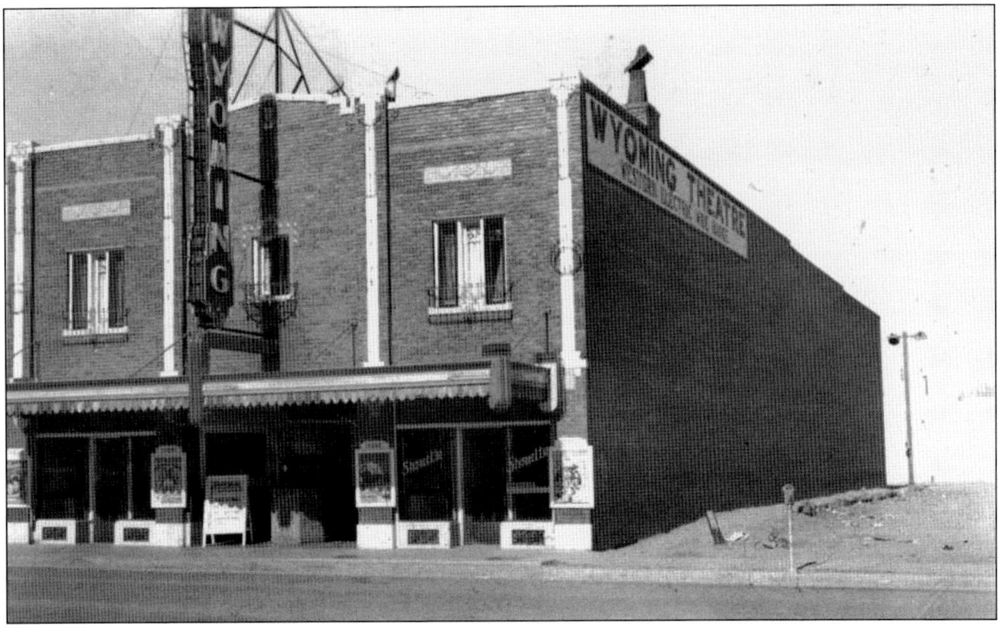

This c. 1924 photograph shows the Wyoming Theater. It was originally built in 1928 by Harry McDonald at 126 East Twentieth Avenue, and silent movies with piano accompaniment were the first to be shown there. Patrons would sit in expensive box wicker love seats with curtains for privacy. A remodel installed more traditional seating for the "talkies." When it was at capacity, the theater could seat up to 700 people. The pillars, window wells, wrought iron, statues, box office, and tiles are still original. Torrington also had two other movie theaters—the Lyrig and the Torrington Theater. There is an upper and lower theater now. (Homesteaders Museum.)

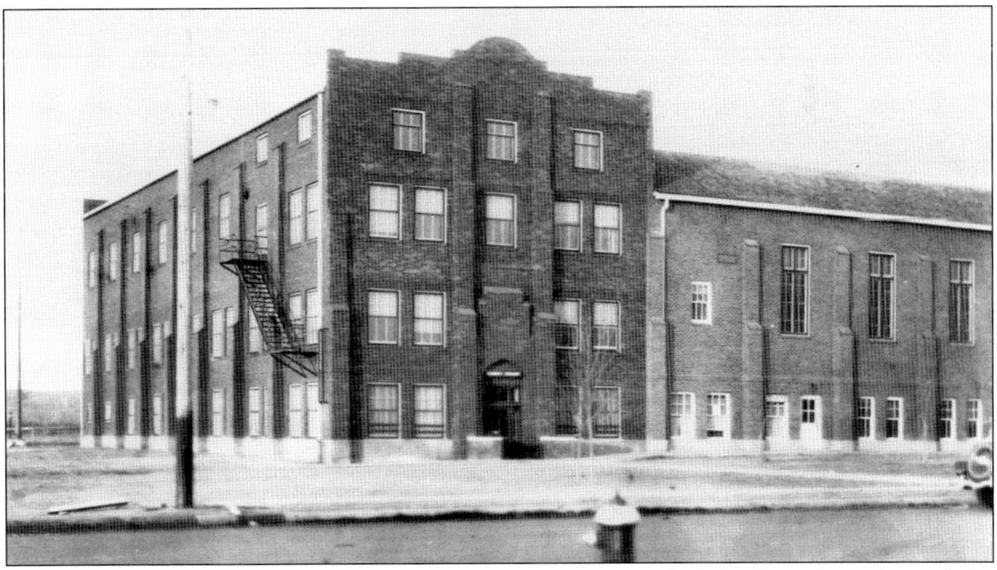

This January 24, 1939, photograph shows the Torrington High School on the right and the new junior high school on the left. The building had been a Works Progress Administration project. The high school was a U-shaped configuration, and the new building on the south closed off the courtyard. The new three-story building added considerable space for classrooms. (Homesteaders Museum.)

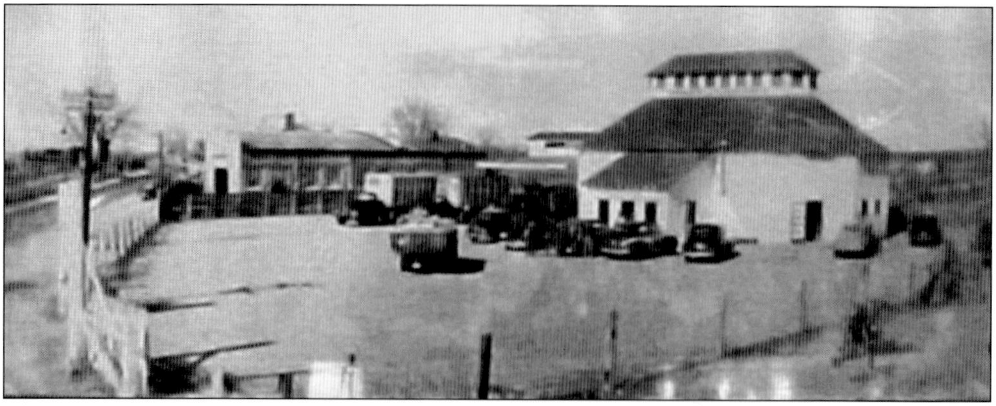

The Torrington Livestock Commission Company sale barn is pictured around 1939 or 1940. This business was first established in 1934 by Fred Petsch of LaGrange. He sold it to Roy and Bus Petsch, who then sold it to Mac Swanson and his son Dick. L.W. Maxfield purchased the business in August 1949. Through the years, he remodeled the buildings and yards and installed a ring scale. During his tenure, the sale barn became the largest auction facility in Wyoming and ranked third to fifth in the nation. Maxfield's two sons, Mike and Lester Jr., and Oliver Dicken took over the business in the late 1970s with Dicken as the auctioneer. Mike and Dicken bought out Lester in the late 1970s, and in 1989, they sold a half interest to Shawn and Lex Madden. Mike retired in 1999, and Dicken died in 2002, leaving the Madden brothers as owners. It is estimated that during the fall, up to 19,000 heads of animals are sold per week at the sale barn today. (Both, Homesteaders Museum.)

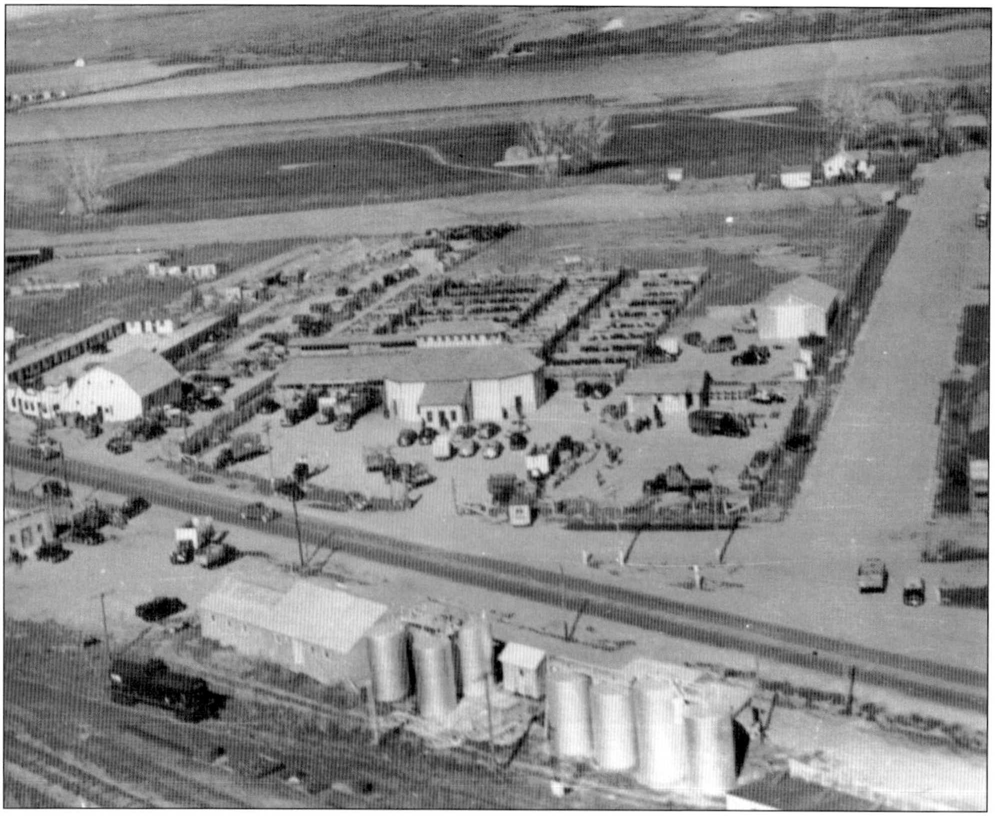

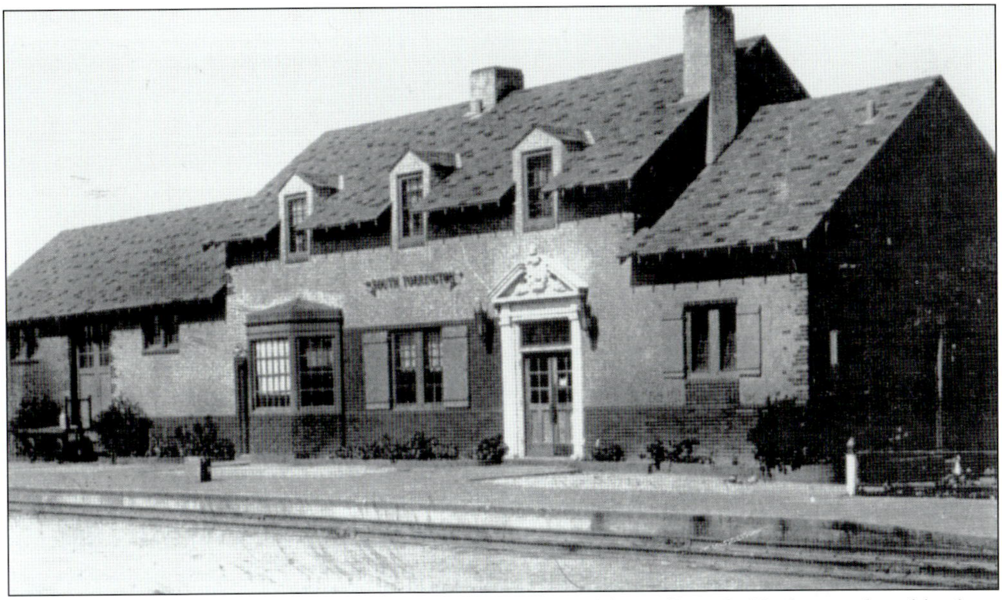

The South Torrington Union Pacific depot was designed by Gilbert S. Underwood and built in 1926. The building's architectural style is Mission Revival and Spanish Colonial Revival, and it was originally planned as a combination passenger and freight depot. The ground level housed the freight and baggage room, a holdover room and record room, an agent's office, a passenger waiting room, bathrooms, and a hallway leading to the upstairs apartment. A basement included a storage room and a furnace room. The upper floor contained living quarters for the station agent, including a living room, two bedrooms, a kitchen, and a bathroom. The railroad line was to serve the Holly Sugar Refinery nearby. By 1928, the railroad was extended to serve as a cutoff from the Union Pacific branch along the North Platte River to the main transcontinental line, known as the North Platte Cutoff. This 1940 photograph shows the South Torrington Union Pacific depot. (Homesteaders Museum.)

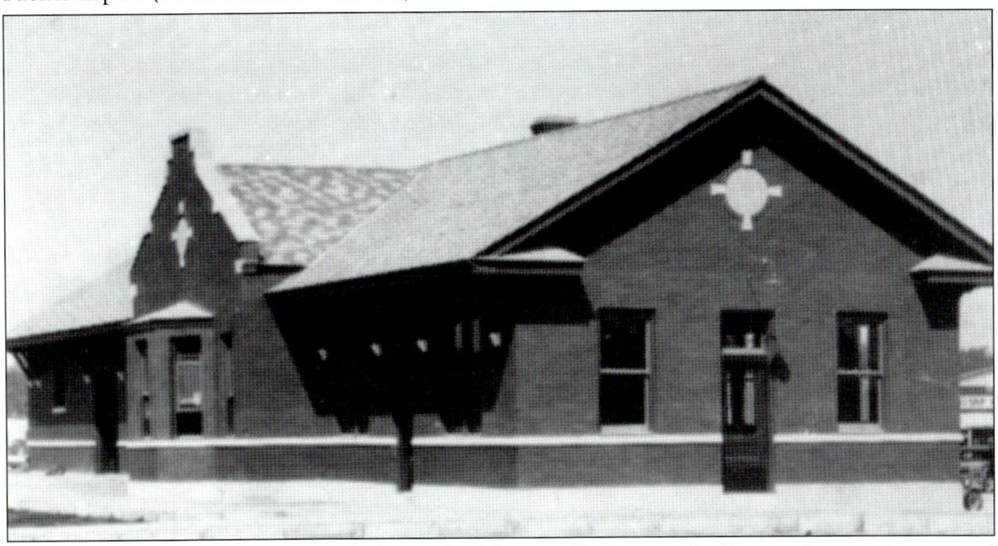

Operating in 1930, this photograph shows the Chicago, Burlington & Quincy depot as it appeared in 1940. The depot was used as both a passenger station and for freight loading and unloading. It was torn down in 1996 to build a Hardee's hamburger restaurant. (Homesteaders Museum.)

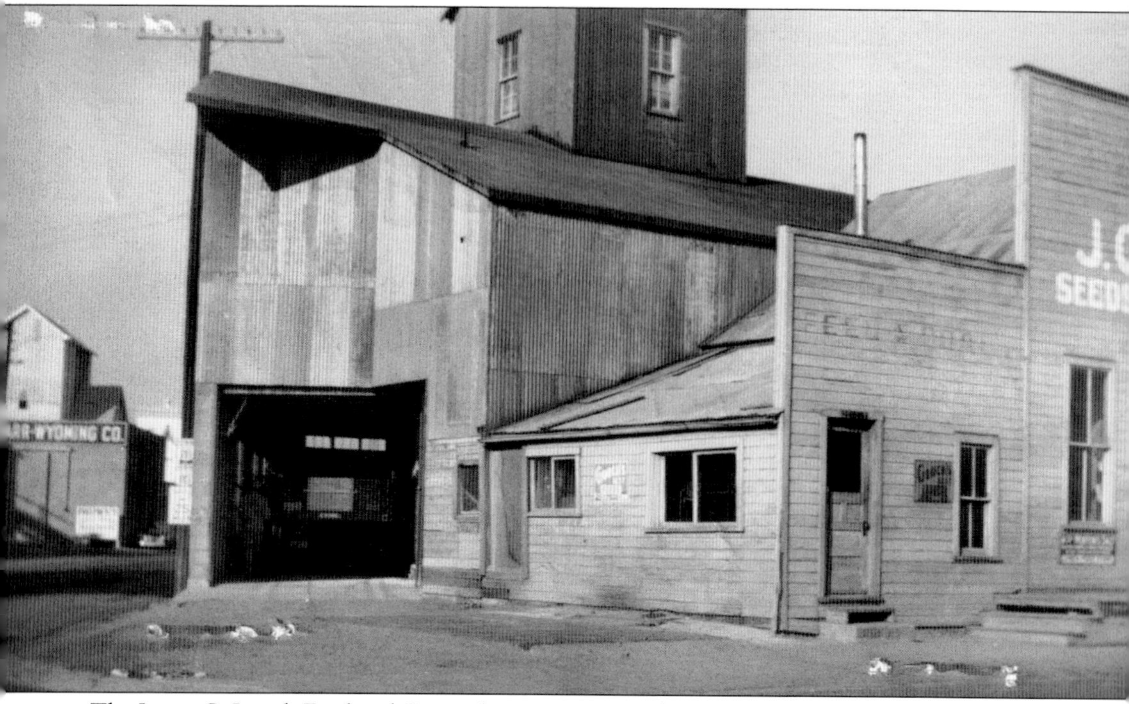

The James C. Lynch Feed and Grain elevator is pictured in 1946; however, the Lynch Feed Store had been in operation since at least 1916. In the background, the Farr Wyoming Company elevators can be seen. Another feed mill and elevator, the Z&W Mill, was a bit farther west on Highway 26. It is the only one still operating at its original location. (Homesteaders Museum.)

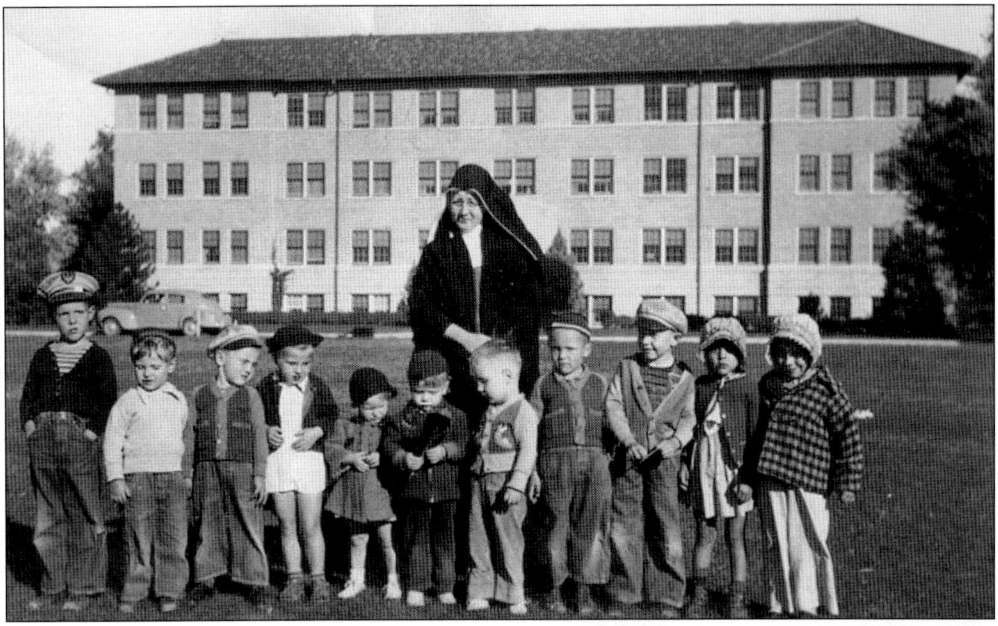

Sister Annette and the nursery are shown in front of St. Joseph's Children's Home on November 2, 1944. (Homesteaders Museum.)

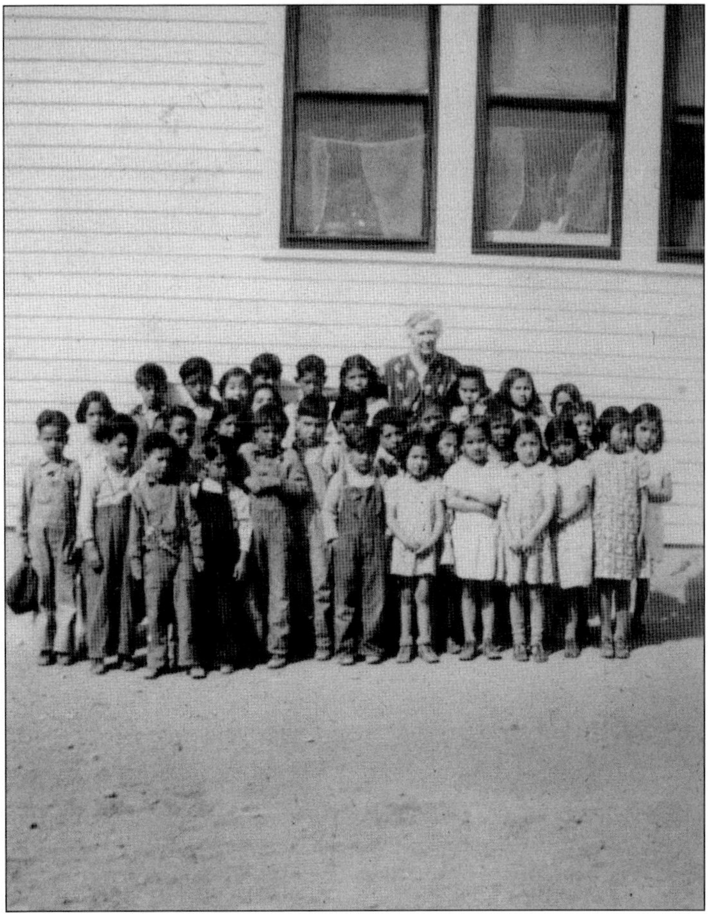

South of the Holly Sugar Factory was the Columbia School, which was specially built for the children of Mexican migrant workers. The teacher was Juanita Patton of Lingle. The building was later used as headquarters for the prisoner of war camp. (Wyoming State Archives, Department of State Parks and Cultural Resources.)

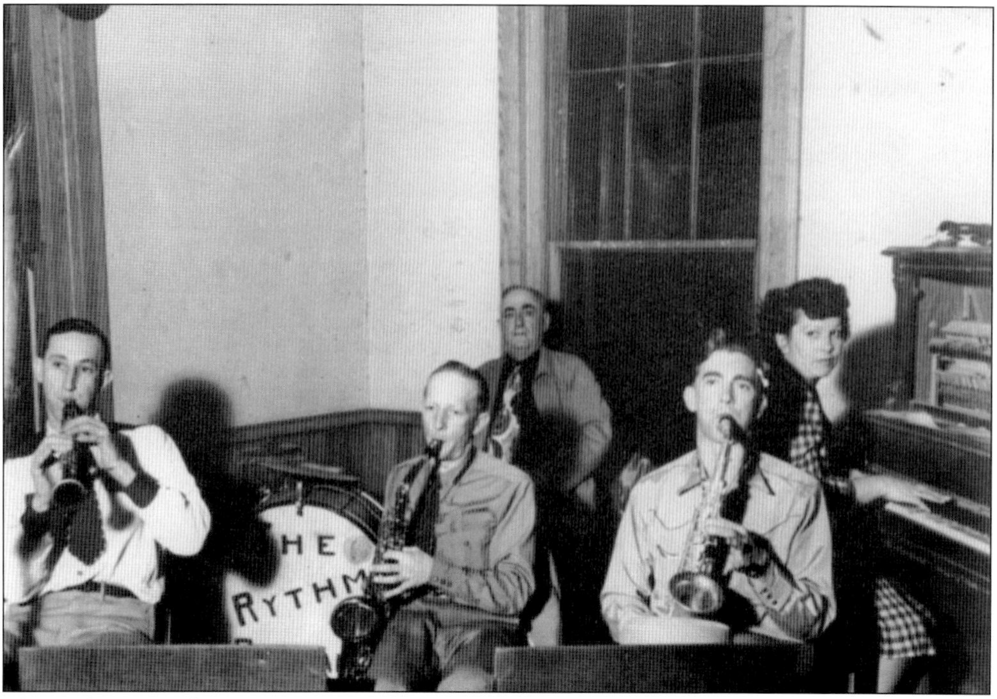

The Rythm Rascals were a very popular band for Saturday night dances in the Yoder area from 1943 until the blizzard of 1949; after the blizzard, Louis Arnold Jr. got married and started farming. They played mostly requests from their repertoire of trendy music. Van Gurney played the clarinet, Kerby Tremain played the saxophone, Louis Arnold Jr. played the coronet and accordion, Fay Morey played the piano, and Leo Arnold played the drums. (Homesteaders Museum.)

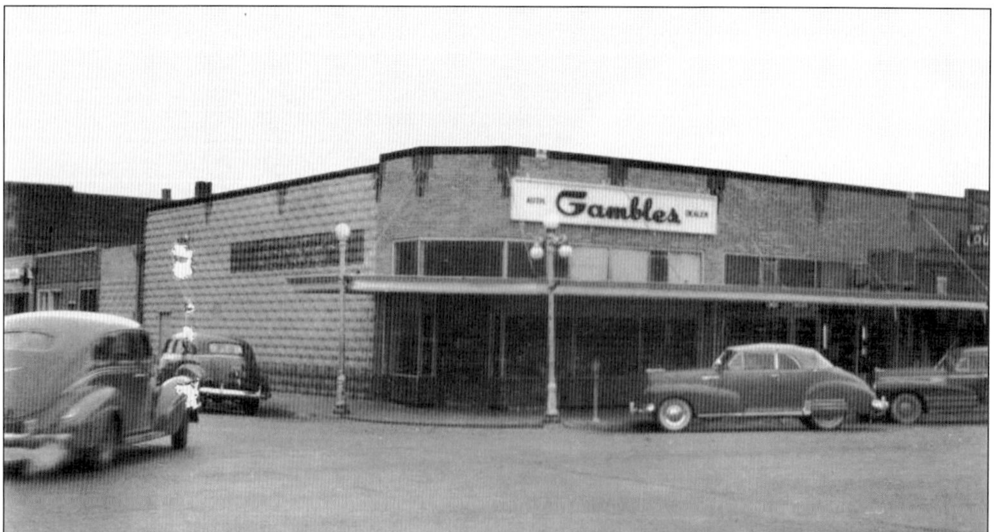

This 1947 photograph shows Gambles Hardware. It was located at the corner of Main Street and Nineteenth Avenue. Torrington Office Supply and the Scrapbooking Creative Zone are currently located at this site. Robert Erickson owned the Gambles store, which sold guns, appliances, and hardware. Later, the building housed the Montgomery Ward store. (Homesteaders Museum.)

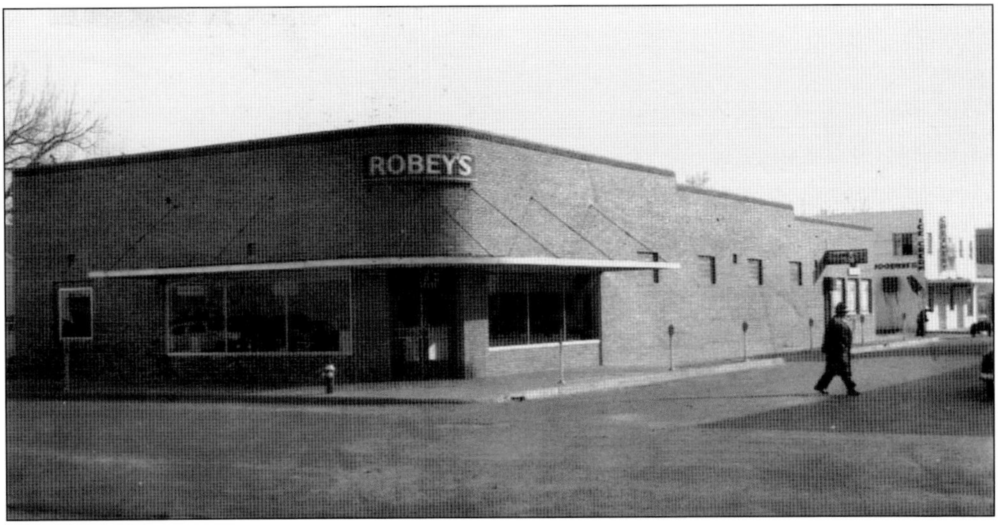

This 1948 photograph shows Robey's Market. The building was constructed in July 1946. Later, the grocery store was sold to James Biffar, who called the business Biffar's Super Market. The building now houses the Goshen County Library at 2001 East A Street. (Homesteaders Museum.)

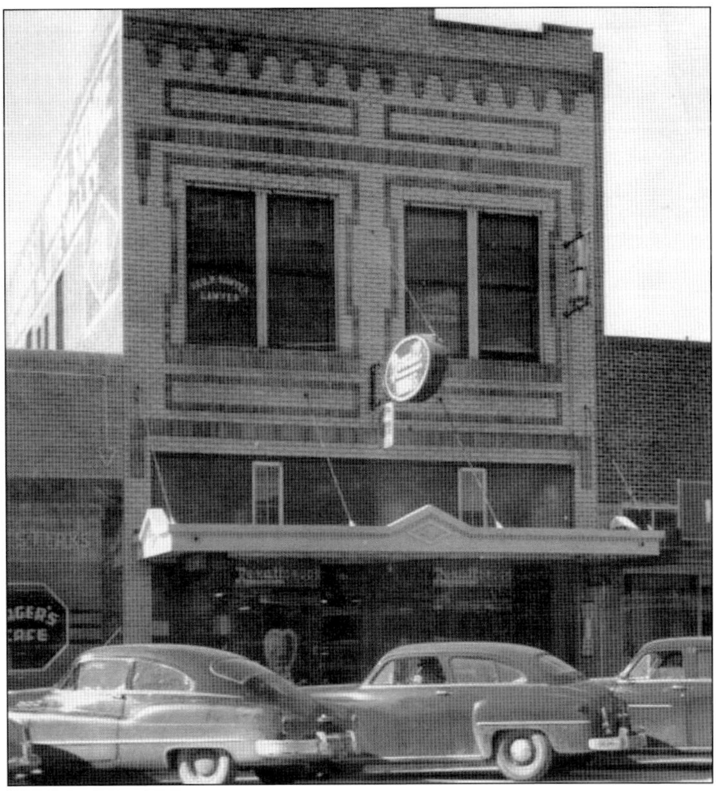

In 1948, this building at 1930 Main Street housed Sager's Café and the Kellam Drugstore. Upstairs housed the law firm of Sawyer & Sawyer, which included John and his son George. In the back of these offices was the Masonic temple. In the building to the north was Gamble's Hardware and Appliance. (Homesteaders Museum.)

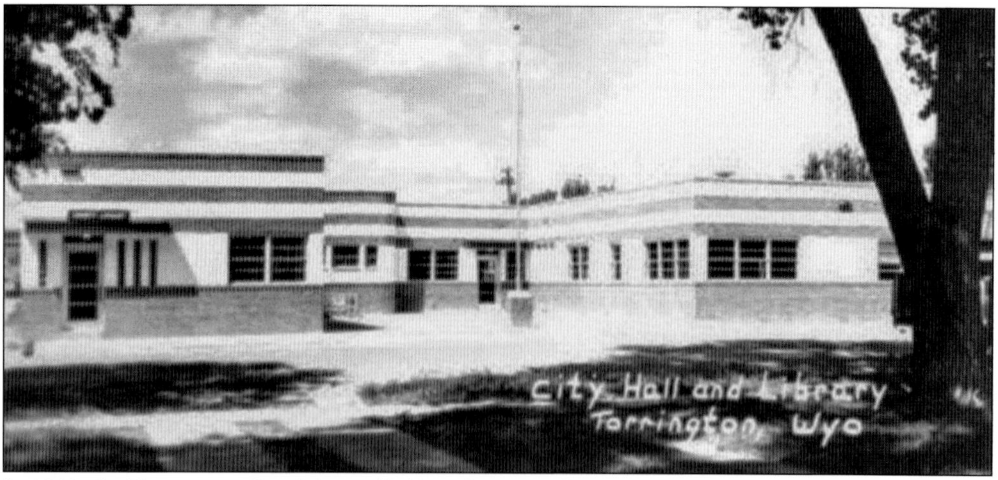

In 1949, the Torrington City Library (left) and City Hall (right) were housed in the same building at the corner of Twentieth Street and East A Street. Notice the open courtyard in the middle, which was subsequently filled in for police offices. The building was designed by architect C.F. Pillsbury of Denver and built by W.N. McCreery and Bill Dean. The south wing was a library that had 10,000 volumes of books with Mrs. F.B. Redfield (Aileen) as librarian. It opened for use on September 2, 1948. On the north side of the building were separate public rest rooms, known to be commodious and modern, that were intended for the benefit of rural women who were visiting the city. Until 2009, an attendant sat in the women's section to help with children while their mothers did the shopping. In 2010, the city hall and police station moved to their new space in what was known as the Lincoln Elementary School. (Homesteaders Museum.)

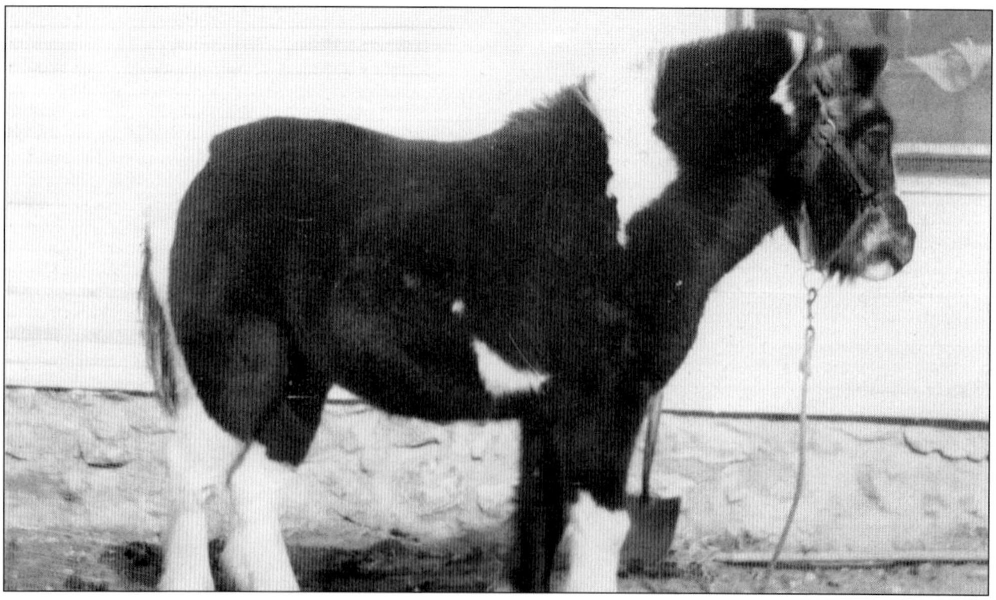

This may not be a true homesteader, but from the time period was circus horse Babe, who was 52 at the time of her death on June 14, 1958. Velda Childers bought the small, half-starved, black and white Shetland horse from a man in Edgemont, South Dakota, who had purchased Babe for his son. At that time, Babe was about 20 years old. Childers taught the horse many tricks, including getting the mail—which was tied with a string—out of the mailbox and returning to the house with it. Tourists came from all over to see this phenomenon. (Homesteaders Museum.)

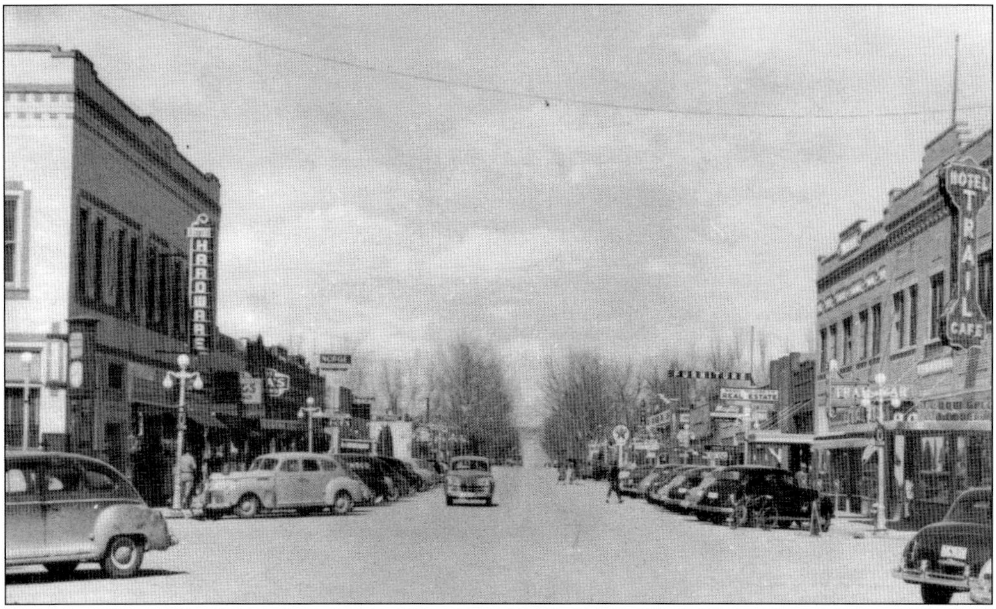

Pictured in 1949 is Main Street looking north from Twentieth Avenue. (Homesteaders Museum.)

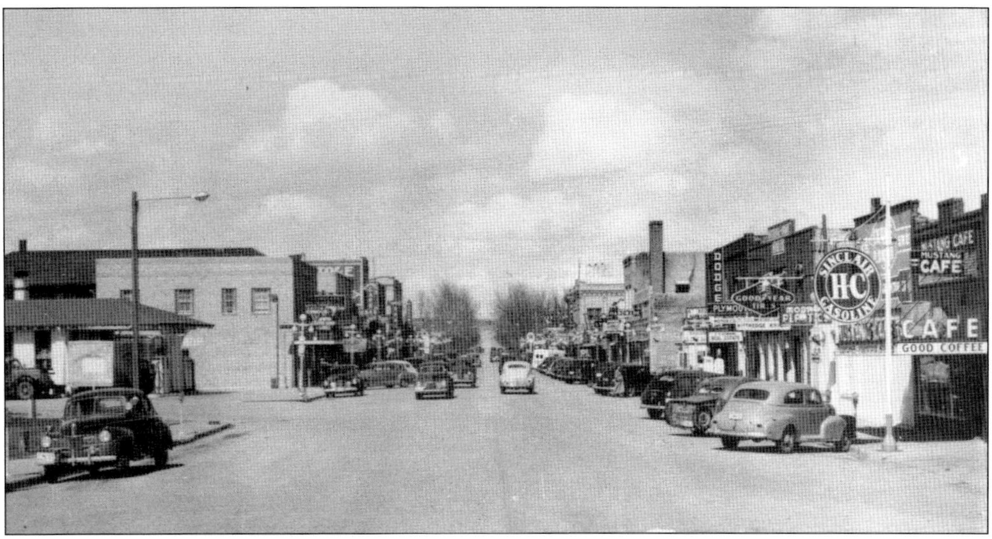

Pictured in 1949 is Main Street looking north from depot. (Homesteaders Museum.)

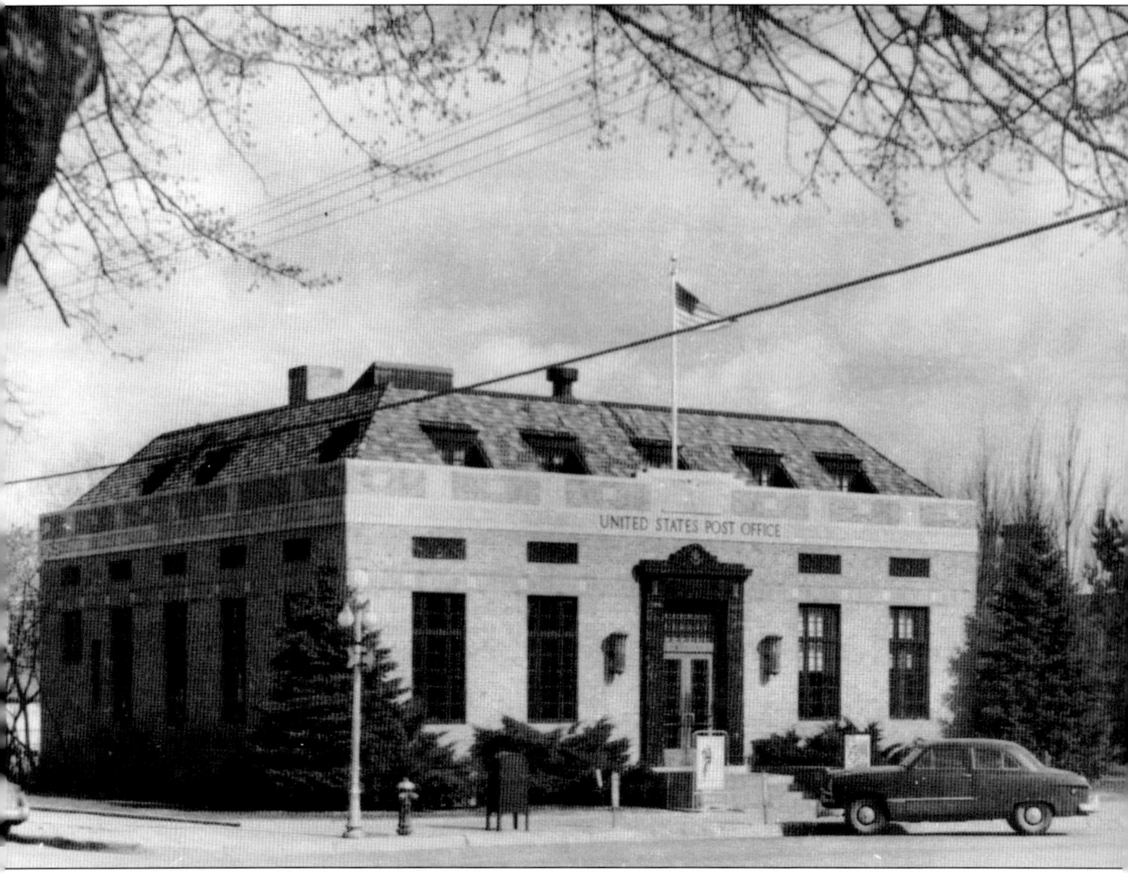

Located at 2141 Main Street is the Torrington branch of the US Post Office. This was the sixth location for the post office, and this building opened for business in June 1933. This picture shows how the building looked in 1952. (Homesteaders Museum.)

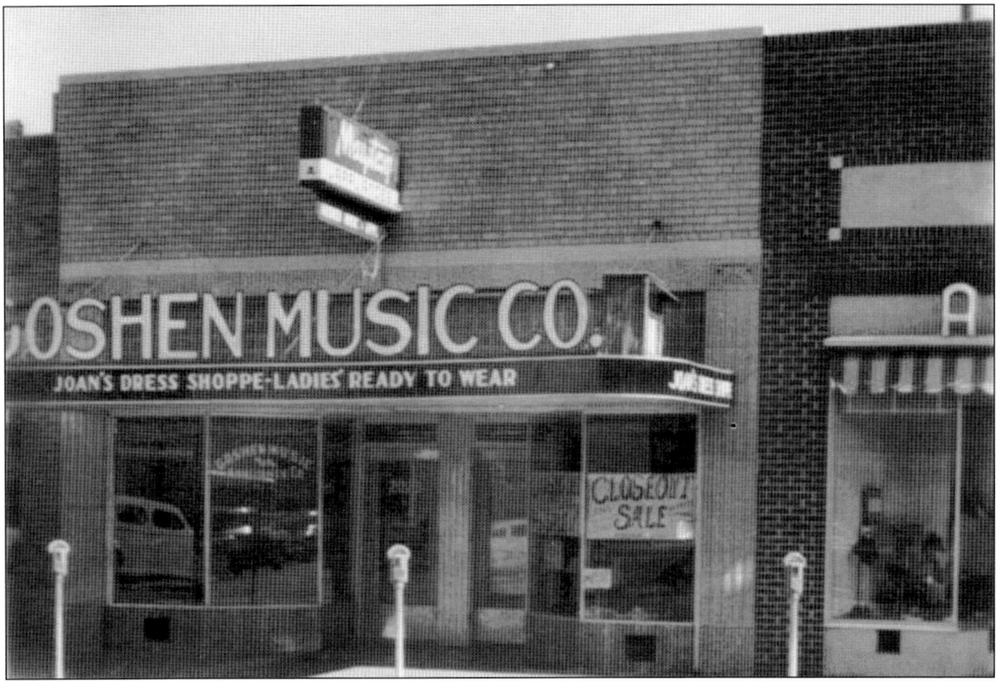

In 1941, W.A. Gibson owned the Goshen Music Company at 2029 Main Street. The building also housed Joan's Dress Shoppe, which sold ladies' ready-to-wear. The music shop evolved into a business that also sold appliances. (Homesteaders Museum.)

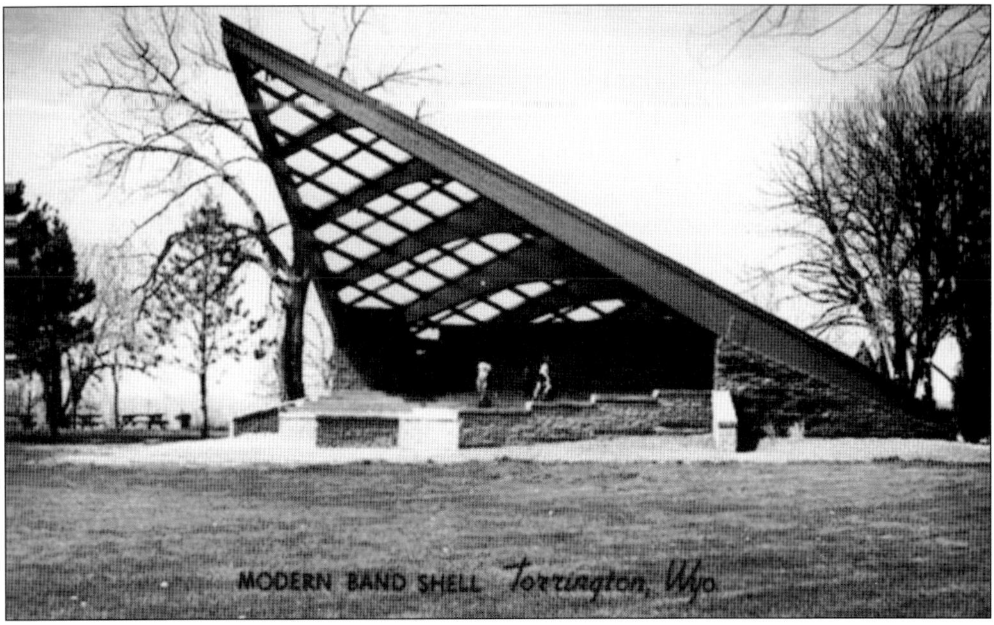

The modern band shell is pictured in 1953 at Pioneer Park. During its tenure, bands from Scottsbluff, Nebraska, and Torrington, Wyoming; the Army band from Rapid City, South Dakota; and the National Guard band, among others, performed there. The acoustics were said to be excellent. When it was discovered in 1987 that some of the timbers were rotting, the city council voted to tear down the structure; however, it took a bulldozer to push it down. (Homesteaders Museum.)

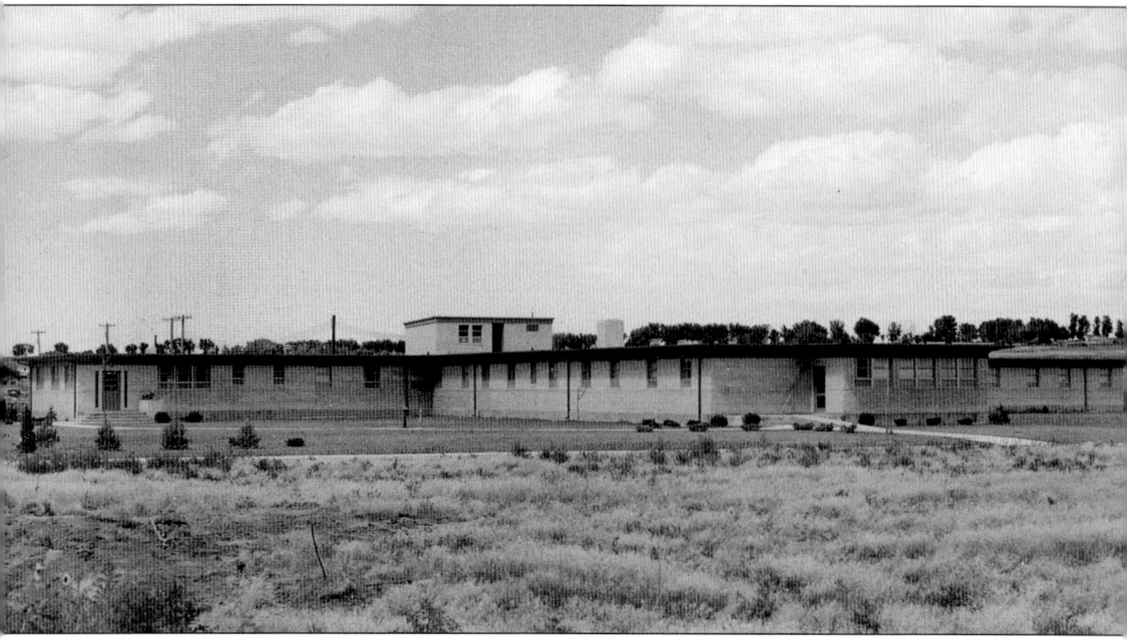

The Spiegelberg Building Company of Laramie began construction on the Goshen County Memorial Hospital in April 1949 at a cost of $303,703. There were 50 beds in the new building. It was located at 2017 East D Street. (Homesteaders Museum.)

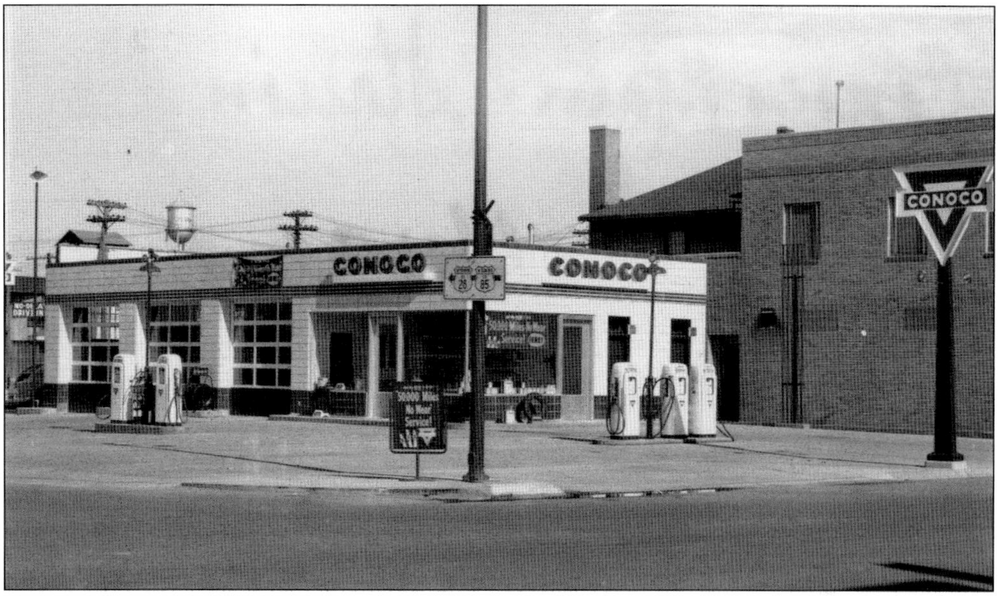

This is not the first building to be on the corner of Main Street and Highway 26 and 85, but in 1952, Barney McCone operated the Conoco service station here. (Homesteaders Museum.)

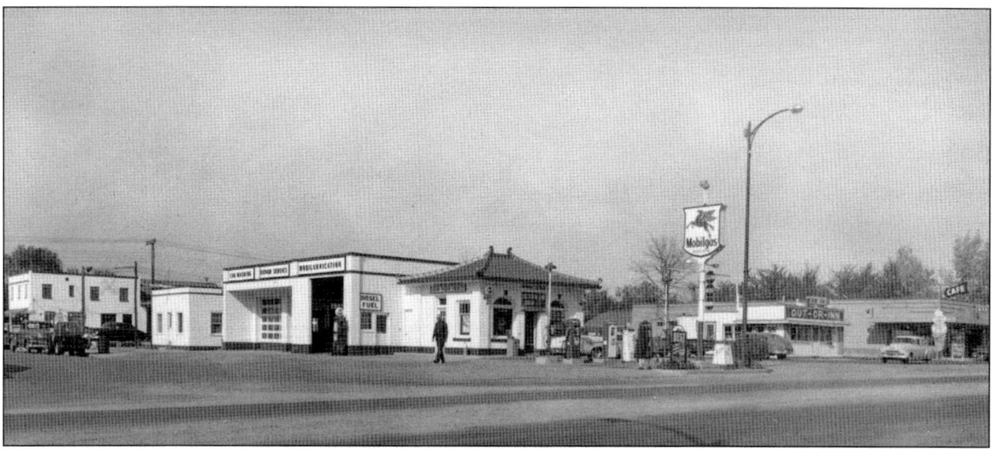

Pictured in 1955 is Fred Dunbar's service station. It was at 1502 South Main Street, where the Trail Bar is now. Dunbar had been a mechanic for the previous owner. (Homesteaders Museum.)

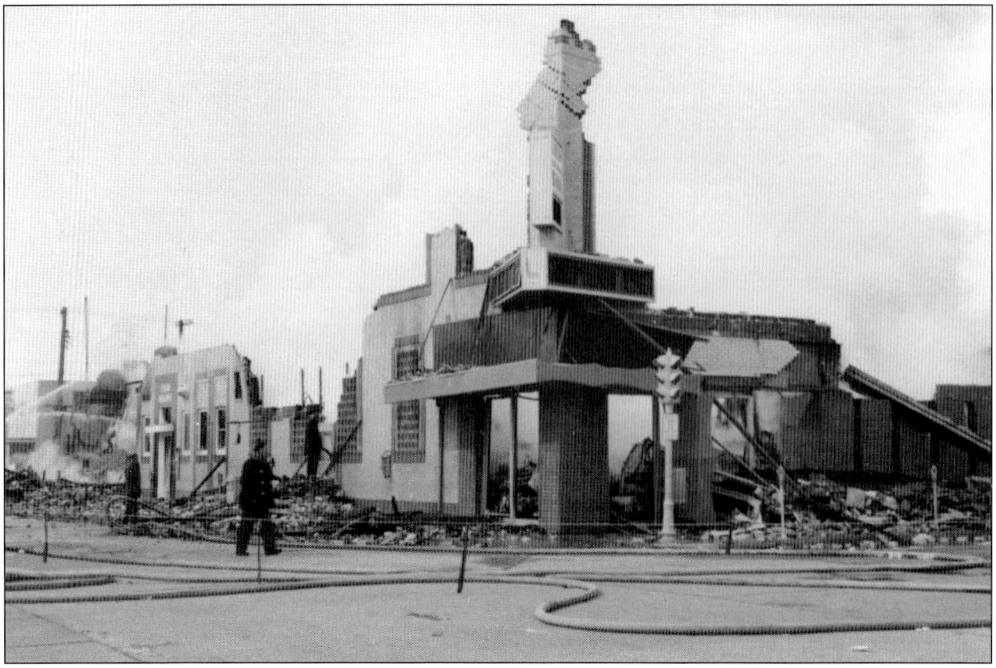

A fire erupted from a gas leak in the early hours of February 22, 1969, totally destroying the W.O. Eaton Building. The Citizen's National Bank, as well as Edelman's Drugstore, were a total loss from the fire, but no firefighters were hurt. The bank had received its charter on January 31, 1918. Edelman's was never rebuilt, but John Vandel opened a drugstore, Vandel's, to replace it. Vandel Drug is still operating at 2041 Main Street. (Both, Homesteaders Museum.)

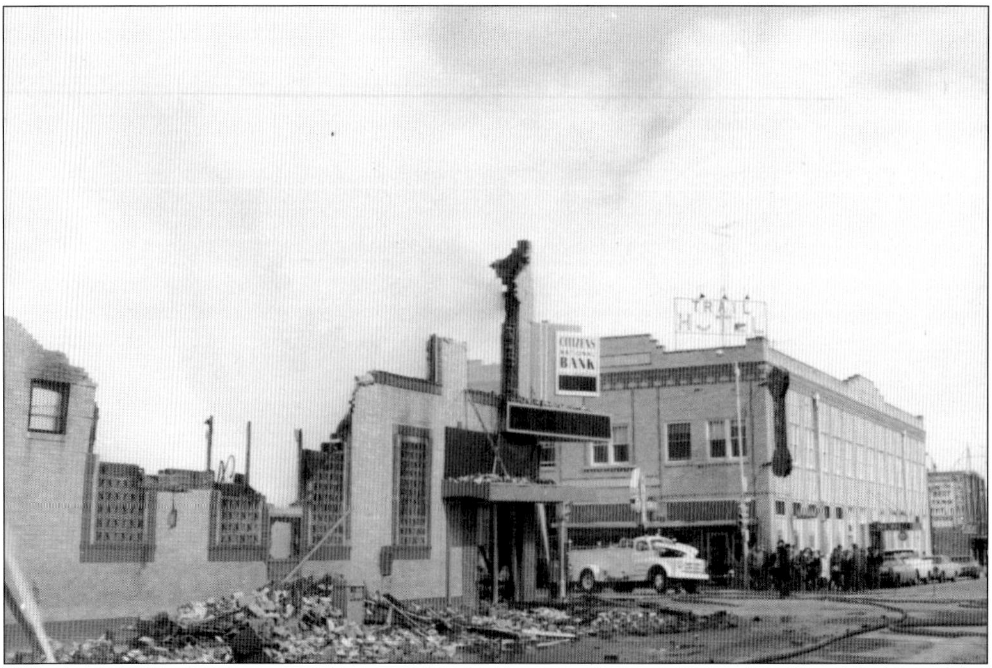

Bibliography

Goshen County History Book Committee. *Wind Pudding and Rabbit Tracks, Volume I*. Torrington, WY: Platte Valley Printers, 1989.

———. *Wind Pudding and Rabbit Tracks, Volume II*. Torrington, WY: Platte Valley Printers, 1993.

Hodgson, Don. *The History of Goshen County*. Torrington, WY: Eastern Wyoming College, 1980.

———. *The Search for Community in Goshen Hole*. Torrington, WY: Eastern Wyoming College, 1982–1983.

hometownchronicles.com/wyoming.htm

Johnson, Elizabeth Wilkinson. *Editor Trails, Rails and Travails*. LaGrange, WY: City of LaGrange, 1988.

www.wyomingtalesandtrails.com

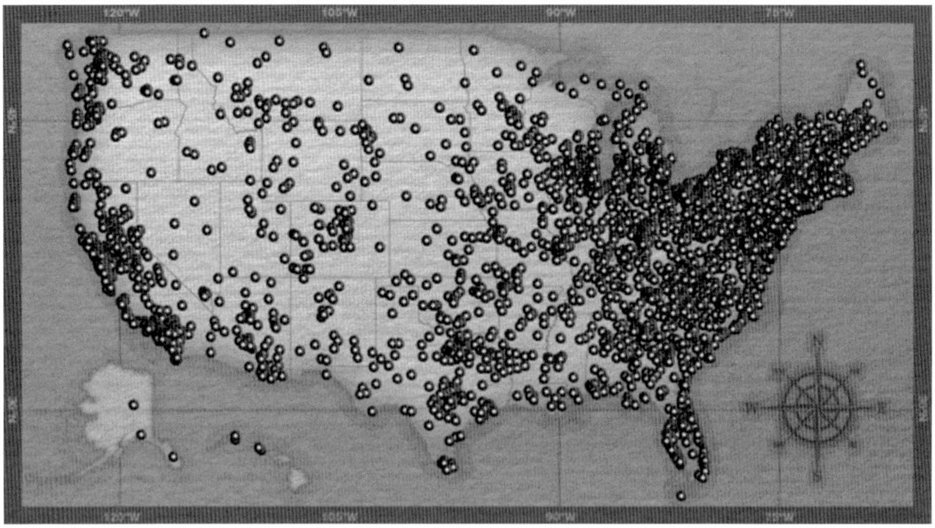